Age, Gender, and Work

Edited by Julie Ann McMullin

Age, Gender, and Work
Small Information Technology
Firms in the New Economy

UBCPress · Vancouver · Toronto

21 20 19 18 17 16 15 14 13 12 11   5 4 3 2 1

Printed in Canada on FSC-certified ancient-forest-free paper
(100% post-consumer recycled) that is processed chlorine- and acid-free.

___

Library and Archives Canada Cataloguing in Publication

  Age, gender, and work : small information technology firms in the new
economy / edited by Julie Ann McMullin.

Includes bibliographical references and index.
ISBN 978-0-7748-1971-8 (bound); 978-0-7748-1972-5 (pbk.)

  1. Information services industry – Employees. 2. Small business. 3. Age and
employment. 4. Sex role in the work environment. 5. Women computer industry
employees. 6. Corporate culture. I. McMullin, Julie Ann

HD8039.I37A34 2011	331.11′91004	C2010-906508-5

___

e-book ISBNs: 978-0-7748-1973-2 (PDF); 978-0-7748-1974-9 (epub)

Canadä

UBC Press gratefully acknowledges the financial support for our publishing program of
the Government of Canada (through the Canada Book Fund), the Canada Council
for the Arts, and the British Columbia Arts Council.

This book has been published with the help of a grant from the Canadian Federation
for the Humanities and Social Sciences, through the Aid to Scholarly Publications
Programme, using funds provided by the Social Sciences and Humanities Research
Council of Canada.

The author acknowledges the assistance of the J.B. Smallman Publication Fund,
and the Faculty of Social Science, The University of Western Ontario.

UBC Press
The University of British Columbia
2029 West Mall
Vancouver, BC V6T 1Z2
www.ubcpress.ca

Contents

List of Tables / vii

Preface and Acknowledgments / ix

Part 1: Key Concepts and Methods / 1

1 Gender, Age, and Work in the New Economy / 3
Julie McMullin and Heather Dryburgh

2 Methods / 18
Emily Jovic, Julie McMullin, and Tammy Duerden Comeau

Part 2: Gender Projects and Regimes / 33

3 Firms as "Gender Regimes": The Experiences of Women in
IT Workplaces / 35
Gillian Ranson and Heather Dryburgh

4 Variants of Masculinity within Masculinist IT Workplace Regimes / 59
Tammy Duerden Comeau and Candace L. Kemp

5 Negotiating Work and Family in the IT Industry / 81
Ingrid Arnet Connidis and Candace L. Kemp

Part 3: Age Regimes and Projects / 111

6 Generational and Age Discourse in IT Firms / 113
Julie McMullin, Emily Jovic, and Tammy Duerden Comeau

7 Aging and Age Discrimination in IT Firms / 133
Julie McMullin and Tammy Duerden Comeau

8 Conclusion: Inequality Regimes and New Economy Work / 159
Emily Jovic and Julie McMullin

Contributors / 173

Index / 175

Tables

2.1 City/regional representation of case study firms / 19

2.2 Time frame for the case study fieldwork / 21

2.3 WANE data sources / 22

2.4 Interview participation, survey response, and partial completion rates / 25

2.5 Firm characteristics / 27

2.6 Sample characteristics / 29

2.7 Interview sample characteristics: Occupations / 30

2.8 Interview sample characteristics: Occupations by gender and age / 31

3.1 Classification of firms as gender regimes / 39

5.1 Percentage of distributions of small IT firm workers for Canada and the United States / 89

5.2 Division of household tasks and child care: Online survey data for small firms in Canada and the United States / 90

Preface and Acknowledgments

This book is about whether and how gender and age structure work and influence workplace cultures within small information technology (IT) firms. This was a central research question in the Workforce Aging in the New Economy (WANE) project, the study from which the data used in this book are drawn.

The book is organized into three parts, which are followed by a concluding chapter. Part 1 provides the context by introducing key concepts used throughout the book, providing an overview of the IT landscape, and detailing the methods used for the WANE project. Part 2 focuses on how gender structures work and influences workplace culture in small IT firms, and Part 3 does the same for age. Finally, a concluding chapter ties the three parts together by summarizing the key findings and commenting on how the chapters have elucidated the relationships between age, gender, and paid work.

This research was supported by a grant from the Initiative on the New Economy (INE) program of the Social Sciences and Humanities Research Council of Canada with additional support from Research Western and the Faculty of Social Science at Western (Julie McMullin, principal investigator). Thanks go to all of the WANE project co-investigators, students, post-doctoral fellows, and other project associates whose work over the past seven years made this book possible. Special thanks go to Emily Jovic and Catherine Gordon, WANE researchers and doctoral students in the Department of Sociology at the University of Western Ontario, who proofread, reference-checked, and formatted the chapters.

Age, Gender, and Work

Part 1:
Key Concepts and Methods

The two chapters in Part 1 set the stage for the rest of the book. In the introductory chapter, "Age, Gender, and Work in the New Economy," the information technology industry is introduced as an example of the new economy but one in which the workers are disproportionately young men. Descriptive data are discussed to locate male, female, older, and younger workers in the small IT firms in our study. Concepts that are central to the book – including workplace culture, life course, and inequality regimes and projects – are discussed and defined. Chapter 1 concludes with a brief overview of the chapters in the rest of the book. Chapter 2 provides more context for the rest of the book by describing the WANE study methodology.

1
Gender, Age, and Work in the New Economy
Julie McMullin and Heather Dryburgh

In Canada, as in most other Western countries, there is a lot of talk about new economies and whether individuals are well enough trained for their nations to compete globally in this new, knowledge-based world of work. As it has evolved, the "new economy" concept refers to changes in the way that paid work is conducted, due primarily to advances in information technology, the innovative implementation of these technologies in the workplace, globalization, and the commodification of knowledge (Castells 1996; Ranson 2003). This book contributes to the literature on the new economy by examining work and employment relations in small and mid-sized,[1] highly skilled, information technology (IT) service firms, an industrial sector that may be considered a benchmark case of a new economy industry.[2]

Globalization, though an elusive concept, is often invoked as a key feature of knowledge economies (Castells 2000). Generally, the globalization of paid work refers to the idea that we are now living and working within a global economy in which national boundaries that once framed production processes have eroded. Linked to other trends – including a rise in flexible work, individualization, and the retrenchment of welfare states (as discussed further in Chapters 5 and 8) – this process has been facilitated through advances in information technologies and transportation systems so that merchandise produced in China, India, and the Philippines is available for purchase in many parts of the world, and service centres for multinational businesses (e.g., IBM) can, in theory, be located anywhere on the globe. There have been extensive debates over whether globalization has been a good thing or a bad thing for individuals and for nations (Ranson 2003). Although some individuals and countries have benefited from globalization, there is little doubt that it has led to increased polarization between nations, individuals, and firms that are considered valuable and those that are not (Castells 2000). At the same time, risk has been more widely dispersed, so that individuals and groups that were traditionally sheltered from job insecurity (e.g., men and the middle class) have lost their jobs or been required to work in non-standard employment as a result of globalization (Beck 1999).

The "risk" concept as it is used here and in the subsequent chapters is grounded in the work of Ulrich Beck. According to Beck, we now live in a risk society where

> the collective patterns of life, progress and controllability, full employ-
> ment and exploitation of nature that were typical of the first modernity
> have now been undermined by five interlinked processes: globalization,
> individualization, gender revolution, underemployment, and global risks
> (as ecological crisis and the crash of global financial markets). The real
> theoretical and political challenge of the second modernity is the fact
> that society must respond to all of these challenges simultaneously.
> (1999, 2)

In Beck and Willms's conceptualization (2004, 140), global risks are "systemic, unpredictable, uncertain and infinite." Unlike the relatively predictable risks in old economies, the risks in new economies are more widespread and unpredictable. Within the realm of paid work, risk is thought to be pervasive in new economies, where work is precarious and unpredictable (Kalleberg, 2009).

The IT industry is an example of an industrial sector where national production boundaries have become increasingly eroded, where firms need to compete globally both for product sales and for skilled, relatively well-paid workers, and where work is thought to be uncertain and un-predictable (Duerden Comeau 2004). Large multinational IT firms such as IBM, Microsoft, and Google dominate the industry, employ hundreds of thousands of workers worldwide, and have been the subjects of extensive research in relation to the organization of work. Yet small and mid-sized IT firms, which make up the majority of IT businesses in many Western countries such as Canada, England, the United States, and Australia, have received little research attention in this regard. Hence, in this book we consider the global character of the IT industry and what it is like to work in small and mid-sized IT firms cross-nationally. To do so, we examine data from a sample of these firms in Canada, Australia, England, and the United States.

It is not only the global character of the IT industry that influences what it is like to work in IT firms but also the fact that, in each of our study countries, highly skilled IT workers are predominantly, and dis-proportionately, young men. In Australia, 77 percent of highly skilled IT employees are under the age of forty-five, which compares with 72 percent in Canada, about 75 percent in the United States, and 80 percent in the United Kingdom. Men comprise 81 percent of highly skilled IT workers in the United Kingdom, 80 percent in the United States, about 75 percent in Canada, and 78 percent in Australia (Brooke et al. 2004; Craft Morgan, Marshall, and Maloney 2004; de Hoog et al. 2004; Downie et al. 2004; Duerden Comeau 2004). In this book, we consider the implications of the age and gender demographics of the IT industry by asking how age and gender influence the structure of work and employment relations for IT workers in small and mid-sized IT firms.

The WANE Project

In 2002, the Social Sciences and Humanities Research Council of Canada funded our international project entitled Workforce Aging in the New Economy: A Comparative Study of Information Technology Employment (for more details about the project, see www.wane.ca). The broad objective of WANE was to study the intersection of workforce aging and the restructuring of work in the new economy within the IT industrial sector.[3] In particular, we were interested in examining the nature of work within the industry and how employment relations and human resource practices shape and are shaped by the life-course transitions of workers. Indeed, the life-course perspective influenced our project both conceptually and methodologically (see Chapter 2). According to Elder, the life-course perspective guides the identification of research problems and research designs by making "time, context, and process more salient dimensions of theory and analysis" (1995, 104). For the purpose of our book, two of Elder's life-course principles relating to time and context are particularly relevant: "life-course transitions" (see especially Chapters 4 and 5) and "linked lives" (see especially Chapter 5). Life-course transitions reflect the timing and sequencing of lives and typically involve a change in status. Hence, the school-to-work transition generally happens in early adulthood and involves a change in status from student to employee. The linked-lives concept refers to the idea that such transitions are rarely carried out by individuals in isolation from others. Rather, decisions about life-course transitions are influenced by partners, parents, co-workers, and children (Elder 1995; McMullin and Marshall 2010).

Besides life-course issues, the WANE team was interested in how gender and aging affect the working lives of employees in a typically young, male profession. To examine these issues, a team of researchers from several countries conducted case study research in small and mid-sized IT firms.

The data for our project come from forty-seven small or medium-sized IT firms dispersed across Australia, Canada, England, and the United States (see Chapter 2 for study design and methodology). Data collection involved face-to-face interviews ($n = 399$), web-based surveys ($n = 452$), observation, and human resource policy documentation. Although we do not have a representative sample of IT workers, we do have a unique opportunity to consider gender and age within IT firms of similar size in several countries. More importantly, intensive data provided by multiple members from the same firm allow for a case study analysis that reveals different perspectives on a parallel work experience.

Small IT Firms in a Big IT World

Small IT companies around the globe benefited from the period of immense growth and profit in the information and communication technologies sector in the 1990s. Canadian ICT employment over this period increased dramatically, and the number of employees in computer services grew by a staggering 95.9 percent between 1994 and 1999. In the computer services design and related services industry (the subsector of ICT work that this study is about), total Canadian employment reached a high of 193,505 employees in 2001 and took a moderate dip to 182,551 in 2002. Although comparable data are not available in our other study countries, industry experts have pointed to the global character of this business cycle, and its significance was noted by every firm in our study (see Chapter 2 for details).

The crash of NASDAQ (a technology-heavy stock market) and the massive layoffs at IBM, Nortel, and other multinational IT firms made headlines in 2000 and 2001 and resulted in a bust in the IT business cycle felt across the globe. Less publicized were the layoffs of workers in small firms and the fact that many small IT firms did not survive the downturn in the industry. Clearly, job insecurity, industry volatility, and the associated risks of working in the IT field at this time were high. It was timely, then, that the fieldwork for the WANE project began in 2003. Many of our study companies emerged out of the ashes of the layoffs and company closures associated with the IT bust, thus providing us with a unique glimpse at the meaning of risk among employees and owners in these firms.

As noted above, risk, in relation to new economy work, has recently gained a lot of currency in sociology through the work of Ulrich Beck and others. But empirical assessments of the risk involved in working in or owning small, new economy-type firms are lacking. Is this risk any different from the risk associated with working in any other small firm? If so, how is it different? How is risk influenced by gender and age? As the chapters in this book show, risk in IT employment is heightened by the requirement to update and maintain skills in an industry where the currency of certain skills changes rapidly. This has implications for how IT employees experience work on the basis of both age (see Chapters 6 and 7) and gender (see Chapters 3 and 4) and for how they negotiate their work and family commitments (see Chapter 5).

Locating Women and Men in Paid Work

Workplaces are not gender neutral (Acker 1990, 147). In fact, many workplaces resist accommodations for women and instead require that women fit into a structure of organizational rules and expectations developed around the "worker" who, until recently, has probably been a man and often still is a man in the context of small IT firms. Rothman (1994) points out that, while liberal feminism worked well to defend women's rights to enter male worlds and to earn equal pay for equal work, it does little to defend women's rights to be women. Given the risky context of IT work and the male-dominated nature of IT occupations, then, we wanted to know how women were making a place for themselves in small and mid-sized IT firms. Risks for workers in such firms included working in companies that were often surviving month to month, hoping to keep their operations going and sometimes unable to pay workers on time. In this climate, accommodations for employees were minimal or sometimes impossible.

Men made up a higher proportion of the employees in the firms we studied than did women, mirroring the national context of IT work in all of the study countries. In our final sample, men comprised about 71 percent of our interview respondents and 73 percent of our survey respondents (see Chapter 2 for more detail). Not surprisingly, in all the study countries women were much more likely than men to report that their treatment in their current and prior jobs had been unfavourably affected by their sex (15 to 37 percent of women and 0 to 2 percent of men). Thus, not only were these women working in a risky IT field, but they had also faced challenges to working in IT because they were women. Consistent with national data, women in our sample reported lower incomes than men (see also WANE country reports at www.wane. ca). In Canada, this was true despite women's equal or longer working hours compared with those of the men we surveyed. In all the other countries, women earned less individual income on average but were also much more likely than men to work fewer hours.

Despite these challenges, women's reported perceptions of their pay, benefits, and job security were fairly positive. The women we surveyed in Australia stood out because they were more likely to have very positive perceptions of their jobs, pay, benefits, and security compared with surveyed men from Australia, and they were somewhat more likely to say their pay was related to an assessment of their job performance.

In Canada and the United Kingdom, the picture of pay and job security was mixed; job security was perceived to be good for greater proportions of women than men surveyed in both countries. When it came to assessment of pay, however, gender differences were smaller in Canada compared with the United Kingdom. Canadian women and men (as well as Australian men) we surveyed were among the least likely of IT workers in the four countries to agree their pay was good. Their comparative dissatisfaction with their pay makes sense given that only about one-third of Canadian respondents indicated their pay was related to an assessment of their job performance. One of the challenges of working in a risky context is that pay can be affected by many factors, including contracts, project deadlines, and so on. In Canada, risk associated with pay appeared to affect women and men fairly equally. In the United Kingdom, though a slightly greater share of women reported good fringe benefits and job security, men we surveyed were more likely than women to agree their pay was good, despite being less likely than women to say their pay was related to an assessment of their job performance.

Gaining permanent employment and having added responsibilities, such as supervising the work of others, are markers of career progression. Our survey data showed that, in all the regions, women were more likely than men to be permanently employed.[4] Despite achieving permanent status, surveyed women were much less likely than men to supervise others in all the regions except Canada. Working in small to mid-sized companies can be a challenge for those looking for career progression and development.

Relative Age: Locating Older and Younger Workers in Paid Work
Just as workplaces are not gender neutral, so too they are not age neutral (McMullin, Duerden Comeau, and Jovic 2007; McMullin and Marshall 2001; McMullin and Shuey 2006; Segrave 2001). There is much complexity, however, in identifying age-based biases in paid work, in part because what is meant by older and younger varies along several dimensions.

We know, for instance, that women are considered older workers at younger ages than are men (Rodeheaver 1992). If a job requires physical strength, co-ordination, or stamina, then workers may be defined as old at relatively young ages. In professional sports, this variation is evident: professional golfers may play on the senior tour when they reach fifty, gymnasts are considered old when they are in their twenties, and professional hockey and baseball players are considered old at thirty-five. Finally, the age at which a worker is considered old probably varies depending on the age structure of the occupational or industrial group. Other things being equal, the age at which a worker is defined as old varies with the proportion of older workers in a particular occupational or industrial group. Hence, medical specialists or judges may not be considered older workers until they are well into their sixties, whereas information technology professionals may be considered old when they are in their early forties.

Our survey data for the IT firms studied show that the majority of workers in all study countries are under the age of forty. Between 25 and 30 percent of the employees in the IT firms are in their forties, between 8 and 15 percent are in their fifties, and only between 1 and 3 percent are in their sixties.

How does the age composition of IT employment influence the age at which workers are considered old and the experiences of older IT employees? In one study of displaced software engineers, Fraser (2001, 136) noted that in the industry "there's a tremendous fascination with twenty-year-olds. There's a saying if you're in your thirties, you're expendable. If you're in your forties, you're unhirable." Our preliminary work suggests that this depiction is accurate and that workers are considered old at quite young ages, usually by the time they are in their early forties. As the owner of one of our Australian study firms says (see Chapter 6 for further details),

> if you're going to do innovative programs, you have a "use-by" date, and I would suggest that that's grown considerably to what it was, but I doubt very much whether you're really going to get people at the cutting edge above forty. And I would suggest that real innovation is going to happen below thirty. (2203003, man, age fifty-six, owner, Australia)

Hence, we paint a picture of the location of "older" and "younger" workers in the IT firms studied using forty as the old age marker but noting that it is somewhat arbitrary.

Our data indicate that in Canada and the United Kingdom younger workers are more likely than older workers to agree that their pay is good, but in Australia and the United States the reverse is true. In all study countries, older workers are more likely than younger workers to agree that they are paid fairly, and with the exception of Canada older workers are more likely than younger workers to agree that their pay is associated with job performance. In all of the study countries, older workers are much more likely than younger workers to believe that they are paid fairly, which is perhaps tied to the fact that younger workers report that they earn less than older workers.

In the United States and the United Kingdom, older workers are less likely than younger workers to agree that their fringe benefits are good, but in Canada and Australia there is no difference in this regard. This may point to similarities and differences across countries in health care delivery, which may weigh more on the minds of older workers than younger workers. With the exception of Australia, older workers are less likely than younger workers to agree that their job security is good.

Again with the exception of Australia, older workers are more likely than younger workers to work more than forty hours per week. As one would expect, in all of the study countries older workers are more likely to supervise others than are younger workers. Workers in the United States and United Kingdom versus those in Canada and Australia are generally more likely to report that they are permanently employed, and older respondents in the United States and United Kingdom versus those in Canada and Australia are more likely to report that they are permanently employed; especially in Canada, older workers are less likely than younger workers to report that they are permanently employed.

Our data also show that younger respondents are more likely than older respondents to believe that youth plays a role in being treated unfavourably at work. This is particularly pronounced in Canada, where over a quarter of younger workers believe they are being treated unfavourably in their current jobs because they are too young and over a quarter also believe they were treated unfavourably in their prior jobs because they were too young. Interestingly, about 10 percent of older workers in all of the study countries reported that they were treated unfavourably in a prior job because they were too young, whereas between 5 and 14 percent of older workers in the study countries reported that they were treated unfavourably in a prior job because they were too old.

In summary, age and gender influence various aspects of IT work. What emerges are complex pictures of the advantages and disadvantages of being a man or a woman, old or young, within a risky and dynamic employment setting. Throughout the chapters of this book, we shed light on these complex pictures through in-depth qualitative analyses of IT firms and the individuals within them.

Gender and Age Relations in Paid Work

Although the discussion above provides a useful glimpse at the location of men and women and older and younger workers in the IT firms studied, there is more to the story of gender and age in paid work than can be gleaned from this description. Gender and age relations are bases of social inequality that emerge simultaneously as both structural and individual features of social life (McMullin 2010). At a structural level, gender and age relations are characterized by power relations in which certain groups (e.g., women, youth, old people) are excluded from some privileges and opportunities in society while others (e.g., men and the middle aged) are not. At an individual level, people "do gender" (West and Zimmerman 1987) and "do age" in their everyday interactions with others and through these interactions either reconstruct gender and age relations or gradually modify them. Hence, gender relations structure paid work and unpaid work in such a way that there remains a wage gap, a glass ceiling, and an imbalance in the domestic labour performed by women and men. Yet women and men negotiate their paid and unpaid labour within the context of families and firms and in interaction with one another. In this way, they do gender and simultaneously reconstruct and perhaps work to gradually alter the gender structures that reproduce inequality in paid work.

Older and younger adults have lower rates of labour force participation than middle-aged adults, and when they are unemployed they remain so for longer periods of time (Adams and Walsh 2007; McMullin and Berger 2006). Age discrimination and age stereotyping in paid work have been problematic for decades (McMullin and Marshall 2010; Segrave 2001), yet age as a basis of inequality in paid work is rarely taken seriously. Joan Acker, for instance, suggests that, "currently, age seems to be a significant basis for inequality, as are certain physical inabilities. I believe that although these other differences are important, they are not, at this time, as thoroughly embedded in organizing processes as are gender, race, and class" (2006, 445). Unlike Acker, we argue in this book that age is "thoroughly embedded in organizing processes" in paid work.

Inequality Regimes

Drawing heavily on the work of Acker (2006, 443), we define "inequality regimes" as loosely interrelated *inequality projects* that result in and maintain patterned discrepancies in the rewards and privileges that people enjoy. Inequality projects refer to the practices, processes, actions, and meanings that connect social structures with everyday experiences (Acker 2006; Omi and Winant 1994). Gender regimes (see Connell 2002) and age regimes are examples of inequality regimes, and gender and age projects are examples of inequality projects; these projects occur at both the structural level and the interpersonal level. People make assumptions about others on the basis of their gender and age and interact with them accordingly. It is through structural and interactional gender and age projects that gender regimes and age regimes become "common sense" (Omi and Winant 1994), conventional (Giddens 1993), or deep structures (Sewell 1992). In other words, it is through our experiences with gender and age projects that we internalize gender and age classification schema and make assessments about our own gender and age identities and those of others.

In the context of paid work, inequality projects implicate individuals in the production and reproduction of inequality as they construct, reproduce, and gradually transform gender and age relations within firms through their daily interactions. Thus, personal attitudes and identities, which are dynamic and changing, can influence the structure and evolution of organizations such as workplaces. On this ground, then, inequality regimes are not static; rather, they transform over time, in response to interactions among individuals, shifting social and economic circumstances, and as a result of human agency and interaction. The nature of the inequality regimes and the character of gender and age projects enacted by individuals are influenced by and, in turn, influence workplace culture.

Workplace culture is a concept that is used frequently in this book and refers to a shared system of practices, knowledge, traditions, attitudes, and values that workers use to manage and understand their daily interactions. According to Gary Alan Fine (2006, 3), "workplaces have distinct cultures, and more significantly, local cultural themes shape the identity of those who labor on the shopfloor ... From a social-psychological perspective, a single 'occupation' may incorporate alternative identities that can be constructed by workers according to their local cultures." Hence, workplace cultures can vary significantly depending on the specific characteristics of firms and the individuals who do gender and age within them.

Gender Projects and Regimes
In Part 2 of this book, we examine whether and how gender projects and regimes emerge in IT firms. The chapters in this section show that gender

projects shape the character of IT firms such that the firms emerge as gender regimes. Drawing on R.W. Connell's concept of gender regimes, Gillian Ranson and Heather Dryburgh show in Chapter 3 how pervasive sex-segregated employment is within our case study firms and how workplaces organize around particular gender regimes. They identify four gender regimes that may classify most of these firms. These gender regimes emerge out of the daily gender projects in which individuals within the firms engage.

The most common is the *masculinist gender regime*. Firms in this regime employed very few women, especially in highly skilled technical jobs and managerial positions. Their workplace cultures are organized around masculine activities. Recruitment is geared to "fit" within the masculine workplace culture, and where women were employed in managerial or technical roles they conformed to a male ethos of work. The masculinist gender regime stands in contrast to the *benignly paternalistic gender regime*. This type of gender regime is characterized by little employment of women but with women holding managerial and technical positions. Leadership in these stable, financially secure firms was by older "family men," and work relationships were collegial and supportive. In *benignly maternalistic gender regimes*, firms employed or tried to employ more women in supervisory and project management positions than was true in the other firms, and the organization of work and the workplace culture tended to be more feminine and maternal. Finally, only one firm in our study could be described as having a *balanced gender regime*. In this firm, two of the four partners and six of the ten employees were women, and older, more experienced workers were valued. There was much emphasis placed on work-life balance and workplace flexibility, which benefited both the men and the women in the firm.

Tammy Duerden Comeau and Candace Kemp take this analysis further in Chapter 4 by showing how there are sub-regimes within the masculinist gender regime that create environments that disadvantage women and older workers. For instance, they identify firms that may be characterized by *entrepreneurial masculinity*, in which workers are expected to be entrepreneurial themselves, work exceptionally long hours, and be highly committed to the firm – clearly a situation that is better suited to younger, single workers, often men. Like the benignly paternalistic firms identified in Chapter 3, firms sometimes take on a traditional familial character in which there is a father figure, and women in the firm work in supportive capacities. This characteristic is often combined with a *brotherhood* style of masculinity, where the exclusion of women, older workers, and men who just "don't fit in" is typical. Masculinity takes on a *craftsman*-like character in yet other firms where value is placed on skill and the rejection of bureaucracy.

In Chapter 5, Ingrid Arnet Connidis and Candace Kemp consider the gender projects at play in the firms studied as women and men enter different life-course stages, especially the transitions to marriage and parenthood. Framed within the idea that individualism is a gender project linked to globalization, Connidis and Kemp show that the firms within the masculinist gender regime value the "unencumbered worker" (Acker 2006, 448). The global rise of individualism and its importance in small IT firms leads to fewer women being employed in small IT firms, a gender project in which opportunities favour men over women.

Age Projects and Regimes

In Part 3, our focus turns to the issue of age and how age projects and regimes emerge within the context of IT employment. In Chapter 6, Julie McMullin, Emily Jovic, and Tammy Duerden Comeau explicitly consider the relationship between age and generations of IT workers. They ask whether generational discourse is invoked to create workplace cultures that favour certain ages of workers or generations in other countries as well as Canada (see also McMullin, Duerden Comeau, and Jovic 2007). Results in this chapter show that IT workers mobilize "generational" discourse and draw on notions of "generational affinity" with comput-ing technology (e.g., the fact that people of different ages are immersed to varying degrees in different computing technologies) in explaining the youthful profile of IT workers and employees' differing levels of technological expertise.

Julie McMullin and Tammy Duerden Comeau consider age relations and ageism more explicitly in Chapter 7. Computing technology, and the ability of older workers to adapt to it, have comprised a significant component of ageist assumptions. Research has shown that older workers are generally characterized as less technologically adept and less interested in new technologies. In spite of the pervasive nature of these stereotypes, little research has examined whether and how these stereotypes manifest in high-skill computing work and whether discriminatory practices based on age are evident in the field. The chapter shows that ageist attitudes and negative stereotypes about older workers' abilities to adapt to and train on new technologies influence hiring practices. It also shows that workers who would be considered young in other industries (those in their thirties) are often considered old in this industry. Assumptions about older workers' abilities reinforce and legitimate discriminatory hiring practices, thereby leaving older workers highly vulnerable to unemployment and redundancy in the IT industry.

Finally, in Chapter 8, Emily Jovic and Julie McMullin draw on the results of the preceding chapters to conclude that small and mid-sized IT companies produce and reproduce gender- and age-based inequalities. Exemplary workers within this industry are young men who not only are unencumbered but also are seen as naturally better able to do the work required of IT professionals. The importance of "fitting in" in the workplace cultures of these firms heightens the extent to which the exemplary worker is idealized. Although this will not come as news to scholars in the field of gender studies, the fact that age is implicated in these processes of exclusion, and the fact that age and gender intersect in this regard, suggest that more attention must be paid to relative age as a basis of inequality in paid work.

Notes

1 Most of the firms in our study were small, employing between four and twenty people. All employed fewer than 250 people, thus corresponding to the widely held definition of small and mid-sized enterprises (SMEs) (European Commission 2005).

2 Because we were interested in highly skilled knowledge work that is characteristic of new economy employment, our primary focus is on the service subsector of IT firms that is involved with consulting and the development of software and computer systems (Duerden Comeau 2003, 1). Employment in software and computer services constitutes close to half of information and communication technologies (ICT) employment in Canada (Industry Canada 2006).

3 Our focus is on one industry within IT or ICT services: namely, the computer design and related services industry. In Industry Canada data, total ICT services typically include software publishers, telecommunications services, cable and other program distributors, Internet service providers, data processing, hosting and related services, and often ICT wholesaling. Where possible here, we use the term "IT," reflecting our interest in the computer design sector (NAICS 54151) of ICT services.

4 The way that firms made use of contractors varied across the study sample; decisions about whether they should be considered as employees of individual firms, and therefore included in the sample, may also have varied across the study countries.

References

Acker, J. 1990. Hierarchies, jobs, bodies: Theory of gendered organizations. *Gender and Society* 4, 2: 139-58.

–. 2006. Inequality regimes: Gender, class, and race in organizations. *Gender and Society* 20, 4: 441-64.

Adams, T., and S. Walsh. 2007. *The organization and experience of work.* Toronto: Thomson Nelson.

Beck, U. 1999. *World risk society.* Cambridge, UK: Polity Press.

Beck, U., and J. Willms. 2004. *Conversations with Ulrich Beck.* Trans. M. Pollak. Cambridge, UK: Polity Press.

Brooke, L., L. Rolland, E. Jones, and C. Topple. 2004. *The Australian information technology workforce and industry context.* WANE International Report 3. London, ON: University of Western Ontario, Workforce Aging in the New Economy (WANE).

Castells, M. 1996. *The rise of the network society.* Cambridge, UK: Blackwell.

–. 2000. Toward a sociology of the network society. *Contemporary Sociology* 29, 5: 693-99.

Connell, R.W. 2002. *Gender.* Cambridge, UK: Polity Press.

Craft Morgan, J., V.W. Marshall, and M. Maloney. 2004. *The U.S. information technology workforce in the new economy.* WANE International Report 2. London, ON: University of Western Ontario, Workforce Aging in the New Economy (WANE).

de Hoog, A., K. Platman, P. Taylor, and A. Vogel. 2004. *Workforce ageing and information technology employment in Germany, the Netherlands, and the United Kingdom.* WANE International Report 4. London, ON: University of Western Ontario, Workforce Aging in the New Economy (WANE).

Downie, R., H.B. Dryburgh, J.A. McMullin, and G. Ranson. 2004. *A profile of information technology employment in Canada.* WANE International Report 1. London, ON: University of Western Ontario, Workforce Aging in the New Economy (WANE).

Duerden Comeau, T. 2003. *Cross-national comparison of information technology employment.* WANE International Report 5. London, ON: University of Western Ontario, Workforce Aging in the New Economy (WANE).

Elder, G.H. Jr. 1995. The life course paradigm: Historical, comparative, and developmental perspectives. In *Examining lives and context: Perspectives on the ecology of human development,* ed. P. Moen, G.H. Elder Jr., and K. Luscher, 101-40. Washington, DC: American Psychological Association Press.

European Commission. 2005. *The new SME definition: User guide and model declaration.* Brussels: European Commission Publications Office. http://ec.europa.eu/.

Fine, G.A. 2006. Shopfloor cultures: The idioculture of production in operational meteorology. *Sociological Quarterly* 47, 1: 1-19.

Fraser, J.A. 2001. *White-collar sweatshop: The deterioration of work and its rewards in corporate America.* New York: Norton.

Giddens, A. 1993. *New rules of sociological method: A positive critique of interpretative sociologies.* 2nd ed. Stanford: Stanford University Press.

Industry Canada. 2006. *Canadian ICT sector profile.* Information and Communications Technologies Branch, Industry Canada, Ottawa. http://strategis.ic.gc.ca/.

Kalleberg, A.L. 2009. 2008 presidential address: Precarious work, insecure workers: Employment relations in transition. *American Sociological Review* 74: 1-22.

McMullin, J.A. 2010. *Understanding social inequality: Intersections of class, age, gender, and ethnicity in Canada.* Toronto: Oxford University Press.

McMullin, J.A., and E. Berger. 2006. Gendered ageism/age(ed) sexism: The case of unemployed older workers. In *Age matters: Re-aligning feminist thinking,* ed. T. Calasanti and K. Slevin, 201-24. New York: Routledge.

McMullin, J.A., T. Duerden Comeau, and E. Jovic. 2007. Generational affinities and discourses of differences: A case study of highly skilled information technology workers. *British Journal of Sociology* 58, 2: 297-316.

McMullin, J.A., and V.W. Marshall. 2001. Ageism, age relations, and garment industry work in Montreal. *Gerontologist* 41, 1: 111-22.

–, eds. 2010. *Aging and working in the new economy: Changing career structures in small IT firms.* Camberly, UK: Edward Elgar.

McMullin, J.A., and K.M. Shuey. 2006. Ageing, disability, and workplace accommodations. *Ageing and Society* 26: 1-17.

Omi, M., and H. Winant. 1994. *Racial formation in the United States from the 1960s to the 1990s.* 2nd ed. New York: Routledge.

Ranson, G. 2003. Understanding the "new economy": A conceptual journey. WANE Working Paper 3. London, ON: University of Western Ontario, Workforce Aging in the New Economy (WANE).

Rodeheaver, D. 1992. Labour market progeria: On the life expectancy of presentability among working women. In *Gender and aging,* ed. L. Glasse and J. Hendricks, 99-110. Amityville, NY: Baywood Publishing.

Rothman, B. 1994. Beyond mothers and fathers: Ideology in a patriarchal society. In *Mothering: Ideology, experience, and agency,* ed. E.N. Glenn, G. Chang, and L.R. Forcie, 139-57. New York: Routledge.

Segrave, K. 2001. *Age discrimination by employers.* Jefferson, NC: McFarland.

Sewell, W.H.J. Jr. 1992. A theory of structure: Duality, agency, and transformation. *American Journal of Sociology* 98, 1: 1-29.

WANE country reports. http://www.wane.ca.

West, C., and D. Zimmerman. 1987. Doing gender. *Gender and Society* 1, 2: 125-51.

2
Methods
Emily Jovic, Julie McMullin, and
Tammy Duerden Comeau

Research Design

To address the broader WANE study objectives (see Chapter 1), a case study research design was employed whereby multiple data sources were used to establish an in-depth understanding of a given research problem in a particular context (see Marshall 1999 for an overview of our approach). This method allows for the consideration of multiple points of view that, when taken together, permit a better understanding of the relationships among members in a given organization (Ragin 1987, 1994, 2000). Thus, the intensive data provided by multiple staff from the same firm reveal different perspectives on parallel work experiences. A key strength of this case study approach is its ability to "produce a description of the complexity of social life" (Marshall 1999, 380). Comparing cases informs us about how different types of institutions and institutional arrangements work and how they affect relationships among their members. We can assess the link between social, economic, and political processes and institutional arrangements in the workplace and their ultimate effects on workers. Case studies do not provide a statistically representative sample, so cross-national and cross-company comparisons must be made on an "interpretive basis" (Marshall 1999, 387). This means that case study analyses must be informed by theoretical and contextual considerations.

In WANE, a case is broadly defined as an IT firm. Criteria were established for firms to be eligible for participation in the study. First, they needed to comprise mostly software-related IT occupations. This often, but not always, corresponded to specific industry codes.[1] Firms had to be in operation at least one year and have four or more staff. The conditions of participation could not compromise data collection. Thus, firms were required to support employee involvement in the study, provide access to human resources (HR) documents, and in most cases allow

Table 2.1

City/regional representation of case study firms

Team	City/region
Australia	Melbourne, Sydney, Brisbane, the Gold Coast
Canada	London, Ottawa, Calgary
England*	Cambridgeshire, West Midlands, London, Southeast England, Southwest England
United States	North Carolina (NC) – Research Triangle Region, Florida (FL) – Tallahassee

* This team was also involved in a case study of a German IT firm. Researchers in Germany and the Netherlands conducted a further eight case studies in those countries.

researchers to observe on-site for a predetermined amount of time. A focus on smaller businesses was salient as very little research on IT work has considered small to medium-sized enterprises (SMEs), which are prevalent in all of the study countries. In 2001, for example, 96 percent of firms in Canada and 93 percent of computer services businesses in the United Kingdom employed fewer than ten people (Bjornsson 2001; Da Pont 2003). Similarly, in Australia, 88 percent of IT firms employed only up to four workers, and 29 percent of IT workers were employed in small firms in 2001 (Brooke et al. 2004).

Within each country, IT firms were further targeted on other criteria suited to the particular region and industry context. Geographical location was a primary and effective means of seeking participants, for convenience and cost effectiveness and because of the proximity and, in some cases, association of researcher postsecondary institutions with sector "hot beds" – regions in which there is a relatively high concentration of IT activity. Table 2.1 outlines the cities and regions from which the case studies were selected in each country. In some regional contexts, particularly Australia and England, case firms were also monitored in order to maximize heterogeneity beyond the baseline conditions outlined above. Criteria in this regard included IT subsector, firm ownership arrangements and management structures, and the demographic composition of staff (e.g., gender, age).

Such variation in the selection of firms in the sample creates a potential for bias since some may have been specifically targeted or are particularly sensitive to certain workforce issues. This would be problematic if the aim of the study was to illustrate broader trends and to generalize these findings to the IT industry as a whole; however, the intent here is to use mixed methodology to document experiences and processes relating to IT work at one point in time. There is the opportunity to consider working in the information technology sector from the perspectives of employees, managers, consultants, and owners in firms of similar size across four countries. Thus, for our purposes, this type of sampling is appropriate.

Case Study Sampling, Key Informants, and Company Access

National teams developed sampling strategies that were best suited to the particular contexts and contours of their locations and industries. Thus, potential participant firms were approached in ways that varied by national region. Despite the existence of country-specific industry classifications, there were few, if any, comprehensive listings available for IT businesses. As a result, research teams used a number of strategies to identify samples of firms. City and IT business directories, media coverage, and business and personal networking with key informants were employed to varying degrees to define sampling frames and to recruit participant firms in each national region. Teams in Canada and the United States relied largely on a sampling frame strategy and key informants; Australia and England employed media releases, IT business directories, key informants, and a business information kit.

In Canada, a sampling frame was defined in each locale (London, Ottawa, Calgary) using city and IT business directories ($n = 178$). Then a series of short, sampling frame telephone surveys ($n = 100$) was conducted in spring 2004 to gain access to firms and to learn more about the local IT landscape. Data were collected at this stage to inform regional IT context and case firm eligibility. Sampling frame respondents, usually firm owners or senior management personnel, were asked basic questions about the firm (e.g., how long the firm had been in business, what products or services it provided, etc.), its workforce (e.g., number of employees, demographic composition), and the IT field in general (e.g., subcontracting, skilled worker shortages). They were also asked if they would be willing to be contacted again about involvement in case studies and/or key informant interviews. Virtually all of the Canadian case firms were recruited through this sampling frame interview process; one case came from a contact list provided by one of four key informants.

The US NC team also employed a similar sampling frame methodology, drawing on regional professional association directories. Those who completed a sampling frame survey ($n = 59$ in NC) and whose firms were eligible (see criteria above) were asked if they would participate in a key informant interview; snowball sampling was used to recruit additional key informants. In-person, key informant interviews ($n = 46$)

Table 2.2

Time frame for the case study fieldwork

Region	Case study start	Case study end
Australia	October 2004	March 2006
Canada	September 2004	October 2005
England	May 2004	May 2005
United States	July 2004	February 2006

were conducted with industry representatives and business executives in order to learn about their perspectives on IT employment and workforce aging issues. These interviews also aided in the identification of firms that might be suitable for, and amenable to, participation in case studies. Because there were far fewer IT firms in the Tallahassee region, the US FL team directly recruited off a regional listing of IT firms.

Australia took a different approach to recruitment, forgoing the sampling frame interview method. Instead, the team used print media releases to raise awareness about the study and disseminated study information to local business councils and technology networks. A formal business information kit was created for distribution through these various channels, and interested parties returned an enclosed "expression of interest" form to the team, which initiated the case study process. Many Australian case firms were therefore self-selected into the project; additional firms were tapped through referrals and social contacts.

For its research in England, the UK-based team employed media releases and an information kit. It also enlisted the help of the UK employer organization for the IT sector, which circulated details of the study to its members. One firm was recruited in this way; the rest were approached directly through cold-calling using contact information from technical directories, listings, and recommendations. Case firm recruitment in the other European countries employed media releases, personal contacts (the Netherlands), and formal networks (Germany).

Negotiations with potential case study firms began in mid-2004, and fieldwork continued through early 2006. Table 2.2 shows the general time frame for the case study-related fieldwork in each country.

In most cases, negotiations entailed a series of telephone conversations and eventually a meeting between the research team leader and the company executive – usually the firm owner(s) and/or senior management. Owners and managers who agreed to have their companies participate in the study signed a case study agreement form on behalf

Table 2.3

WANE data sources

Type of data	Description and format
Observational notes	Typed/handwritten notes recorded after each visit *Format:* electronic documents
Archival data	Publicly available sources such as newspaper articles and websites as well as firm-specific policy and documents *Format:* mix of print and electronic
In-depth interviews	Face-to-face interviews *Format:* tape- or digitally recorded and transcribed; electronic documents
Web surveys	Self-administered, online questionnaire; quantitative data compiled by hosting firm, MSI *Format:* quantitative data sets (i.e., SPSS) and individual electronic report summaries

of the firm, outlining mutually determined parameters of participation. Typically, firms agreed to supply employee contact information, access to HR policies, and employee participation time. In return, the research teams pledged to provide participating companies with first access to international research reports. Feedback reports were also provided to each firm in Canada and the United States and to the larger English firms.

Data Collection
An ongoing requirement in our case study method was to establish a detailed context for each case, and this was accomplished by collecting data from a range of sources. Table 2.3 summarizes the primary sources of information and their formats.

Whenever researchers entered a firm, they took *observational notes* about the environment and how work was structured. These notes were recorded after most company visits, including negotiations and interviews. *Archival data* were also collected for each case study company from publicly available sources such as business trade journals, magazine or newspaper articles, and company websites, as well as firm-specific newsletters, human resource policy documents, annual reports, and collective agreements. Where applicable (not all firms had such information available), HR documents and policy-related material were provided by the CEO or administrative/HR staff. Finally, we conducted both *in-depth, qualitative interviews* and self-administered *web surveys* with managers and employees at each case study firm.

In-depth interviews were conducted with company executives, human resource managers, and employees in various occupational groups. Respondents were asked about their personal histories and experiences with IT work, and managers were also asked about their views of the IT field in general. As well, demographic attributes (e.g., gender, age, job title, tenure at firm, family status) were gathered from the interviews for each participant. The number of interviews targeted at each firm depended largely on characteristics of the organization, such as number of employees and occupational groups. For many of the firms, particularly the smaller ones, all employees and managers were invited to take part. In some cases, however, research teams solicited a particular profile of respondents using characteristics such as age, gender, occupational role, or length of tenure; in other cases, management made autonomous exclusions – such as those in certain roles (e.g., non-IT positions) or contract workers.

The firm provided contact information for potential participants, usually most or all of its employees, and qualitative interview invitations were delivered to each person. Employees were then contacted by telephone or email to see if they were interested in participating. If an individual declined the request, there was no further attempt to involve that person. For those who agreed, a convenient time was arranged for an interview. Most interviews took place in a private office or meeting room at the respondent's place of work; occasionally, they occurred in a coffee shop, off work premises, or via telephone at the discretion or preference of the interviewee. In some cases, a company liaison facilitated the scheduling. Interviews were recorded on tape and/or digitally. They generally lasted for about one hour but ranged from thirty minutes to more than three hours. The Canadian team conducted twenty-four additional interviews – eleven with contract workers, eight with former large-firm workers, and four with key informants. As well, US researchers completed thirty-five key informant interviews alongside their case firm interviews.

Managers and employees were invited to complete a self-administered web survey. The online strategy suits this project as IT professionals are well versed in computers and web applications. We would have provided a paper version of the survey if that was the preference; none of the respondents made this request. Invitations to participate in the web survey were typically distributed following the in-depth interview;

in some cases, they were emailed to respondents beforehand or without an interview at all. Each person was given a unique ID and password that were used to access the survey. Respondents were generally sent an introductory letter by WANE researchers, followed by a series of automatically generated email reminders.

The web survey solicited information about demographic characteristics, work history, attitudes about older and younger workers, nonstandard employment practices, and so on. Retrospective questions about life-course transitions, using well-established procedures that map out the timing and sequencing of individual lives, were also included (Marshall et al. 2001). Web surveys took approximately forty to sixty minutes to complete and could be filled out at the discretion of respondents from any location with Internet access. An important feature of the survey was the ability for respondents to complete it in stages, over days or weeks, as required. The qualitative and quantitative components of this research are complementary, with the former providing information on meaning and process and the latter providing data that allow us to describe, contextualize, and, to a limited extent, generalize about the nature of work in IT firms.

Management input and logistical considerations meant that not all employees in all firms were targeted for inclusion, particularly in larger companies. Across the 47 case study firms in four countries, there were 399 in-depth interviews and 452 web surveys (49 of those were partial completions). There was significant, but not perfect, overlap between the interviews and web surveys: 45 percent of respondents did both; 23 percent completed an interview but no survey; and 32 percent filled out a web survey only. This variation reflects both participant- and researcher-initiated selection processes. Table 2.4 shows how the interviews and surveys are divided among the four countries.

The overall participation rate for the interviews was 86 percent, ranging from 81 percent in Canada to 100 percent in England. This figure represents the number of viable interview transcripts (i.e., electronic failures are excluded) out of the total number of eligible participants in each country. As noted previously, both researcher considerations and management dictates meant that not all employees at all firms were invited to participate. The participation rate reflects both direct and soft refusals from potential interviewees as well as those who may have agreed but did not participate for whatever reason. The English team engaged in negotiations with managers and requested interviews once they were on-site, which served to augment their participation rate.

Table 2.4

Interview participation, survey response, and partial completion rates

	Region		Interviews		Surveys	
	#	Participation rate (%)[1]	#	Response rate (%)[1]	# Complete	Partials (%)[2]
Australia	91	82	81	22	69	15
Canada	141	81	107	60	94	12
England	61	100	125	75	117	6
United States	106	90	139	50[3]	123	12
Total	399	86	452	46	403	11

1 Participation and response rates are calculated using the number of interview transcripts/ survey records out of the number of *eligible* respondents at each firm; eligible respondents are those who were invited to participate in the study.

2 The heading "Partials" refers to the proportion of incomplete survey records (i.e., those who completed at least the first section but not the entire survey; does not include question non-responses).

3 One US case, a medium-sized firm of more than 100 staff, experienced complications with data collection because company officials had not fully bought in to study participation, and the project never really took off in that location. Removing these cases from the US response rate yields a cleaned rate of 67 percent. Responses from this company remain available for analysis.

The overall survey response rate was 46 percent and ranged from a low of 22 percent in Australia to a high of 75 percent in England. These rates were influenced by lower participation in larger firms, where nearly all employees received a survey invitation yet had little or no contact with the research team. In smaller firms, most or all employees were interviewed. This response rate was also impacted in certain firms where management thought there was too much overlap between interview and survey content. Most respondents ($n = 403$, or 89 percent) completed the survey in full; regional partial completion rates were between 6 and 15 percent.

Ethics

Research involving people and under the auspices of a postsecondary institution must be approved by an ethics review board. Prior to entering the field, research teams from each national region were required to submit an application for ethics approval at their home institutions. This process aims to preserve the personal rights and dignity of participants by minimizing risks and outlining best practices for gaining consent and preserving the confidentiality of all data collected over the duration of the study.

Consent forms were signed by all case study participants. On this form, respondents were informed that they could refuse to answer any questions asked and could decide to end participation at any point. For telephone interviews, informed consent was sought verbally. All ethics protocols were followed. Participants (both firms and individuals) are identified by ID numbers, and transcripts have been blinded to eliminate traceable information such as surnames, products, websites, client names, and associated business names. Further, information provided by employees was not revealed to their employers.

In terms of data storage, all audiotapes, written records, transcribed interviews, notes, and other relevant information are kept in locked filing cabinets in locked offices. All project data are stored on a secure server, and tapes will be destroyed after analysis. The web-based survey is housed on a secure site requiring password access. Only the principal investigator, co-investigators, their research staff, and the company responsible for administering the web survey have access to raw data.

Data Management

The WANE team contracted a private firm, MSI International, to process the web survey responses and to provide data sets, open-text responses, and a methodology report. As the data from the self-administered online surveys came in, researchers produced summary statistics such as frequencies, means, and cross-tabulations.

For the qualitative data, all in-depth interviews were transcribed verbatim, entered into a qualitative data analysis software package (Nvivo), and coded by identifying meaningful themes and trends. The transcripts were coded in Nvivo using very general categories, or "housekeeping codes," which were intended to provide some basic organization to a large volume of data (Lofland and Lofland 1995). There are six broad categories of codes reflecting the proposed research questions – (1) employment relations, (2) diversity (e.g., gender, age, ethnicity, class), (3) life-course transitions, (4) human resources management, (5) current employment, and (6) health – and twenty separate housekeeping nodes or containers of interview text within the larger categories.

To facilitate comparative case analysis, the research team developed a case study document template. This template was designed to address the five proposed research objectives, to provide a description and history of each case study firm, and to consider policy implications. A case study report was written for each case study firm. Additional comparative analyses are being conducted by pooling within-country case studies and examining differences and similarities across geographical regions, size of

Table 2.5

Firm characteristics

	Region				Total	
	Australia	Canada	England	US	#	%
Firm size						
4-20	9	17	4	7	37	79
21-99	1	1	2	3	7	15
100-250	1	0	1	1	3	6
Firm age						
<5 years	2	4	3	2	11	24
5-10 years	5	6	2	6	19	40
11-20 years	2	7	1	3	13	28
21+ years	2	1	1	0	4	8
Firm specialization						
Software/web development	6	13	7	9	35	75
Systems analysis/support	1	1	0	1	3	6
Consulting/business	4	4	0	0	8	17
Other	0	0	0	1	1	2
# Case study firms	11	18	7	11	47	

firm, type of firm, and so forth. In this way, we can look for explanations first within firms, then within the context of a single region (Australia, Canada, England, United States), and then within the multiple contexts of region, size, type of firm, and other factors that emerge as relevant.

Sample Characteristics: Firms

From mid-2004 through early 2006, forty-seven firms took part in the study, with 586 unique individuals participating in interviews and/or web surveys, responding to questions on a wide range of topics. To formulate a descriptive snapshot of the sample of IT firms and workers in this study, a sample profile was compiled using demographic variables and individual- and firm-level information collected during the course of the fieldwork. Table 2.5 presents a firm-level profile broken down by country of size/number of employees, age of operation, and company specialization. Keeping with the project's interest in understudied small and mid-sized businesses, the majority of case study firms (*n* = 37, or 79 percent) were small, employing just 4 to 20 people. Seven firms employed between 21 and 99 workers, and three had between 100 and 250 staff.

Pinpointing how long these firms had been in business proved challenging because many had experienced an assortment of mergers, divisions, and name changes. Thus, the reported year of inception may vary on these terms. From the data on offer, firms were in operation on average 9.8 years; however, nearly half were less than 8 years old. Three-quarters of the firms were involved with software and/or web development. Six percent of the firms focused on systems analysis and support functions, and 19 percent were involved in consulting, business, or other endeavours.

Sample Characteristics: Participants

Demographic attributes collected during in-depth interviews help to provide a snapshot of the IT workers in our study. Table 2.6 contains a sample profile by country of selected demographic characteristics of those who participated in the interviews (I) and web surveys (S).

Survey and interview samples overlap considerably, and their descriptive statistics correspond closely; for illustrative purposes, the interview data will be discussed here. Although we make no claim that the sample is representative of the IT industry as a whole, the profile is comparable to reports of industry and labour force composition (e.g., Gunderson, Jacobs, and Vaillancourt 2005 for Canada). In particular, our sample reflects industry trends in the distribution of gender (male dominated) and age (generally younger than overall labour force averages).

Interview participants ranged in age from 19 to 63, with a mean of 38.4 years. In England and the United States, respondents were, on average, slightly older (40 years) compared with those in Canada and Australia (approximately 37.4 years). Labour force statistics from Canada indicate a mean age for IT workers of 36.4 years, with an even lower average (35.4 years) for private-sector firms (Gunderson, Jacobs, and Vaillancourt 2005). Interest in workforce aging issues among the research teams, and potentially among some of the respondents themselves, may have contributed to a slightly higher average age of participants. The sample was male dominated – nearly three-quarters (71 percent) were men; the proportion of women (29 percent), though low, was comparable to industry averages (e.g., 27 percent in Canada; Gunderson, Jacobs, and Vaillancourt 2005). Most of the respondents (73 percent) were either married or in common-law relationships; 20 percent were single/never married, and 7 percent were separated, divorced, or widowed. More than half (56 percent) were parents. A small proportion of respondents (12.6 percent) were identified as visible minorities. There were considerable regional differences in this designation, with Australia and the United States having higher proportions of visible minorities in their samples compared with Canada and England.

Table 2.6

Sample characteristics

Interview/survey		Australia		Canada		England		US		All regions	
		I	S	I	S	I	S	I	S	I	S
N		91	81	141	107	61	125	103	139	399	452
Age (in years)[1]	mean	37.6	38.1	37.2	37.4	40.0	37.8	40.0	38.7	38.4	38.0
	median	37.0	35.0	37.0	38.0	39.0	36.0	41.0	38.5	38.0	37.0
	range	21-61	23-62	19-62	20-63	22-63	21-64	23-63	20-63	19-63	20-64
	% age 45+	27.6	27.9	24.8	19.8	33.3	27.4	33.3	28.7	28.9	25.8
Gender	% female	40.7	34.8	23.4	23.4	26.2	23.1	26.4	30.6	28.6	27.5
	% male	59.3	65.2	76.6	76.6	73.8	76.9	73.6	69.4	71.4	72.5
Marital status	% married/cohabiting	75.9	75.7	65.9	68.1	71.2	73.7	80.8	71.4	72.8	72.1
	% single/never married	17.7	20.1	25.2	22.3	20.3	19.5	13.1	23.0	19.6	21.3
	% separated/divorced	6.3	4.3	8.9	9.6	8.5	6.8	6.1	5.6	7.5	6.4
Parental status	% with children	45.9	45.7	54.4	51.1	67.9	51.7	61.6	47.6	56.4	49.3
Minority status[2]	% visible minority	17.6	5.8	6.4	9.6	6.0	5.1	20.7	15.4[2]	12.6	9.4

1 For the interviews, "age" was reported at the time of the interview; for the surveys, "age" was calculated as at 2005 using the respondent's birth year; this is reflected in discrepancies in age range.

2 US survey respondents were asked a filter question – "are you Spanish/Hispanic/Latino" – followed by a "select all that apply" race question; all other regions were asked, "are you a member of an ethnic/visible minority group?"

Table 2.7

Interview sample characteristics: Occupations

	Australia	Canada	England	US	All regions	N
Occupation						398
IT/technical role %	48.4	41.8	37.7	36.2	41.2	164
IT/other role %	14.3	14.2	14.8	34.3	19.6	78
IT/management role %	19.8	17.7	23.0	17.1	18.1	75
Non-IT role %	9.9	13.5	13.1	6.7	10.8	43
CEOs/presidents %	7.7	12.8	11.5	5.7	9.5	38
Contractor %	7.8	12.1	0	0	6.3	398
Job tenure (in years)						388
mean	5.2	5.3	7.5	3.3	5.1	
median	3.0	4.0	7.0	2.0	4.0	
range	0-29	0-21	0-30	0-19	0-30	
N	91	141	61	103		

In addition to demographic characteristics, occupational data were collected in the surveys and through descriptive information contained in the in-depth interviews. From the surveys, 80 percent of respondents reported working in one of twenty-six IT/technical roles, while 20 percent held non-IT positions. Interview respondents were asked about their jobs and tasks, and ten broad occupational categories were distilled from this more detailed qualitative data. These job groupings were further refined into IT/technical roles (programmers, engineers, technicians), IT/other roles (analysts, other), non-IT roles (administration, HR, sales/marketing), management (IT managers), and CEOs/presidents. Most respondents (79 percent) worked in positions that entailed a considerable technical component – programmers, engineers, technicians, analysts, and IT management. Table 2.7 contains a sample profile by country of occupation-related characteristics of the workers who were interviewed. Australia and Canada included some contract workers in their samples, while England and the United States did not. In some cases, based on the nature of their employment relationship, these workers would have been excluded from the original contact list by firm management. Finally, for job tenure, respondents were employed with their firms for a mean of 5.1 years. There was some regional variation, with English employees more likely, on average, to have longer tenures (7.5 years) and American workers shorter ones (3.3 years).

Table 2.8

Interview sample characteristics: Occupations by gender and age

	Gender		Age	
	Women	Men	<45	>45
Occupation				
IT/technical role %	27.2	46.8	49.1	27.5
IT/other role %	33.3	14.1	19.1	19.3
IT/management role %	12.3	21.5	19.1	17.4
Non-IT role %	23.7	5.6	6.0	19.3
CEOs/presidents %	3.5	12.0	6.7	16.5
Contractor %	8.0	5.6	7.1	3.7
Job tenure (in years)				
mean	4.5	5.4	4.0	7.8
median	3.0	4.0	3.0	5.5
range	0-26	0-30	0-17	0-30
N	114	284	267	109

Given the skewed composition of the IT workforce in general, it is also worthwhile to consider the distribution of occupational roles by gender and by age. In Table 2.8, the same job roles are broken down along these lines. Generally, men are concentrated in the technical (47 percent) and management roles (22 percent) and as upper management/owners (12 percent). Women are less prevalent in these jobs; however, they are overrepresented in the IT/other category (33.3 percent), which includes titles such as business analyst and technical writer, and more importantly in the non-IT roles (24 percent), such as administrative assistants and human resources personnel. Thus, though the female composition of the sample is comparable to overall IT labour force statistics, women in this study were somewhat underrepresented in the technical roles.

Study Design and Methods

The WANE project offers qualitative and quantitative data from an international sample of information technology firms and workers. This methods chapter reviewed the WANE research objectives, case study research design, sampling, ethics, data collection and management, and preliminary analysis techniques for the larger study, and provided a summary of some of the basic characteristics of the participating firms and individuals. Methodological specifics for analyses contained in each chapter, such as coding conventions or analytical processes, are taken up separately in the relevant chapter.

In all of the chapters, participants and firms are identified by unique numeric identifiers, which are consistent across all publications that use WANE data. This approach allows readers to track the use of data across publications.

Note

1 For example, North American Industry Classification System (NAICS) code 54151 – Computer Systems Design and Related Services – and Australian and New Zealand Standard Industrial Classification (ANZSIC) code 783 – Computer Services Industry.

References

Bjornsson, K. 2001. Computer services: Strong employment growth and low labour productivity despite high labour costs and a highly-educated labour force. *Statistics in focus: Industry, trade, and services,* Theme 4-11/2001. (Catalogue KS-NP-01-011-EN-I.) European Union/Luxembourg: Eurostat/European Commission.

Brooke, L., L. Rolland, E. Jones, and C. Topple. 2004. *Australian country report.* WANE International Report 3. London, ON: University of Western Ontario, Workforce Aging in the New Economy (WANE).

Da Pont, M. 2003. Building the perfect system: An analysis of the computer systems design and related services industry. *Analytical Paper Series – Service Industries Division, Statistics Canada.* (Catalogue 63F0002XIE-No. 45.) Ottawa: Statistics Canada.

Gunderson, M., L. Jacobs, and F. Vaillancourt. 2005. *The information technology (IT) labour market in Canada: Results from the Software Human Resource Council (SHRC).* Ottawa: Government of Canada, Sector Council Program.

Lofland, J., and L.H. Lofland. 1995. *Analyzing social settings: A guide to qualitative observation and analysis.* Belmont, CA: Wadsworth.

Marshall, V.W. 1999. Reasoning with case studies: Issues of an aging workforce. *Journal of Aging Studies* 13, 4: 377-89.

Marshall, V.W., W. Heinz, H. Krueger, and A. Verma, eds. 2001. *Restructuring work and the life course.* Toronto: University of Toronto Press.

Ragin, C.C. 1987. *The comparative method: Moving beyond qualitative and quantitative strategies.* Berkeley: University of California Press.

–. 1994. *Constructing social research.* Thousand Oaks, CA: Pine Forge Press.

–. 2000. *Fuzzy-set social science.* Chicago: University of Chicago Press.

Part 2:
Gender Projects and Regimes

This part of the book focuses on how gender structures paid work and influences workplace cultures in small information technology firms. Although age is considered to a certain extent, these chapters primarily examine gender projects and gender regimes as they relate to the experiences of workers in small IT firms. In Chapter 3, the authors develop a typology of gender regimes that reflects the workplace cultures within which the IT firms in this study can be placed. This and the subsequent chapter show that gender regimes enshrine workplace cultures often on the basis of various types of masculinity that, in turn, influence the experiences of the men and women in the firm. Chapter 5 considers, in greater detail, the implications of these gendered workplace cultures on men and women who are juggling work and family responsibilities. This chapter shows that working in IT can be particularly challenging for men and women as they enter different life-course stages, such as marriage and parenthood, which come with competing time demands.

3
Firms as "Gender Regimes": The Experiences of Women in IT Workplaces
Gillian Ranson and Heather Dryburgh

Women and men working in the new economy in the 2000s experience work within a context that is exciting and challenging at the same time as it is fraught with risk, uncertainty, and job insecurity. For women working in the male-dominated IT sector, the gendered social context and its cultural expressions and meanings are additional realities of working life that require navigation. This chapter looks at how women in four countries experienced working in small to mid-sized IT firms in the early 2000s. What we are learning is that the social contexts of risk and uncertainty in such firms challenge and hold out promise to women and men in different ways. We find that IT work experiences for women are mediated by the framework of the historical context, women's location in work (and particular workplaces), and their places along life-course trajectories.

Several important studies of occupational gender segregation have examined the roles of historical change and social context in the level of gender concentration in certain professions, such as medicine and dentistry (Adams 2004; Witz 1992). Like these professions, in the case of IT, the rapid changes over the past two decades suggest that the historical context should be considered for its influence on the gender composition of workers in IT. For this reason, we draw attention to a few key events and outcomes of the significant change that occurred during the early 2000s in the IT sector in the regions we studied.

One of the early activities of the WANE project was to map the contours of IT employment in all the project regions. We found that the proportion of women in IT occupations was small in all regions. In the early 2000s, not only were women much less well represented in IT occupations than in the labour force as a whole, but also their representation in IT had declined for all of the study countries except Australia. The United States, for example, saw a decline in women in IT from 41 percent to 35 percent between 1996 and 2002 (Craft Morgan, Marshall, and Maloney 2004; Duerden Comeau 2004). In addition, women in all of the reference countries tended to cluster in the less technical and lower-paying IT occupations (Downie et al. 2004).

In all of the WANE countries, financial returns to women IT workers in the early 2000s were, on average, less than those to men, even though they were almost as likely as men to be working full time (Duerden Comeau 2004; Finnie 2002; Habtu 2003). Habtu's (2003) analysis of 2001 Canadian census data, for example, showed that women IT workers had lower median earnings than men ($41,100 compared with $47,100). Similar disparities were found in the other study regions.

Despite women's concentration in particular IT specializations, and an ongoing gender wage gap, in general the 1990s comprised a period of improving IT work conditions, increasing wages, and an inflow of both men and women workers (see WANE country reports at www.wane.ca). For example, throughout the 1990s, the demand for IT workers was so high that the Canadian government provided funding incentives to open up more spaces in computing education. The result was that computer education in universities, colleges, and private technical accreditation courses expanded significantly. Women tended to enroll in increasing proportions in community college and private programs, whereas the proportions of men taking up university computer science spaces grew through this period (Dryburgh 2000). In the United States, college degrees in IT fields of study also increased significantly between 1999 and 2001 (IT Workforce Data Project 2003), a time when the OECD documented the growing international migration of IT workers to countries with IT labour shortages (OECD 2002).

Despite the increased supply of IT workers resulting from these initiatives, the unemployment rate was still lower for IT workers than for other workers during that period (Duerden Comeau 2004), so jobs were plentiful. People with IT-related university degrees were only one source of workers for the IT sector during the boom period. Many IT workers entered IT occupations without computer science or other IT-related degrees or diplomas. In that period of high demand for workers, experience was highly valued and was often sufficient to secure an IT job (Dryburgh 2000).

For all of the countries in this study, the early 2000s brought a period of economic bust for IT companies. Many failed, and others survived by taking drastic measures such as massive downsizing or outsourcing. In the boom period, the increase in skilled immigrants was not seen as problematic, but since the bust there were increasing fears that immigrants were competing for jobs with domestic workers (Duerden Comeau 2004). The IT bust meant that more IT workers were looking for work, so demands for formal education became more common. The lack of formal IT education may be a factor in explaining women's lower incomes and declining representation in IT work in Canada, as women were more likely than men to have entered IT work via non-traditional routes (Downie et al. 2004).

The context for IT changed during this time, which meant that trained workers faced a different employment outlook, many finding jobs in small, struggling IT firms that survived or started after the bust. In fact, small IT companies prevailed in the ICT sector after the bust. Over 93 percent of computer service businesses in England had fewer than ten employees at the turn of the century, and in Australia in 2001-2 an estimated 88 percent of IT firms had fewer than five employees (Duerden Comeau 2004). Similarly, in the United States, 78 percent of computer systems design and related services firms employed fewer than five workers, though mid-sized firms still employed the majority of IT workers in the United States in the early 2000s (Bureau of Labor Statistics 2004). In Canada, over half of IT workers worked in small and mid-sized firms at that time (Da Pont 2003).

The promise of secure, interesting, and highly paid jobs in IT during the boom period gave way to job insecurity and higher risk for employees during the bust. Interestingly, though, professional occupations in IT continued to enjoy high status, and the majority of IT professionals were permanent employees (Craft Morgan, Marshall, and Maloney 2004; Platman 2003; Wolfson 2003). Risk appeared to be an acceptable or necessary part of IT work, however, because IT professionals tended to change jobs at a higher rate than other workers. For example, in 2001 in Australia, 70 percent of IT workers had worked five years or less in their current positions (Duerden Comeau 2004).

In the historical context of post-boom small to mid-sized IT firms and a tighter labour market, IT workers were vulnerable on several fronts. Immigrants and new graduates increased the competition for jobs, outsourcing was becoming an increasingly common strategy for employers, and employers were becoming more demanding when it came to educational requirements (Platman 2003). At this unique time in the history of the IT industry, we might expect women to be especially vulnerable.

IT Firms as Gender Regimes

Women's experiences in IT are also a product of the individual firms that employ women. In the WANE study, we made comparisons between women and men in each of the study countries and among women across all four countries, based on their individual experiences in a range of different workplaces. There were eighteen small and mid-sized firms in Canada, ten in the United States, ten in Australia, and six in England. For each workplace, semi-structured in-person interviews and field notes, along with the survey information, were used to generate case study reports on each firm. These reports, and the interviews with the individual women, allowed us to explore women's experiences in IT employment at the level of the workplace.

The most striking commonality, across almost all of the firms, was the small proportion of women in each. This is not surprising given the aggregate figures noted earlier about women's participation in IT employment. But its significance at the level of the individual workplace is profound. It suggests a scenario, repeated in firm after firm, in which lone women, or women in small numbers, are working in organizations that are owned, led, and numerically dominated by men. Most of the women in our study were working on men's turf and usually on men's terms. On a daily basis, gender played into work arrangements and workplace interactions in ways that significantly shaped participation in and experience of IT work. Workplaces, in other words, were also gender regimes.

"Gender regime" is a term coined by sociologist and gender scholar R.W. Connell (2002) to describe the way in which gender plays out in ongoing groups and institutions, including work organizations such as the firms in our study. It takes account of how work is divided (and who is recruited to do it), how power is distributed, how symbolic representations of gender are drawn on, and how the emotional climate is managed. Differences among workplace gender regimes are a useful signpost to the different experiences of women and men in whatever workplace positions they occupy. In this section of the chapter, we use "gender regime" as a device to classify our case study firms in each of the four study countries.[1] This classification appears in Table 3.1. Because more than 40 percent of the case study firms and more than a third of the women interviewed for the study were in Canada, we begin with the dominant Canadian classifications, using them as templates against which to assess the gender regimes of firms in the other study countries.

Table 3.1

Classification of firms as gender regimes

ID #	Country	Age of firm (years)	# FT, non-contract	# Women	Age range	Gender regime
102	Canada	3	4	0	27-35	Masculinist
106	Canada	4	10	1	20-33	Masculinist
111	Canada	14	21	2	23-47	Masculinist
112	Canada	4	14	1	19-62	Masculinist
114	Canada	10	12	2	29-45	Masculinist
117	Canada	5	14	1	25-36	Masculinist
205	Australia	9	5	1	24-26	Masculinist
401	England	13	9	1	29-46	Masculinist (with woman in leadership role)
502	US	4	8	1	25-43	Masculinist (with woman in leadership role)
504	US	4	13	1	24-43	Masculinist
107	Canada	6	5	1	28-58	Benignly paternalistic
108	Canada	20	7	2	33-60	Benignly paternalistic
113	Canada	9	12	6	25-43	Benignly paternalistic (with woman in leadership role)
116	Canada	3	12	2	41-62	Benignly paternalistic
118	Canada	10	7	2	22-43	Benignly paternalistic (with woman in leadership role)
207	Australia	7	69	21	24-47	Benignly paternalistic
208	Australia	27	16	4	25-62	Benignly paternalistic
402	England	8	24	10	29-46	Benignly paternalistic
403	England	27	16	2	24-58	Benignly paternalistic
404	England	2	65	15	22-63	Benignly paternalistic
507	US	8	14	? 2+	20-45	Benignly paternalistic (with woman in leadership role)
204	Australia	4	14	10	23-60	Benignly maternalistic
210	Australia	16	22	8	19-55	Benignly maternalistic
407	England	7	7	1	30-50	Benignly maternalistic
115	Canada	5	10	6	34-48	Balanced

The Masculinist Gender Regime

The gender regime that was most common in the Canadian firms was the one we call "masculinist." Firms with masculinist gender regimes shared most of the following characteristics:

• Women were numerically negligible; some firms in this category employed no women, or only one, in an administrative support capacity.
• Women were mostly absent from core, high-skill, technical work and from management.
• Workplace culture was geared to male interests and activities.
• Recruitment practices were aimed at employees who would "fit in" with this workplace culture, so women continued to be excluded.
• Where individual women did occupy key managerial or technical roles, they accommodated, rather than challenged, the dominant male ethos, positioning themselves as "one of the boys."

In Canada, six of the eighteen case study firms included in this chapter were variations on the masculinist gender regime. For example, in Firm 111, a twenty-one-employee software development firm, there were only three women, and all were in administrative or client support positions. The client services department, in which two of the three women worked, was also segregated in a separate office. The exclusively male development and marketing departments occupied the bigger and airier office space, which included the lunch room. This was the locus of a masculine brand of socializing that tended to keep the women away. One of the (male) programmers commented with a laugh, "lately, it's just been the development crew, I guess. I guess everybody else is scared of us ... [to] come and hang out with us" (1191120). One of the women in client services, recounting talk and behaviour at a recent company event, commented, "it's very guyish here" (1191094).

The "guyish" workplace culture of Firm 111 was evident in Firm 112 as well. The workplace culture of the latter firm – a fourteen-person software development company – was characterized by its thirty-seven-year-old male president as "very laid back" and "the young guy type [of] environment," with *Maxim* magazines lying around, a fridge that "probably has beer in it," and recreational diversions, including mini-car racing, a putting green, a dartboard, and video games (1112146).[2] This firm had one long-term woman employee, a quality assurance analyst who was highly regarded by the president. In a telling description of her place in the firm, he described her as "kind of my right-hand man on the development side" (1112146). At the time of the case study, this woman was on a year's maternity leave. Her replacement was another woman without formal IT training who had done intermittent temp and freelance work for the firm and had a family connection to one of the partners. She commented, "when K. decided to go on maternity leave, they considered me not because I'd had any training doing what she does but just because they knew me, knew my work, and figured I could handle the job" (1112081). In hiring this woman as a replacement, the partners were not hiring anyone who would challenge the workplace culture. She spoke of past work experience in both female- and male-dominated workplaces and said she much preferred working with men, who were "more easygoing," compared with women, who were more serious, "very competitive," and sometimes "petty" (1112081).

In both of these workplaces, and others like them in the study, survival for the rare women employees required them to position themselves in particular ways with respect to "the boys" (Ranson 2005). The long-term employee and "right-hand man" had clearly adapted to the workplace culture. Her replacement's conscious aligning of herself with men rather than women as co-workers was likely to do the same.

Also, future hiring to higher-level technical or managerial jobs in these workplaces was likely to be restricted to men. This was partly because of the informal, network-oriented, relationship-based way in which recruitment tended to be handled. The president of Firm 112 said that, when a new position came up, "we would typically ask the staff here if they knew anyone who was appropriate." He added, "I've been able to find the people that I need just in relationships that I have in the industry to date, and it's worked out very well" (1112146). In Firm 111, gendered stereotypes about IT workers were also likely to come into play. One of the firm's younger male programmers commented, "well, it's like we're actually doing some work with a company in [the United States], and the developer that we'll be working with is a woman. And I'm like, wow, a woman developer, like, you don't see it, you don't. I think that's the first woman developer that I've seen. Or, and I haven't even seen her, just heard about really" (1191159).

Although the workforce in many masculinist firms was young, and usually white, there were variations in terms of family structure. In Firm 106, a ten-person web design and communications company, where the only woman – the wife of the CEO – was the office manager, nine of the ten were in their twenties, but seven of the ten were married. Two had children, and at the time of the field research the only accommodations to parenthood that the firm needed to make were flexibility around doctors' appointments and a few days off at the birth of a child – accommodations that might work for fathers, but would be unlikely to work for mothers. In the same vein, one characteristic of "family friendliness" noted by the president was the fact that spouses with children frequently dropped in to visit. In these firms, as in many others in the study as a whole, family friendliness took a particular, male-oriented form and often translated as flexibility to compensate for occasional long hours of work.

Versions of the masculinist gender regime occurred in all of the other study countries as well. In the United States, two of the case study firms could be readily identified in this way. Indeed, the most extreme form of the masculinist gender regime appeared in Firm 504, a thirteen-person software development company where the only woman was also the only African American. This firm, like others of its type, was founded by a group of men who had a history of working together in other companies before starting this one. Their employees were mainly young men in their twenties. Many of the stereotypes about IT workplaces and IT workers played out in this firm. The availability of futons and air mattresses for employees working through the night to meet deadlines spoke to the workplace culture (and the expectation) of long work hours; ping-pong and foosball were among the stress relievers. The workplace culture was loud and jokey but also competitive – a good example of the "men's club" social settings described by Bird (1996). One male re-spondent commented, "it's not a 'we all nurture each other' type [of] environment ... You pick on each other, and you're competitive." He continued, "there's very little positive feedback, let's put it that way" (5504060). The sole woman in this firm, employed there for less than a year, was acutely conscious of what she described as her "outsider" status – though she was inclined to attribute it more to her race than to her gender. She had a university degree in computer science but was working in a technical support position, alongside programmers whose educational background was probably not too different from her own. This seemed to worry her less than it might have; her view of women in support positions was somewhat essentialist and inflected with the biblical perspective of women as men's helpmates. With a history of post-2000 layoffs from IT-related jobs, and concerns about the security of her present position, she was taking on much more menial jobs in the workplace, such as cleaning up and washing dishes, to make herself indispensable. "As a woman, you can use your womanly characteristics to improve the company," she commented. "So that's what I'm trying to do" (5504112).

Many of the Australian firms, for the reasons noted earlier (see endnote 1), were not easy to classify by gender regime. But one did offer a clear example of a masculinist gender regime, from yet another perspective. Firm 205, a virtual marketing firm, offered interactive advertising services. There were five employees covering four key roles: the CEO, the technical director, the account services director, and another account manager. All four of the key roles were occupied by young men under thirty. The firm also employed an outer network of contractors. Firm 205 provided a glimpse of the pervasiveness of men's professional and personal networks that are well known to exclude women. Here members of the young male executive workforce were generally university recruited, following the CEO's plan to "poach schools for like-minded individuals" (AUS205K1); two members of the group were completing further studies at the time of the case study research. The twenty-four-year-old CEO co-owned the firm with his father, whom he acknowledged as his mentor. There was an atmosphere of male sociability in this firm too, with music playing on Fridays and all of the employees "head[ing] off to the pub together" (2205003). But there was also an interesting example of competition between different masculinities – the executive/managerial and the youthful/sporting – in a single setting; the young CEO had recently needed to pay attention to some contract developers who were arriving at work at midnight and then leaving at 5 a.m. to go surfing. From all of the foregoing, perhaps it is not surprising that there is no information available on the firm's one woman employee, who was not interviewed. From the context of other interviews and the case study report on the firm, it seems safe to assume that she was in an administrative support position; her absence from all discussion about Firm 205 is significant.

In England, one of the case study firms, Firm 401, offered a clear example of a masculinist gender regime – but its version was entirely different from those discussed so far. Firm 401, an e-learning software development firm with a total staff of nine (six of whom were founder-partners), had been formed out of another company that had gone bankrupt. The sole woman, at forty-six the oldest staff member, was one of the six founders, all of whom were very good friends. Conscious of gender issues in a way that many token women are not, she offered an unusual perspective on a masculinist gender regime that she herself had helped to create and to which she remained deeply committed. In this firm, she was very much a "conceptual man" (Ranson 2005); as she commented, "I've survived as a woman because I've not behaved like one" (4401068).

The thirteen years of this firm's history also offered some insights into the way that firms as gender regimes undergo transitions as their employees enter different life-course stages. The masculinist regime in this firm had evolved from the sort of young men's workplace culture described earlier to a less frenetic and more family-oriented one as five of the six partners had children. The original foundation of trust between the partners had endured; they rotated the position of director and over the years had supported one another through a variety of personal crises and transitions. But the firm remained very much a men's workplace. Its woman partner spoke of occasional "ranting, screaming" arguments and an informal workplace environment characterized by bad language and jokes offensive not just to women – "we offend everything." In this context, she commented wryly, "in the flames of gender hell, I'm going to pay for what I've sat and listened to" (4401068). With its sole woman classed, in her own words, not as a woman but as a friend among friends, this workplace too was a men's club. The "friendship-based" way of working that she described was likely to exclude all but a select few. "I think the way we are is very difficult for people to come in to us, to work with us," she said. "Whenever we talk about getting other people in, I'm thinking, you know, what will they make of us? And ... it will change us" (4401068).

As Firm 401 makes clear, the presence of women, even in leadership positions, does not necessarily feminize a workplace. The competition for contracts in many start-up firms, along with the high pressure of project deadlines and the financial insecurity of an unstable marketplace, to say nothing of the more widespread male domination of the IT industry, seemed to produce a climate in other firms as well where women took to "managing like a man" (Wajcman 1998). Managerial masculinities are both discourses and models of behaviour that women too can appropriate. Firm 502 in the United States (described in detail in Chapter 5) was another example of a masculinist gender regime with a woman – in this firm the only woman – as CFO and co-founder. This eight-person high-tech firm was made up of employees with university degrees in IT; recruitment explicitly favoured "workaholics" without family commitments.

The Benignly Paternalistic Gender Regime

In three of the Canadian firms, the prevailing gender regime could best be described as "benignly paternalistic." These firms, like those already described, were also male dominated, but the women in them had a different status from those in more masculinist workplaces. The benignly paternalistic firms shared most of the following characteristics:

- Leadership was by older men who were also recognizably "family men."
- Women were few but positioned in key technical roles, not restricted to administration or support.
- Firms were (usually) in stable, profitable niches, with more financial security.
- Work relationships were collegial and supportive.

One version of the benignly paternalistic gender regime was evident in Firm 108, a seven-person software development firm with a history of more than twenty years in a specialized niche in the transportation industry and a workforce made up mainly of employees in their thirties with partners and children. Two women played key employee roles in the firm. One was a highly trained programmer with an Eastern European university degree and Canadian technical college training who had been with the firm for seven years. The other was the office manager, a fourteen-year employee who functioned as a kind of "office wife." Behind the scenes was the actual wife of the founder and president, herself a co-owner of the firm. She had been trained in the health field, and her involvement with a union led (at the employees' request) to her participation in the development of the company's fledgling human resources handbook. The president's family loomed large in the firm, and the president, and other employees, considered the firm to function like a family. Certainly, part of its public face, as exemplified in the company newsletter sent to some 1,500 clients, was very homey. Produced by the office manager, it contained birth announcements, recipes, and jokes alongside more technical material.

In this firm, too, recruitment was geared to ensuring that new employees fit the firm's social culture – but here the workplace culture to be preserved was that generated by a small, friendly, ethnically diverse, and decidedly non-macho group, working by choice in close physical proximity, with specialized responsibilities but ready to lend a hand when others were overburdened. Women were just as likely to fit in as men. As the female programmer put it, "it's a small company, everybody knows everybody, right? And their families. We can just talk, you know? So you feel a bit like family" (1108068).

From her perspective, there were limitations to Firm 108 as a workplace, but they related more to the size of the firm than to the work itself. "There is no career here, right? That's it. You are where you are. There's no ladders to climb." This employee had made a conscious decision to settle for considerable workplace support and collegiality, generally regular hours, and the flexibility she needed as a mother, instead of the higher-paced (and higher-paid) option of work in a larger company, where a "career" in her terms might have been possible. She commented, "I like the company, I like the people ... I got used to everything, and I'm okay here" (1108068).

A different version of the benignly paternalistic gender regime appeared in Firm 107, a cutting-edge consulting company with a founder-president, four full-time permanent staff (one of whom was a woman), and six contractors (three of whom were women). As a consulting company, with employees and contractors working off-site on projects in client organizations, the firm did not have a workplace culture of its own. The gender regime manifested itself more in the president's own company philosophy, the way in which he organized and staffed contracts, and his relationships with contractors and particularly employees.

Technologically, this was a leading-edge company; the senior employees were advanced IT practitioners, experts in their individual fields. Part of the president's commitment to their professional development was the requirement that they attend at least one conference annually, often to present papers. All of the study participants in this firm spoke warmly of the president; interviews with the women suggested that he respected their abilities and was demonstrably willing to advance their career interests.

The sole woman among the four employees was university trained and had brought several years of high-end technical work experience into the firm when she had joined it eleven years earlier. The technical excellence and mentoring so strongly encouraged by the president allowed her to "do a lot of writing and go to a lot of conferences." She also presented tutorials, all as an outgrowth of the firm's consulting expertise. "I've elevated my visibility internationally," she said. "Like, I'm, anyway, not that I'm this great guru, I'm not ... I am a step up from just kind of being a worker or whatever ... So [Firm 107] is open to that, and, you know, there's a lot of support for that kind of thing" (1107107).

She earned in excess of $100,000 and was one of two senior employees who strategized with the president – and, in her words, pushed him – about the firm's direction. In broader terms, what she pushed against were the constraints and boundaries established in firms like this one, where one strong and fairly charismatic man with a vision of how things should run was the final authority. The paradox, though, was that this environment, largely the creation of the owner, gave her the experience and confidence to challenge him. Two of these challenges were personal;

gendered in almost classic terms, they add detail to the meaning of benign paternalism.

The first challenge occurred when she went on maternity leave. He was not willing to top up her salary. His semi-joking words about this in our interview were "I'm not going to pay you $120,000 to go have a baby. I mean, if you do two of those, I'm broke." And he pushed hard to get her back to work before her six months of leave were up. She started back a little sooner than she had planned but resisted coming back full time until she was ready and the baby was a year or so old. Several years later he could say, in the context of accommodations to the individual needs of employees, "[she] has a young daughter, so we know that, when we hold meetings, we've got to be done by five" (1107029).

The second challenge occurred more recently. Her mother died at a time when she was being urged to take over the lead on a major project. Back at work but grieving ("I can't even think back to how bad I felt then"), she argued for another employee, capable but less senior, to take the lead ("he's the better candidate, let's build him up"). She described this story's conclusion:

Finally, I had to overrule [the president] and say, "I'm having a meeting with [the client representative] and telling her it's going to be [the other employee], because no matter how much you tell me I have to do it I can't, and you're not listening." ... We talked about it fairly recently again, and he really, and he is very sensitive, he says, "I'm sorry. I missed that." (1107107)

One point illuminated by these challenges is the extent to which in benignly paternalistic gender regimes, like those in Firms 108 and 107, both of them small companies, workplace interactions and negotiations are deeply personal and link directly to the personality and management style of the leader as a "father figure." From the perspective of women working in such firms, the chinks in the paternalistic armour – the cultivation of mutually respectful working relationships and the willingness to be open to new ways of doing things – make it benign and potentially woman friendly.

Benignly paternalistic gender regimes along the lines described for the Canadian firms were most clearly evident in three firms in England and three firms in Australia. In England, for example, Firm 402, a twenty-four-person software development company, appeared to be a larger version of family-oriented Firm 108 in Canada. In the English firm, female family influence worked through the part-time human resources manager, the wife of one of the two owner-managers. Although the most senior positions in Firm 402 were occupied by men, the firm's ten women covered a diverse range of occupations; the market development manager and three of the six software developers were women. The workforce was stable, and more than half were forty-five or older. Although not all management interactions were benign – the sexism of the technical director was raised in one interview – in general the firm appeared to be a calm, professional, well-organized workplace. The human resources manager spoke of her commitment – and, given the family relationship just noted, presumably the commitment of the owners – to "make sure that their workplace is right, that they've got everything they need for their comfort and safety" (4402289). The female market development manager commented, "there is very much a community feel to this company. I think it takes a lot to get accepted if you're coming into it. Once you're accepted into the company ... they're very happy to have you here ... I feel like I'm at home here, whereas I haven't felt like that before at other companies" (4402133).

If Firm 402 in England resembled Firm 108 in Canada, there were echoes of Canada's Firm 107 in Australia's Firm 208, a sixteen-member consulting firm with four women employees. This firm was in its twenty-seventh year of operation at the time of the case study. Like Firm 107, it had a single owner with strong ideas about how things should be run. These ideas were often traditional; he insisted on a formal dress code, for example, and according to one of the senior women employees he "hated his secretary wearing trousers" (2208045). But in other ways, he was much more enlightened, allowing employees to accommodate family and other responsibilities with flexible scheduling and acknowledging and rewarding special achievements among employees. Interviews with two of the firm's four women – a fifty-one-year-old senior consultant with the firm for twenty-five years and a twenty-five year old employed with the company for four years and newly appointed to the job of business development manager – indicated a workplace that was open and friendly. They also suggested an owner who had the last word, but with whom negotiation was possible, and who had employees' interests at heart. The support that they in turn were willing to give him was best demonstrated during the high-tech downturn of 2000-1, when, also like Firm 107 in Canada, all employees took a pay cut to keep the company going. The female business development manager, a new employee at the time, explained, "I guess because it's all very much a, a very family sort of company, everyone understood." She also commented, "the whole culture is that people stay around a long time and, and really care about each other" (2208149).

Among the US firms in the study, the model of the benignly paternalistic gender regime led by men was more elusive. For example, Firm 503, a software development company with seven full-time employees (two of them women), was owned by two brothers. It was decidedly paternalistic but not necessarily benign, especially as far as women employees were concerned. The case study report on the firm noted that employees spoke of family relationships within the company but that most families have "challenges." In this case, the perception was that the "patriarchs" had become more preoccupied with ensuring the firm's financial future than with day-to-day management and involvement in their employees' lives. The two women interviewed in this case study also spoke, however, of the owners' conservative views about women and the "double standard" between women and men in the firm. A more progressive leadership style seemed to exist in Firm 501, another privately owned software development company – but here there were no full-time women employees to describe the gender regime from their perspective. The firm had four full-time employees, two part-time moonlighting contractors, and a part-time human resources and accounting person (the only woman). The firm's owner, whose history included management of other IT firms, had strong views about mentoring and professional development, but his firm was still too much in post-2001 start-up mode to be able to implement them. In this firm, the absence of women as full-time employees appeared to be accidental rather than intentional; there was nothing to suggest that women would not do well, and with some financial stability and growth they might yet be hired. The gender regimes in both of these US firms point to the broader problem of financial insecurity and pressure of work in small start-up companies, a problem that can overwhelm the best management intentions with respect to providing optimal working conditions and a good work-life balance.

As with the masculinist gender regimes described earlier, there were also examples in the study of benignly paternalistic gender regimes in which women, not men, were the leaders. Here "managing like a man" took on a different form from the masculinist version described earlier, but women were "father" rather than "mother" figures in the firms they led. For example, in the United States, Firm 507, a fifteen-employee technical support firm, was another benignly paternalistic gender regime, even though the CEO (one of three partners) was a woman. In this firm, she had one of the highest levels of technical expertise and was acknowledged warmly as an accessible, accommodating manager. Her commitment to work-life balance was tangibly reflected in the spare office being used as a nursery for the (female) part-time general manager's baby. The "paternalism" in this firm was reflected not so much in managerial style as in its sharp hierarchy of skill and education; outside the top tier of management, most employees were technicians who had left blue-collar jobs to start a second career in IT. All the technicians were men. Here too, though, the absence of women was not intentional. Female technicians had been hired in the past, but at the time of the case study research they were not presenting as candidates. The CEO commented, "I cannot find good, strong, female techs. They're much more in sales. They're much more in systems development. They're very strong ... They just, they're not engineers ... At least, they don't come to me as engineers. Maybe they're just so good they go somewhere else" (5507C2 ID1).

In Canada, Firm 113 was an example of a firm with a woman as a leader and a gender regime that seemed to be benignly paternalistic in spite of, not necessarily because of, her presence. Firm 113 was a place-ment agency for IT contractors but also had a database administration arm and a software development arm. The woman leader was one of the firm's three partners, all of whom (along with some other colleagues, now departed) had set up the firm as a means to deal more honestly with contractors than they themselves had been treated and to give them a better deal. These values may have distinguished Firm 113 from other firms in the cutthroat environment in which they were working, but they could not be attributed to the presence of the woman partner. Another (male) partner had the original idea and did the groundwork to establish the firm. And though there was a higher proportion of women among the full-time employees, they were in lower-paying, less highly skilled technical and administrative support positions.

The woman partner also specialized in the placement side of the business, while the other two partners had more technical roles. In many ways, the gender regime in play closely resembled the benignly paternalistic regimes described earlier. Like those firms, there were no *Maxim* magazines or putting greens visible in Firm 113, and there was considerable flexibility and support for family responsibilities. But an-other note also sounded in the woman partner's interview. She spoke of preferring to work with men rather than women, who tended to be "gossipy." "It's easier when there's like a bunch of guys," she said. "It's true. Maybe people don't want to hear that, but it's true" (1113003).

There were echoes here of the sole woman who was a partner in Firm 401 in England and who helped to create a gender regime that was actually masculinist. Such women, in leadership roles but more inclined to align themselves with men than women as employees and co-workers, were unlikely to become champions of other women working in IT.

Similar reservations applied to Firm 118, a "body shop" offering permanent and contract placement services for IT workers. In the city where the firm was located, the placement industry was highly competitive and aggressive, and this firm, with six contractors on staff at the time of the case study, was a small player. The firm's woman president described a breathtakingly detailed and gruelling daily schedule that included two hours of work by cell phone during her daily commute. She suggested that being a woman allowed her to avoid the power struggles common in similar male-run agencies; men were "more relaxed" with a woman – "it's almost, you have to rely on your intuition and the touchy-feely side of it" (1118006). But the nature of the employer-employee relationship, in which the employer takes a cut of the fee earned by the employee in a client site, may be viewed as exploitation by employees over time – and this was in fact the perception of the one female contractor currently working in the firm. Other contractors spoke more positively of the president's personal dealings with them, but the nature of the business made these relationships much more expedient and instrumental than relationships in conventional workplaces.

The Benignly Maternalistic Gender Regime

The gender regimes in the firms described so far attribute much to the power, and the person, of the leader. In most cases, in the WANE firms, leaders were men whose various styles helped to create the two different versions of managerial masculinity we have singled out. In the rare case study firms in which women were leaders, they tended to appropriate the same managerial discourses, and the gender regimes in their firms did not appear to be transformed by a feminine presence at the helm. There were three clear cases, though, where women did make a difference and where "benignly maternalistic" seemed to be the best description of the firm's gender regime. These firms shared most of the following characteristics:

- A woman carried out most of the project management and employee supervision in the firm, in two cases in close co-operation with a (male) CEO.

- This supervision and oversight had a distinctly feminine, maternal flavour.
- Women were either present in the firm in appreciable numbers, working across the range of its activities, or explicitly targeted for recruitment.

For example, Firm 407 in England was a seven-person software development firm catering to a specialized niche market in which a key role was played by the female customer service manager (also the sole employee to have a financial stake in the firm). Interviews in this firm suggested the extent to which she worked in partnership with the owner; her position in the firm extended well beyond the daily routine of project management and employee supervision. Philosophically she shared, and in practical terms she implemented, the approach to human resources advocated by the firm's founder. This approach produced an environment in which employees could set their own hours and work from home if need be (two employees and the owner were permanently home based). It also meant that attention was paid to psychological well-being. For example, the company's branch office moved out of the customer service manager's home to conventional office space in a neighbouring town to accommodate the needs of a young employee who struggled with the isolation of working from home by himself. She commented:

> So the working arrangements are what I've organized really, which is – I've experienced the inflexibility of larger organizations, and I felt quite strongly, [the owner] and I felt quite strongly, that you're not just the person you are while you're in the office, you have a whole life, and that we wished to be more accommodating of people. (4407006)

Part of this flexibility was explicitly geared to making the firm more welcoming to women employees, though none had so far been recruited.

The maternalistic character of the gender regime in Firm 210, in Australia, was due to the approach of the female general manager. In her style, and in her relationship with the firm's owner, she was a counterpart to the customer service manager just described. The Australian "matriarch" was in charge of the firm's human resources, among many other responsibilities. The wife of a minister, she regarded much of this work as "pastoral care," claiming that she knew "far too much" about all the employees (2210006). This firm was characterized by a remarkably diverse workforce and recruitment in which friendship, family relationships, and the opportunity to lend a helping hand had all, at different times, played a part.

Of all the small and mid-sized firms in the study, only one, in Australia, was not only owned and managed by women but also had significantly more women than men as employees. Firm 204 was co-owned by two women, one of whom had stepped back from direct involvement in the firm some weeks before the case study. The remaining owner/managing director was a thirty-two-year-old woman without formal IT training who had developed a relatively low-tech content-management system for websites targeted to the home business market. Of the firm's sixteen employees, twelve were women. Most had been hired less than twelve months prior to our fieldwork, and most had little or no background training in IT. One woman, newly hired to a sales position, had been running a beauty salon. She commented, "I've learnt so much in two and a half months I can tell you! ... I could type on a computer and could turn one on ... not too much else, Internet, that's it. Now I'm doing all sorts of things that I've never dreamed of" (2204224).

With few skills, the employees were highly dependent on the managing director, who was the main trainer and go-to person in the firm. Her tendency to hire untrained people if she thought they had the right attitude and could fit in with the workplace culture could be construed as benevolent in that, as the case study report noted, the firm was "a 'secure' pad for candidates seeking new skills and experiences that potentially could leverage employees to the wider marketplace." But remuneration was poor, and other human resource policies were poorly handled – several employees had yet to sign employment contracts. The women interviewed for the case study spoke warmly of the "family-like" workplace culture and the flexibility – but their employment options, in most other IT workplaces, would have been limited or non-existent.

The Balanced Gender Regime

Of the gender regimes described so far, perhaps the best that could be said is that, in a resoundingly male-dominated environment, some were the kind in which some women could do well. In most cases, women were not working on equal terms with men, across all levels of the firm. One of the Canadian firms (115) was a marked contrast not only to the other Canadian firms but to firms in the other study countries as well. The interviews conducted in this firm, and summed up in the case study report, point to a gender regime that can best be described as "balanced." This balance was demonstrated in the following characteristics:

- Two of the four partners were women, and one was the major shareholder and CEO.

- The CEO was highly trained technically (PhD level).
- Six of the firm's ten employees were women, and all ten collectively represented high levels of technical training and expertise.
- There was an appreciation for older and more experienced workers.
- There was an explicit attention to workplace flexibility and work-life balance, to which both men and women subscribed and from which both benefited.

Like some other case study firms, Firm 115 was still on somewhat shaky financial ground, having been formed in the wake of the post-2000 high-tech downturn. So salaries were on the low side. The compensation was a demonstrable flexibility with respect to work arrangements and a commitment to work-life balance.

Key to the balance implicit in this gender regime was the fact that gender did not appear to differentiate either partners or employees in terms of their expertise, their influence on the firm's direction, or their responsibilities and interests outside work. Many "snapshots" gleaned from the interviews build up this balanced picture. For example, though the female CEO had no children, she had sporting and other interests outside work that constituted the life dimension in her own work-life balance. Because of these interests, she usually came to work at 10 a.m. and (with the exception of inevitably busy year-end weeks) was committed to keeping work hours within reasonable limits. She commented that neither she nor the other employees wanted to be in one of the "driven start-up modes" where seventy- or eighty-hour weeks were the expectation. "I won't do it, I won't ask anybody else to do it," she said (1115006).

Gender stereotypes blurred in other ways as well. Most employees had children, and men as well as women took advantage of the firm's family friendliness; the one six-month parental leave the company had accommodated was taken by one of the men. Among other accommodations, all employees except the office manager were set up to work at home if need be. One worker with a disability had written into her employment contract that she could work three days a week from home. Employees at every level were recognized and rewarded for significant contributions, with rewards ranging from year-end bonuses to gifts of spa days. There were also intermittent company social events – the week before the field research was conducted they had all gone bowling. The influence of the large company where all the partners (and most of the other employees) had worked before joining Firm 115 also reflected a much more organized approach to employee benefits, which were generally recognized to be very good for a company of its size and stage. Although lacking large company resources for employee training, the partner in charge of human resources noted the firm's interest in doing what it could – initially through small-scale, one-day events – to advance and widen employees' skill bases.

In developing this regime – balanced both in terms of gender and in terms of accommodation to life outside work – this firm had many advantages. It was made up of people with a prior (and successful) history of working together and occupied a highly specialized technical niche in a city where its practitioners were well known. This meant that the firm could not only draw from this extended family for new recruits but also carry over established client relationships. At the same time, there was a conscious attention to equity and respect for all employees that made it stand out.

Conclusion

Since the IT bust in the early 2000s, small to mid-sized IT firms in all of the WANE countries carried out business in an environment of increased risk and uncertainty compared with the boom period of the 1990s. Clearly, the ways in which these firms rose to the challenges they faced at the time of our field research had impacts on the women and men who worked and interacted daily there.

The national data showed that all was not equal in IT workplaces generally across the four countries – compared with men, women were still minorities in IT workplaces, they made less money on average, they were less likely to be in supervisory positions, and they were more likely to work in the non-technical occupations. The survey data also showed that, despite these disparities, women in significant numbers, and for varying reasons by country, were finding satisfying work in IT and were benefiting from permanent employment with good benefits and career development opportunities. Listening to what these women had to say about their experiences, we found that, in many cases, the contradiction between the general gender inequities in IT work and women's reported satisfaction could be explained by the way in which work was set up in their workplaces. Firms responded in many ways to the challenges of the post-boom IT context, and the regimes that characterized these firms had impacts on the men and women working in them.

Considering the experiences of women and the workplaces that employed – or did not employ – women in IT work, the balanced gender regime stands out as an ideal to which companies should aspire. In contrast, the masculinist gender regimes in many other firms in the study suggest a model in need of renovation or replacement. Many of the firms included in this category employed, and were led by, mainly younger men; youth, combined with gender, produced working environments that, at the least, were discouraging to women. So, from a woman's perspective, it is reassuring to reflect on the changes that had clearly occurred in several of the study firms as both the CEO and the firm itself matured. Benignly paternalistic gender regimes were generally led by older men and more stable, financially secure firms (often also with older workers).

Age and experience play out in many ways. In a start-up company, for example, there is less leeway than in a firm whose reputation is solidly established to negotiate project deadlines with clients. But the nature of the work is also a factor in determining the gender regime in play. For example, employees in firms for whom client services comprise a major component of the work have less flexibility than employees in firms selling a product in a secure and clearly defined niche market. Finally, as noted earlier, the stress of competition, in a globalizing economy, may overwhelm the best intentions of individual employers to create welcoming workplaces.

We should also note that, in this context of competition and variable work demands, the mere addition of women to previously male-dominated workplaces will not necessarily produce changes to workplace culture. There are multiple models of managerial masculinities (see, e.g., Collinson and Hearn 1994) that women as well as men often appropriate; the women managers in our study whose style promoted either masculinist or benignly paternalistic gender regimes are examples.

Finally, women's participation in IT firms in the study clearly related to their levels of skill and education. Women did best in the firms to which they brought technical expertise or could package other educational and work experience to fill a gap in the firm's skill requirements. Enterprising individual women were able to do this, in individual firms, but they hardly constituted a significant movement of women into IT workplaces. Indeed, the persistent male domination of IT raises the question of whether women will ever make more serious headway.

One positive sign is that, in the benignly paternalistic gender regimes we described, women were few but often thriving. In the short run, such regimes might be the best option for women since they are likely to increase in number as the current generation of young CEOs, and their firms, move into new life stages. Another positive sign, glimpsed in several of the study firms, was a consciously anti-corporate, more lifestyle-focused approach to work arrangements that was also likely to be more attractive to women workers. Finally, there remains the possibility that those individual women, doing well in spite of their minority gender status, will serve as models for other women. Gender scholars, whose work is informed by a social constructionist perspective, point to the ways that individuals reproduce conventional expectations about gender by conforming to them. But others (Deutsch 2007; Sullivan 2004) call for more attention to non-conformity as a source of change. By entering all levels of IT work and thriving, women would be challenging many stereotypes. By examining the actions of these non-traditional women, "we may be able to identify the conditions under which these actions change normative conceptions of gender, and how and when these new conceptions can take advantage of or even drive institutional change" (Deutsch 2007, 120).

Notes

1 Our focus in this chapter is on the gender regimes that were dominant and read-ily identifiable from the available interview and other case study material. Some firms were less easy to classify. They included those in which there were family as well as workplace relationships among employees and owners and those that appeared to be in a state of transition at the time of the WANE fieldwork. In some firms, including some in which no women were employed, there was not enough information available to assign a classification.

2 A more detailed discussion of the masculinist workplace culture of Firms 111 and 112 is provided in Chapter 4.

References

Adams, T. 2004. *Professionalization in computing-related occupations: Canada, the U.S., and Britain.* WANE Working Paper 8. London, ON: University of Western Ontario, Workforce Aging in the New Economy (WANE).

Bird, S.R. 1996. Welcome to the men's club: Homosociality and the maintenance of hegemonic masculinity. *Gender and Society* 10, 2: 120-32.

Bureau of Labor Statistics, US Department of Labor. *Career guide to industries, 2004.* http://www.bls.gov/.

Collinson, D., and J. Hearn. 1994. Naming men as men: Implications for work, organization, and management. *Gender, Work, and Organization* 1, 1: 2-22.

Connell, R.W. 2002. *Gender.* Cambridge, UK: Polity Press.

Craft Morgan, J., V.W. Marshall, and M. Maloney. 2004. *The U.S. information tech-nology workforce in the new economy.* WANE International Report 2. London, ON: University of Western Ontario, Workforce Aging in the New Economy (WANE).

Da Pont, M. 2003. *Building the perfect system: An analysis of the computer sys-tems design and related services industry.* Analytical Paper Series 45. (Catalogue 63F0002XIE.) Ottawa: Service Industries Division, Statistics Canada.

Deutsch, F.M. 2007. Undoing gender. *Gender and Society* 21, 1: 106-27.

Downie, R., H.B. Dryburgh, J.A. McMullin, and G. Ranson. 2004. *A profile of information technology employment in Canada.* WANE International Report 1.

London, ON: University of Western Ontario, Workforce Aging in the New Economy (WANE).

Dryburgh, H.B. 2000. Women in computing: Alternative routes to computing careers. PhD diss., McMaster University, Hamilton, ON.

Duerden Comeau, T. 2004. *Cross-national comparison of information technology employment.* WANE International Report 5. London, ON: University of Western Ontario, Workforce Aging in the New Economy (WANE).

Finnie, R. 2002. *Early labour market outcomes of recent Canadian university graduates by discipline: A longitudinal, cross-cohort analysis.* Analytical Studies Research Paper Series 164. Ottawa: Business and Labour Market Analysis Division, Statistics Canada.

Habtu, R. 2003. Information technology workers. *Perspectives on Labour and Income* 4, 7: 5-11. (Statistics Canada Catalogue 75-0001-XIE.)

The IT Workforce Data Project. 2003. *The outlook in 2003 for information technology workers in the U.S.A.* http://www.international.ucla.edu/.

Organization for Economic Co-Operation and Development (OECD). 2002. *Information technology outlook: ICTs and the information economy.* Paris: OECD.

Platman, K. 2003. Understanding the European information technology (IT) labour market: An interim report. Unpublished report prepared for the European team meeting of the WANE project, University of Cambridge.

Ranson, G. 2005. No longer "one of the boys": Negotiations with motherhood, as prospect or reality, among women in engineering. *Canadian Review of Sociology and Anthropology* 42: 145-66.

Sullivan, O. 2004. Changing gender practices within the household: A theoretical perspective. *Gender and Society* 18: 207-22.

Wajcman, J. 1998. *Managing like a man.* University Park: Pennsylvania State University Press.

WANE country reports. http://www.wane.ca.

Witz, A. 1992. *Professions and patriarchy.* London: Routledge.

Wolfson, W.G. 2003. *Analysis of labour force survey data for the information technology occupations, final report, June.* Prepared for Software Human Resource Council, Toronto.

4

Variants of Masculinity within Masculinist IT Workplace Regimes

Tammy Duerden Comeau and Candace L. Kemp

Entrepreneurial action, computing and managerial occupations, and business environments have traditionally been staked out as male terrain in a multitude of ways, all of which carry implications for IT firms and the workers within them. In this chapter, we take up Ranson and Dryburgh's classification of "gender regimes" among the WANE case study firms, looking in more depth at those firms deemed "masculinist" and examining how masculinities within these firms intersect and what the implications may be for employment equity and longevity for workers in these firms. As Ranson and Dryburgh point out, masculinist firms – those firms characterized by "male ethos" workplace cultures, few women, and informal, word-of-mouth recruitment practices – are the least conducive to employment diversity and the most in need of policy and reform. Yet this type of firm also evokes prominent cultural images of the "prototypical" IT firm where affiliations between youth, productivity, and technical innovation persist.

Given these affiliations, it is important to examine the nature of masculinist environments and variations between these firms (firms that often act as templates for images of the successful, innovative IT start-up) to assess the implications for workers as these firms evolve. Indeed, we found notable differences between and within masculinist firms over time. As Ranson and Dryburgh note, gender regimes are not static. How workplace cultures and organizational practices shift over time holds varying outcomes for aging owners and workers within these firms. To examine Ranson and Dryburgh's masculinist firms in more depth, we first explore variants of masculinity that have been charted in computing and other workplace environments.

Masculinities in IT

As Ranson and Dryburgh illustrate, the notion of a gender regime is useful for communicating how gender organizes work and action in institutions from task division to workplace culture (Connell 2002). Indeed, Connell's (1987, 2002) conceptualizations of gender have included and inspired explorations of masculinities within various workplace domains. According to Connell (2002, 44), masculinity can be understood as a "configuration of social practices linked to the position of men in the gender order, and socially distinguished from practices linked to the position of women." The nature of masculinity in computing work has its roots in a number of highly masculinized realms, including the military, engineering, and mathematics (Edwards 1990; Faulkner 2000; Hacker 1990; Wright 1996). The dominant themes here are the mastery of technical skills and the sublimation of the social. For example, Connell (1987, 181) describes the professional culture of engineers as a masculinity that is "emotionally flat, centered on a specialized skill, insistent on professional esteem and technically-based dominance over other workers." Here machines and technology are explicitly valued over humans and relationships (Faulkner 2000; Wright 1996). Wright (1996) argues that computing occupations possess a distinct form of occupational masculinity combining elements of engineering and hacker/nerd masculinity. She draws on Turkle's (1984) work to outline the culture of hackers/nerds as "being antisocial, and having no rules except mutual tolerance and respect for individualism, manipulation, and mastery of the computer" (1996, 84).

Studies on management masculinities have highlighted their pluralistic nature (Collinson and Hearn 1994, 2001; Whitehead 2002). Collinson and Hearn (2001) have identified numerous types of managerial masculinity in the corporate environments they examined, including paternalism, authoritarianism, entrepreneurialism, careerism, and informalism. Although paternalism entails a gentlemanly and sometimes benevolent father figure, authoritarianism is characterized by "intolerance of dissent or difference, a rejection of dialogue and debate and a preference for coercive power relations based on dictatorial controls and unquestioning obedience" (Collinson and Hearn 2001, 156). According to Collinson and Hearn (2001, 158), characteristics of entrepreneurial masculinity include keen competition, the endurance of long hours, and immovable work deadlines – a work ethic often spearheaded by younger businessmen though perhaps increasingly taken up in the global arena (Acker 2004). Entrepreneurial masculinity is characterized by the "self-made man and the macho, virile, swashbuckling and flamboyant entrepreneur" (McDowell 2001, 184). Indeed, scholars have found that the term "entrepreneur" itself signals a masculine presence and persona (Ahl 2002; Lewis 2006).

Although more recent studies of gendering in IT settings have emerged (Benn 2007; Peterson 2007), few have focused on differences among men and the implications of workplace cultures for men who cannot meet the dominant forms of masculinity. An exception is Cooper's (2000) study of men working in Silicon Valley IT firms, where she found a form of masculinity that was competitive, valuing "technical skills" more than "athletic ability." In Cooper's analysis, the dominant form of organizational masculinity entailed "men compet[ing] in cubicles to see who can work more hours, who can cut the best code, and who can be most creative and innovative ... Out-machoing someone means being more of a nerd than the other person" (2000, 382). Control of the labour process was rooted in this configuration of masculinity and experienced as internal and identity based: "Being a man" in IT required an all-encompassing commitment to technical work. Even so, the implications of this type of environment among men of different ages and for women were not an area of focus.

Since masculinities are not discrete but merge, wax, and wane over time, there is a need to explore how they intersect within organizations and what the implications are for workers (McDowell 2001). Hegemonic masculinities are those that predominate or are ascendant in given contexts; however, as Connell (2000, 10) points out, "different masculinities do not sit side-by-side like dishes on a smorgasbord. There are definite social relations between them ... Especially, there are relations of hierarchy for some masculinities are dominant while others are subordinated or marginalized." Indeed, age is a dimension of difference and a basis of inequality that may hold particular relevance in computing. As Calasanti (2004, 311) notes, hegemonic masculinity rests on expectations of youthfulness: peak performance and aggressive endurance. As men age, changes in their ability to compete may lead to feelings of marginalization in spite of the status and power that some men experience over time (Calasanti 2004).

In this chapter, we address the intersection of various organizational masculinities in perhaps the most masculine of IT work settings. Drawing on Ranson and Dryburgh's masculinist gender regimes, we explore the implications for workers in terms of workplace equity. In doing so, we use a case study approach examining how the lives of owners and workers shape the nature of workplace culture within the firm. The diversity of masculinities and their intersecting nature have been established, yet few studies have delved into how masculinities actually interact in organizational contexts. We are aided by the life-course perspective and particularly by the concept of "linked lives" (Elder 1998; Elder and Johnson 2003). In this context, the interlinkage of lives means that neither identities nor workplace cultures are formed in isolation; rather, relationships and ties among individuals come to shape both gender identities and workplace cultures in time and place. In regard to configurations of masculinities in changing firms, the life-course events of its members (particularly those in positions of power) often skew the direction and evolution of workplace culture and policy.

Analysis

Although we elected to focus on the ten firms deemed masculinist gender regimes, our initial analysis involved twenty-four WANE firms, including five in Australia, ten in Canada, four in England, and five in the United States. We used a firm-based approach, attempting to understand the firm as a unit of analysis, and analyzed data from each firm before narrowing our focus. Our initial analysis began with a consideration of two IT firms in our sample. Each author read case study reports, employee interviews, and field notes for these firms and made notes on emergent themes, particularly those surrounding workplace culture and practice. Using our emergent themes as a guide, we developed a preliminary coding scheme, which we then applied to our analysis of subsequent firms. We held regular meetings to discuss the coding scheme, including the definition, content, and application of codes. Code development involved returning to the data for clarification, and we refined codes in a reiterative process, particularly when new themes emerged or when our previously created codes did not fit the data. Throughout the analytic process, we worked collaboratively and were constantly verifying and refining codes until we could reach agreement.

Our final coding scheme captures a continuum of masculine workplace cultures as they emerged from our initial analysis. The workplace cultures are as follows: familial, brotherhood, craftsman, entrepreneurial, and bureaucratic. We did not find these workplace cultures to be mutually exclusive. Rather, as described by workers, all firms articulated at least two of these themes. What is compelling about the ten masculinist firms is the variation in workplace culture evident in spite of the replication of intersecting masculinities and organizational forms. As charted by Ranson and Dryburgh, of the ten masculinist firms, six are from Canada, two are from the United States, one is from Australia, and one is from England. The firms range in size from four to twenty-one people, and they range in age from three to fourteen years. The median age of the workers in these firms varies from 24 to 41.5; however, only two of these firms have a median age over 40. Again, characteristic of masculinist firms, only two firms have up to two women employed.

Masculinity Types

Among the ten masculinist firm regimes, the most common intersecting masculinities were those we classify as brotherhood and entrepreneurial. Entrepreneurial masculinity has been variously characterized as a highly competitive, macho ethic – the exhibition of a virile and confident business aura, a drive to succeed and conquer, and a rather unbending attitude to do whatever it takes to complete the project, make the deal, and so on. In its extreme form, completion of work is its ultimate priority. At the conclusion of our analysis, it became apparent that entrepreneurialism in this vein was present to varying degrees in all of our sample firms. Thus, though we discuss entrepreneurialism in our case studies, it is an a priori workplace culture for these firms, many of which emerged from the remnants of failed companies with the determination to succeed at all costs. Brotherhood masculinities can be considered an acceleration and/or exaggeration of like-sibling ties. These ties are based on shared interests, boyish pursuits, and a certain amount of playful banter, competitive, sporty games, and guyish surroundings.

Formalized bureaucracies were largely absent from our firms; however, elements of a rationalized, bureaucratic impulse in relation to policy were integrated with and/or emergent in some entrepreneurial workplace cultures. We have called this type of bureaucratic masculinity "strategic" as it appears to be utilized in efforts to respond to worker insurgence and to selectively enforce discipline and control when needed. These responses tended to involve rationalizing and depersonalizing work processes/procedures and developing policies that insulated the firm to some extent from the idiosyncrasies of individual workers. In contrast, elements of craftsmanship masculinity and the importance of technical skill and problem-solving facilities formed a significant component of some firms' workplace cultures. When present, this impulse exuded most strongly from the workers themselves, with some exceptions. Pride in the ability to innovate, create, and work deeply in technology comprised a significant part of the masculine work identity for some workers, and this component could work either to spur on workers to solve a problem (contributing to the success and buoying entrepreneurial workplace cultures) or, in some instances, to clash with business imperatives and considerations.

Familial masculinities were also present, and they describe work environments that were informal, casual, friendly, and caring to some degree as opposed to formal, corporate environments. In some firms, owners and managers acted in paternal or protective roles, while in others disciplinary authority reigned from parental-type figures. Indeed, in small firms, the lack of separation and the blurred lines of authority, space, and position often lent themselves to mimicking familial-type ties.

The mobilization of these gendered resources both individually by workers and in the organizational context of masculinist firms themselves influenced the pace of work, the value placed on workers, and the activities and workplace cultures in the firms. In what follows, we present our findings using a collective case study approach (Stake 2005). We draw on four firms to illustrate similarities and difference and describe their history, composition, nature of work, and workplace culture. These cases were selected as they best illustrate the varied nature of intersecting organizational masculinities within masculinist gender regimes and their implications for equitable workplace relations. Our case study firms were also chosen because they differ from one another in terms of workplace culture. As a collective, they illustrate varying degrees of entrepreneurialism and its intersections with other masculinities. Further, these cases demonstrate the diversity of workplace cultures within a common masculinist gender regime and operate as cultural snapshots of highly masculine work environments. We begin with a case study of Cytek – a premier brotherhood/entrepreneurial firm that has persisted for more than a decade and evolved from earlier ventures into a staunchly masculinist regime.

Case Studies

Case 112: Cytek

Cytek is a Canadian-based firm that was initially formed in the late 1990s. It is a stable, fourteen-person operation that dominates a highly specialized niche in software application work. Four owners, a younger technical wizard and three older business-savvy entrepreneurs, run the firm. It is among those exhibiting the most masculine of workplace cultures. The median age of employees in this firm is thirty-three, though the ages range from nineteen to sixty-two, and the owners admittedly seek youngish, preferably unattached, workers to perform their highly skilled technical roles and/or those involving travel. Indeed, though they do not specify that they seek men, one of the owner-partners considers IT "a real young guy's game" (1112133, late forties, man) and another says that their office decor is spartan and geared to a younger crowd because "we knew we were going to be hiring younger people" (1112016, late forties, man).

Including the owners, fewer than half of the firm's workers are married (40 percent), and just over half have children (55 percent). The pace of work is rapid, and technical workers in particular are often at the mercy of demanding clients. Entrepreneurial teams and the ethic to "get the work done" are the emphases here, with little concern for clocking hours per se. The owners label the worksite a "boy's club," and a plethora of masculine activities and pursuits makes the workplace culture at Cytek predominantly one of "brotherhood."

The management style at Cytek is "hands off" and flexible, and it promotes a "fun" workplace culture. Activities and environmental surroundings include golf putting, darts, video games, movies, soccer, and football should workers want to take a break. The CEO describes the workplace culture as follows:

> Um, the partners are older guys but still think they're younger guys ... Most people wear jeans to work, they wear shorts to work in the summer ... We've got video games in the back and satellite TV ... It's just very, very laid back and informal, but we get a lot of work done even though it is very casual. (1112146, late thirties, man)

In the case of this firm, though there is diversity in age, those on the older end of the spectrum are the owners, and they decidedly do not want to take on a paternal or particularly authoritative role; rather, they explicitly want to be "one of the boys" and to play along with the young guys. All of the owners have worked in large corporate organizations and do not want to replicate that experience here. According to one owner, managing people is a headache – this venture began with the idea "to primarily just have fun, make enough money to, you know, have a good living, and not have to answer to anybody, and it was a bit of ... a clubhouse, you know, that was the whole attitude this started with. And then the damn thing went off and got successful, and we had to hire other people" (1112133, late forties, man). In this way, the owners reject the title of "boss"; one owner says, "I would kick myself in the butt if I ever heard one of these people saying that I acted like a boss ... You know, [a] little place like this, you shouldn't have to have a boss. Everybody is working towards a common goal, and one person isn't any more important than the other person" (1112016, early sixties, man). Employees agree, and one software engineer in his late twenties notes that the relationship with management/owners is the "same as employee to employee really" (1112107, late twenties, man). The refrain of not wanting to be like a "boss" was a common one among our case firms, where brotherhood workplace cultures predominated.

Like the majority of the staff here, the oldest technical worker, a software engineer in his late thirties, highly values the informal workplace culture: "We're all into sports, so we throw the football around, kick a soccer ball, and stuff like that, so it's fun, it's very easygoing. We've got an Atari game back there, you know" (1112159, late thirties, man). There is less talk among technical workers here of the "joy of technical craftsmanship" and more of the appeal of the fun, casual workplace culture. Indeed, these leisure activities act as a buffer to demanding work requirements. Although the management style is very laid back and flexible, there is a great deal of work and little leeway (if any) on project deadlines and client demands.

Again, the flexibility offered in hours and work direction comes at a price. This software engineer says that work is done on the basis of "who [which client] is yelling at us more."

> It's 100 percent up to me what I do during the day. But come Friday, this and this and this have to be done. If I take, you know, not that I can take three days off at the beginning of the week, but I can do whatever I want to do during the day as long as things get done. And that's really the only stipulation. And when things start to slip, you know, then I guess their binoculars get out on you, and you're under the gun a bit. (1112107, late twenties, man)

Personal time management and taking responsibility for getting the work done are key priorities, and only when deadlines come into question does management tighten its grip and demand results. At the same time, there is little need for such flexibility among the workers as most of them are single men. The firm seeks those who will work with little provocation. As the CEO says,

> I don't impose a lot of structure on the environment because it seems to be working now. And it's very unstructured, where all people know what their responsibility is, they're very committed, and you'll come in here on the weekend, you'll find staff here working not because I asked them to, just 'cause ... they want to. (1112146, late thirties, man)

Still, workers might feel compelled to get the job done; if it takes coming in on the weekend to do it, then that is what they do. One divorced father at the firm appreciates the flexibility when he is with his children but says that, when he is child-free, they can work him "to the bone" (1112159, late thirties, man). This feast-or-famine logic, where there is a sharp dichotomy between working and playing hard, is hardly conducive to long-term work-life balance. As another engineer approaches fatherhood, he expresses a desire to readjust his life priorities. Whether or not the firm will be flexible toward men who want to be active parents and avoid excessive hours is not yet clear; however, traditional notions of motherhood and fatherhood seem to structure how flexible employment conditions are conceived and operationalized at this firm.

Indeed, the fun activities to offset the workload are designed to appeal to a particular type of worker: young, unattached, and male. Chucking foam balls at one another or competing at golf, darts, and Nintendo is not for everyone. The workplace activities are geared to young men. This masculinist organization offers a sharp contrast to the following English firm, which has been in operation for nearly the same amount of time yet undergone a different trajectory in workplace culture and practice.

Case 401: Learning Link
Based in England, Learning Link began nearly a decade and a half ago out of the remains of a failed IT company. At the time of our study, staff members included six original partners and three additional workers employed in technical jobs. The nine workers ranged in age from twenty-nine to forty-three, and only one (a partner) is a woman. Among the most distinctive features of the e-learning company is the rotation of the directorship between partners and subsequent decision making by committee.

As with all other firms examined here, Learning Link's workplace culture reveals entrepreneurialism, but its prevalence has waned somewhat over time, corresponding with the change in the partners' family responsibilities. In the early years, when the six partners ranged in age from twenty-four to thirty-three, and none was a parent, the firm was highly macho, entrepreneurial in terms of workplace culture and practice. The partners put in long hours, worked to tight deadlines, and in doing so made personal, social, and financial sacrifices for the firm's (and ultimately their own) success. According to one of the partners,

> when we started the company, it was very hard, and it was ... more than a full-time job just to keep the company on its feet and solvent, you

know. We'd be calculating it down to the pennies what we could pay ourselves, and some weeks it wouldn't be anything [laughs], you know. (4401055, early forties, man)

Their dedication and ability to deliver (no matter how tight the deadline) made them very popular with clients. Insofar as it has remained client focused and driven, Learning Link has retained elements of entrepreneurialism, but it has evolved into a familial workplace with some elements of subdued brotherhood.

After being together for many years, those at Learning Link share a bond akin to family relations. Yet unlike other firms, where family relationships translate into sibling rivalry and favouritism, there is little hierarchy. Relationships are largely egalitarian. Although they "do get on very well," typical of family relationships, discussions between partners and staff occasionally escalate into "murderous rows" and "huge volatile screaming." Arguments have not held them back but "dragged" them "forward." One partner put it this way:

It's like arguing with the husband and wife ... You have the screaming rows with people you're closest to that you would never have with other people. You take out your frustrations and anger and whatever on the people that you're closest to rather than other people. Because you know that it doesn't matter, that you'll still be stuck together the next day. You know, you're still, you know, mother and daughter, brother and sister, husband and wife, or whatever the next day. (4401068, late forties, woman)

Thus, despite the odd row, partners and other staff members view one another as kin.

Further reinforcing their family-like relations, over time those at Learning Link have shared many life-course transitions and personal experiences, particularly those related to parenthood and the care of a parent. For instance, one of the firm's workers explains that he needed time off to care for his terminally ill parent: "I worked remotely a lot then, and you know I helped my family care for him ... I mean [my colleagues] came down and helped me. They drove me places, they came to the funeral" (4401016, late twenties, man). Perhaps most importantly, by the early 2000s, all but one of the partners had children, and the pressure of this "baby boom" ultimately influenced workplace culture and work practices. At first, the partners were reluctant to support flexible working arrangements, particularly in terms of working at home. The partners soon realized, however, that flexible arrangements (working remotely, variable hours, and part-time work) were one way that they and other employees could negotiate life changes, accommodating their needs and preferences while retaining the workers so indispensable to Learning Link.

Delving further into this case study, however, it seems that workplace culture and relationships are not entirely as cohesive as presented above. The firm's multiple worksites, including working from home and at a client site, mean that face-to-face meetings are relatively rare, and sometimes workers do not "talk to each other for a month." These arrangements lead to less brotherhood, including the daily playfulness, as well as social and physical activity noted in other male-dominated IT firms. Nevertheless, according to one of the partners, when this group gets together, their "certain cultural style" could be interpreted as "unprofessional." For instance, they seem to enjoy "taking the piss out of each other all the time" (4401068, late forties, woman). In other words, they like to aggravate each other on occasion.

Of all the masculinist case study firms, Learning Link's workplace culture holds the most promise for aging in IT. The longevity enjoyed by Learning Link allows us to consider how workplace culture can change over time and how such change can be responsive to the life-course transitions of its members. Over time, the retreat of highly entrepreneurial tendencies in favour of work practices more supportive of work-life balance has positive implications for aging and life-course transitions as experienced by those in the IT industry.

In terms of gender, the relative absence of women in the firm suggests that it may not be a particularly female-friendly work environment. Yet the lone female partner does not feel out of place and is considered part of the team. With both child and parent care responsibilities, she has far more duties than her male colleagues, but the organization of work allows her to manage these duties. As Ranson and Dryburgh point out, her positioning as "one of the boys" has allowed her to operate successfully in this environment.

The family-like relationships that have grown within this group of owners (and workers) are related to the length of their connections and their overlapping lives. Being in it together "for better or worse" has lent itself to a supportive environment – in terms of both workers' responses to one another and workplace practices. As they play out in Learning Link's history, the family-like relationships alongside the playful brotherhood dimensions create one of the more supportive environments for those who wish to remain in IT beyond their youth. In this case, entrepreneurial masculinities have eased, and brotherhood ties have evolved into more familial-based connections. Still, though these developments have benefited the tight-knit group of owners, it is unclear whether this greater flexibility would apply equally to potential new recruits.

Case 111: Web-Based Designs

Located in Canada, our next case study, Web-Based Designs, has been in business for nearly a decade and a half. The early years involved considerable personal sacrifice by the two founders and their families, but the firm has enjoyed success and is planning for continued growth. With twenty-one workers (including owners and managers), the firm is the largest of the small firms in our sample. The company designs web-based products and involves three distinct divisions: client services, sales and marketing, and development. Its current organizational structure involves four key decision makers: the CEO/president, executive vice-president, marketing manager, and head of client services. All are men.

Firm demographics reflect patterns typical of the industry. Of those interviewed, the median age is thirty, with a range of twenty-three to forty-seven years. The two founders are married with children, and four other workers have children. With two women in client services and one in office administration, they are the minority. These elements are characteristic of masculinist regimes. Like all firms examined here, web-Based Designs demonstrates elements of entrepreneurialism. Everyone is aware that the goal is growth. There is evidence of teamwork and drive toward the unified aim of success. Because of its size, organization, and composition, Web-Based Designs represents a firm with a highly pluralistic workplace culture where threads of familial, brotherhood, and entrepreneurial workplace cultures are evident.

Workplace relations at Web-Based Designs are routinely described using familial metaphors. The partnership between the two founders was described as a "successful marriage." However, the early years appear to have been marked by greater periods of equality and compatibility than the present. According to the executive vice-president, "we go through stages. It's not unlike a marriage in that I, you know, we were obviously fairly close friends at the time that we started the company. I wouldn't say we're close friends now. I would say we're good acquaintances. We get along fine, but we do argue" (1191042, early forties, man). The CEO's aggressive outbursts make it difficult to disagree with him, which in many ways has made the executive VP more of a silent partner.

Regardless of the balance of control and the ebb and flow of their relationship, to a certain extent the partners' life-course transitions and their real family relationships have been mutually influential and affected hiring decisions and work allocations. To have some semblance of family life, they got "somebody else to help carry the ball" so that they could eat dinner at their "own kitchen table once in a while" (1191042, early forties, man). Although there is some flexibility for workers in terms of accommodating their life-course needs, their company demographics mean that they have only needed to be flexible with one employee – a single mother. Consequently, the life-course transitions of their employees have not given rise to significant changes in how business is done at Web-Based Designs.

In terms of stewardship, this firm is like a traditional family in which the allocation of resources, space, and rewards is determined top down and influences employee relations. At the broadest level, the founders might be seen as parental figures who favour the developers, giving them preferential treatment over those in sales and marketing and in client services. However, workers bring their own ideas and responses to their co-workers, and the work environment shapes the workplace culture within the firm.

For its part, the client services department is located in a different, smaller, more dimly lit space with its own entrance. This separation alongside differential treatment has led to a strong sense of team among client services representatives as well as resentment and an "us and them" mentality toward the other divisions. According to one employee, "we feel very much as though we do a lot of the work here and get little of the credit" (1191107, early forties, man). The lack of company-supported training for client services has at least one worker, a female trainer, skeptical of having longevity in the firm. In general, the client services team feels disadvantaged, underpaid, and undervalued relative to those in the industry and more specifically those around them. For the most part, this perceived disadvantage has led to bonding and camaraderie among them and competition with others. Yet, for one young male client services employee, the fact that two of his closest co-workers are not men is disconcerting. In his words, "if I call for support, I picture someone sort of like me, generally a young guy" (1191029, early twenties, man). Although his vision of IT reflects the gender composition of the development team and his aspirations for a career in development, at Web-Based Designs the separation between divisions, including their workplace cultures, is a barrier to his inclusion.

Members of the development division are well bonded. Unlike those in client services, this bonding is not a response to their collective treatment. Rather, the programmers have bonded through similar interests, hobbies, and lifestyles. Their brotherhood is representative of those found in other firms as it is articulated in ways that solidify similarities and point out gender and age differences in the workplace, often to the end of exclusion.

Lunchtime at the office is illustrative. Housed in the area occupied by development and the sales and marketing divisions, the lunchroom is considered by most to be the programmers' territory. According to one programmer, "lately it's just been the development crew ... I guess everybody else is scared of us" (1191120, age unknown, man). Typically, there is a cribbage game and "guy" conversation (see Ranson and Dryburgh in this volume).

One of the women in client services ate lunch with the development crew in the past and described her experience thus:

The conversation in that lunchroom was just so guy ... It's all about how much drinking they can do, you know, and this, that, and the other thing, and then, you know, it has verged a couple of times into territory that the guys need to be a little bit careful of. (1191094, early thirties, woman)

Although she indicated that she is not offended by these behaviours, she has ceased going to the lunchroom. As suggested above, she is not alone in avoiding it.

There is a sense of youthfulness and immaturity implicit in this form of fraternal masculinity. Although not necessarily excluded from these goings-on, the development manager, at age thirty-five, considers himself "not young at all" and working in "a young company" with "young people." Moreover, he explains, "for the first time in my life ... I'm realizing that ... I just need to get over the trappings of the young rebel, because I'm not him anymore" (1191146, age thirty-five, man). The fact that he once was a "young punk" similar to the young developers he manages contributes to his understanding, tolerance, and acceptance of this behaviour, all the while excluding himself and being excluded by their antics.

Web-Based Designs demonstrates how workplace practices and cultures can be exclusionary, especially along the lines of gender and aging. The life-course transitions of the partners (namely, marriage and parenthood) have altered their personal approaches to work and to hiring rather than the way work gets done more generally. Hoping to reduce some of their work responsibilities, they have increased the number of employees at the firm. Having employees without substantial family responsibilities supports their personal preferences for organizational growth but also work-life balance. Nevertheless, it remains to be seen how work practices might be altered to respond to changing employee demographics.

The brotherhood workplace culture that has developed among the technical employees, as well as the sibling-like rivalry between divisions, create situations of inclusion and exclusion, based in part on occupation, gender, and age. For instance, the behaviours of the young engineers solidify the bonds between them but create a less-than-friendly work environment for women and older workers. Even those who once identified with the group find its membership somewhat unsustainable as their careers and lives progress.

Case 117: Hightechnik

Hightechnik began four years ago in classic IT start-up fashion as a gleam in the eye of its founder, who gathered up his technically skilled friends and started the firm out of his garage. Now the firm operates out of a snappy downtown office in a large Canadian city where the original "techie" founder has paired up with a practised IT entrepreneur. These two effectively split the tasks of the firm between business and technology; they also practise quite different management styles and personas. The business CEO operates the firm as if it is a large corporation and has recently developed more rigid work guidelines and policies. In contrast, the CTO practises a more flexible work ethic and has tolerance for less conventional work hours. This "disagreement over the level of flexibility" between the two owners is related to the CEO's quest to "maintain structure and discipline" during the growth process (1117175, late thirties, man).

Hightechnik employs fourteen workers and has keen plans to expand in its niche of high-level software engineering for the gaming industry. In terms of demographic profile, the firm is made up almost exclusively of young white men, many with formal computer science degrees, ranging in age from mid-twenties to mid-thirties. Six of the nine employees interviewed are married, and half of those married have young children. Only one young woman works in an administrative capacity; therefore, the gender composition of the workplace is overwhelmingly male. In addition, the tasks of the lone woman employee fall clearly under gender-stereotypical work. Supportive roles have also been played by the wives of both owners in their taking on of occasional contract work when required by the firm. In fact, workers admit that the gender composition of their firm has "gotten worse" (a woman in a technical role left), and it seems that those workers who were most ill suited to the more recent inculcation of bureaucratic procedures and disciplinary measures were winnowed out and/or left voluntarily.

In the midst of this, the firm is highly entrepreneurial and task driven, employing workers with a strong sense of craftsman masculinity and pride in their technical abilities. There is no reference to "family" or familial relations here other than by one worker, who compared managerial tactics and decision making to those of an "abusive parent" (1117032, early thirties, man). What is interesting about Hightechnik is how various masculinities – craftsman, bureaucratic, and entrepreneurial – clash in the workplace culture of the firm. There are many conflicting undercurrents between the imperatives of management and the expectations of workers. The CEO exudes classic bureaucratic masculinity – rationality, discipline, dedication, and commitment – combined with an entrepreneurial competitive spirit. In contrast, many of the programmers bring a "hacker ethic" based on craftsmanship and pride.

The firm carries some of the trappings of an idealized high-tech firm intent on growth – again, the workplace culture cultivated by management is somewhat divided and has evolved over time. The CEO has started and grown successful high-tech firms in the past and has substantial expertise in entrepreneurial ventures – his focus on business strategy and market growth has galvanized the firm, and he is intent on exerting control over growth: "Auditors walk in, and for a company of our size they're actually very surprised at how much fiscal discipline we have. Um, but my philosophy's always been that to be a big company you have to act like a big company from day one. So we do that" (1117175, mid-thirties, man). Operating like a large firm has led to the development and dissemination of a book that outlines several policies related to work processes, hours, and the like. The CEO wants to institute a policy on time off that treats sick days, vacation days, and any time off as all the same, with a "one-size-fits-all" policy limiting days off. There is a strong degree of mismatch between the strategic implementation of policy and the size of the firm:

> It's a small company, but the CEO kind of likes to run it as if it's a big company at times. So I suppose that's one of the things that some of the people didn't like but left. So I don't know, I guess there's things

like, you know, the core hours ... things like sort of acceptable use of computers. (1117045, late twenties, man)

I think they're suited to a larger company than we currently have. I think they're suited to a hundred to five hundred, hundred to a thousand, company as opposed to thirteen people. But you've got to start somewhere ... I mean, we have the policies, they're there, the things we need to enforce, the things we don't we kind of gloss over. (1117110, late twenties, man)

Workers have the sense of being oppressed, and one programmer who referred to the "rebels" who have left suggested that "a lot of people feel that they're, you know, their voice kind of goes unheard." This programmer talked enviously of the lengths that other firms will go to in order to accommodate workers: "You're our employees, we know you guys are going to have to work heavy deadlines for this, we're going to pamper you" (1117019, mid-twenties, man). In contrast to being "pampered," workers at Hightechnik feel underappreciated for what they regard as a prodigious level of skill. The mood in the firm is serious, there are no distractions or jokes among these young men, and generally there is a social distance created between the owners and the workers in spite of their social proximity.

The owners have great difficulty finding workers who are sufficiently skilled to perform the high-level work that they do, and all workers here are highly educated. The firm looks for "problem solvers" and "out of the box" thinkers and compares the tasks performed to that of "climbing Mount Everest." (1117175, late thirties, man)

In spite of the imperative to grow, the firm is not looking for corporate workers but those who will meet the tight deadlines to which the firm must work:

I look for how quickly they think on their feet, how effectively did they think out of the box, how well will they function in a team environment, do they understand what it's like to work in a start-up. Um, because the biggest mistake you can make is to hire somebody who's got that big corporate culture attitude and simply doesn't have the understanding of what it's like to work in a small entrepreneurial organization. (1117175, late thirties, man)

The work structure is entrepreneurial and growth driven; work is done in fluid teams, and in the past a great deal of overtime was common.

In this way, tight deadlines, team sacrifice, and pulling one's weight are second nature to workers here. Indeed, the CEO admits that last year's "crunch times" burned everyone out, and they have now put scheduling in place to try to ameliorate the need to work "eighteen-hour days" and the like (1117175, late thirties, man). In part, changes in the lives of the owners themselves have helped to spur these changes in organizational logic and policy. A senior manager who is expecting a child notes these changes:

> And our [CEO] and [CTO] both have had children in the last six or eight months. Um, and them having children at that time really helps. You can see the way that culture kind of overflows, and there's a lot of flexibility around that sort of thing. So there's, there's flexibility in what has to be done. We're also able to flex our hours ... That's kind of one of the policies, but there's generally, like it's on a case-by-case basis. (1117149, IT manager, early thirties, man)

The arrival of children in the lives of the owners has affected the firm's organizational policies and allowed parents to utilize some flex time. Another father at the firm with an infant takes advantage of this; however, the "case-by-case" distribution of this benefit has meant that those without children are not able to take advantage of this flexibility. Parenthood seems to be the only legitimate reason for occasionally working from home. Again, the strategic use of bureaucratic policies has benefited workers whose lives mimic those of the owners and left other workers disadvantaged in this regard.

The nature of the work itself – craftsmanship and the technical skill that the owners seek and the workers believe they bring – bumps up against the new bureaucratic regime. The employees are aware of their superior skill levels, and all express their love of the work process of "building and fixing." This programmer expresses the joy of this:

> And so there's a construction process, and at the same time you're using your own creativity to come by it, and in order to somehow solve the problem you've really got to pick your brains, you know, get out there, try things you've never really thought of before, and usually in the end there will always be some way of fixing it or building it. (1117019, late twenties, man)

Flexibility and fun in the creative process seem to have been present in the firm's past, but now the firm is bent on growth. In the midst of tight deadlines and relentless work, programmers have come to feel underappreciated. In response to a number of rules and policies but no pay increases, some workers have been described as "rebellious," and three have left in the past six months. This masculinist firm offers a unique example in the early phase of business growth, where craftsmanship masculinities conflict with bureaucratic masculinities all in the midst of life-course changes.

Conclusion

It is clear that masculinities in masculinist IT firms do not exist in static isolation; rather, they are shaped by both owners and workers. Shifts in entrepreneurial masculinity highlight both the intersections and the relevance of linked lives in examining workplace cultures in IT. Entrepreneurial masculinity in its most virulent form makes heavy demands on workers and encourages their highest allegiance to be to the firm. In these firms, variants of masculinity co-exist in different ways, sometimes bolstering and sometimes conflicting with organizational aims and directives. Indeed, in masculinist IT firms, the gender identities taken up and exhibited collectively can influence the workplace culture more strongly than might be evident in large firms (though of course there is a dialectical relationship here).

The familial/sibling workplace culture evident at Learning Link illustrates how initial virulent entrepreneurial masculinity may fade over time as the lives of owners and workers change. The concurrent life-course transitions among owners in this firm enabled a more flexible shift in working arrangements that appear to be more positive for aging and incorporating balance in life and work than those exhibited in other masculinist firms. At the same time, the team's homogeneous age demographic and lone woman suggest some exclusion. They admit that it would be difficult to incorporate new people into their tight-knit group. Further, in the early stages of the firm, all workers accepted and performed according to a rapid entrepreneurial work pace. Nonetheless, among the masculinist firms, this firm represents one of the more flexible, equitable, and less gender segregated along the continuum. In this sense, the "macho" workplace culture and masculinity of the firm have softened or mellowed over time in the face of late parenthood and life-course changes. Still, power relations are equitable here among most workers in the firm – an unusual feature, as is the inclusion of a woman in the firm's partnership.

In contrast, Web-Based Designs illustrates how a traditional familial structure in combination with a strong brotherhood element results in highly divided and poor gender relations in a masculinist firm. Prospects for career movement are limited in departments populated more by women and deemed to be less valuable to the firm. As the programmers articulated it, this form of brotherhood excludes those who are not part of their brotherhood workplace culture, including other men, women, and those who are older. Although formerly part of this brotherhood and in some cases accepting it, enabling it, and lamenting the loss of it, some of the older male workers also feel that they are on the periphery and do not participate, having moved into management. Indeed, tolerance of the often immature brotherhood antics of the programmers reinforces the preference for developers as the favourite children of the firm. This firm illustrates the divided workplace cultures that may develop over time as firms grow, and how brotherhood workplace cultures persist and are renewed by the hiring of ever-younger men to fulfill technical roles.

Yet the brotherhood workplace culture outwardly appears to be one of high solidarity and content employee-owner relationships. Cytek illustrates one of the most masculine workplace cultures. There the mostly older male owners have created or "engineered" something of an oasis where power differences are minimized, work is gender segregated, and play hard/work hard entrepreneurialism reigns supreme. Nonetheless, this firm shows how younger men are also at a disadvantage in brotherhood firms as they face significant pressures to continue to perform in spite of life-course changes, such as partnership, marriage, and children. This organizational arrangement suggests that, as younger men within the firm age, there is less flexibility offered to them in rearranging life priorities. Ultimately, brotherhoods are fun-filled work environments for "brothers," exclusive by design, with operational appeal to attract workers with few outside responsibilities. Firms such as Cytek, where younger workers are pushed to sacrifice balance in their personal lives, have questionable sustainability – what about men who are tired of boyish activities and women who continue to be excluded?

Hightechnik shows that, while in some cases entrepreneurial impulses and craftsman masculinity work well in concert, in instituting tighter restrictions on the work process, craftsmanship can act as a rallying point – the value placed on skill and work in this case spurs workers to resist and reject the imposition of bureaucracy: some by leaving the firm and stirring up dissent, others by considering leaving IT altogether. This firm suggests that the strategic use of bureaucracy by management may increase organizational inequity and result in the loss of workers on the periphery in IT: women and men who are not able or willing to live up to hegemonic masculinities in the firm. Yet shared life-course milestones and like circumstances between owners and workers may lead to preferential treatment for some workers at the expense of others.

Firms exhibiting masculinist regimes share male-dominated environments and restricted opportunities for workers who do not conform to, or cannot adapt to, the masculine aura of the workplace. At the same time, masculinist firms show considerable variance in the mechanics of how masculinities intersect and play out in the workplace culture of the firm. We suggest that persistent "hyper-masculinist" environments provide a cohesive fit for few people. Over time, the "hyper-masculinist" ethos becomes far less attractive and those workers (namely owners) who are able either change their work practices or extract themselves from positions guided by this ethos.

References

Acker, J. 2004. Gender, capitalism, and globalization. *Critical Sociology* 30, 1: 17-41.

Ahl, H.J. 2002. The construction of the female entrepreneur as the other. In *Casting the other: The production and maintenance of inequalities in work organizations,* ed. B. Czarniawska and H. Hopfl, 52-67. London: Routledge.

Benn, E.R. 2007. Defining expertise in software development while doing gender. *Gender, Work, and Organization* 14, 4: 312-32.

Calasanti, T. 2004. Feminist gerontology and old men. *Journal of Gerontology* 59B, 6: 305-14.

Collinson, D., and J. Hearn. 1994. Naming men as men: Implications for work, organization, and management. *Gender, Work, and Organization* 1: 2-22.

–. 2001. Naming men as men: Implications for work, organization, and management. In *The masculinities reader,* ed. S.M. Whitehead and F.J. Barrett, 144-69. Cambridge, UK: Polity Press.

Connell, R.W. 1987. *Gender and power: Society, the person, and sexual politics.* Cambridge, UK: Polity Press.

–. 2000. *The men and the boys.* Cambridge, UK: Polity Press.

–. 2002. Studying men and masculinity. *Resources for Feminist Research* 29, 1-2: 43-53.

Cooper, M. 2000. Being the "go-to guy": Fatherhood, masculinity, and the organization of work in Silicon Valley. *Qualitative Sociology* 23, 4: 379-405.

Edwards, P.N. 1990. The army and the microworld: Computers and the politics of gender identity. *Signs: Journal of Women in Culture and Society* 16, 1: 102-27.

Elder, G.H. Jr. 1998. The life course and human development. In *Handbook of child psychology: Theoretical models of human development,* 5th ed., ed. R.M. Lerner, 939-91. New York: Wiley and Sons.

Elder, G.H. Jr., and M. Kirkpatrick Johnson. 2003. The life course and aging: Challenges, lessons, and new directions. In *Invitation to the life course: Toward new understandings of later life,* ed. R.A. Settersten, 48-81. Amityville, NY: Baywood.

Faulkner, W. 2000. Dualisms, hierarchies, and gender in engineering. *Social Studies of Science* 30, 5: 759-92.

Hacker, S. 1990. The culture of engineering: Women, workplace, and machine. In *Doing it the hard way: Investigations of gender and technology,* ed. D.E. Smith and S.M. Turner, 111-26. Boston: Unwin Hyman.

Lewis, P. 2006. The quest for invisibility: Female entrepreneurs and the masculine norm of entrepreneurship. *Gender, Work, and Organization* 13, 5: 453-69.

McDowell, L. 2001. Men, management, and multiple masculinities in organizations. *Geoforum* 32, 2: 181-98.

Peterson, H. 2007. Gendered work ideals in Swedish IT firms: Valued and not valued workers. *Gender, Work, and Organization* 14, 4: 333-48.

Stake, R. 2005. Qualitative case studies. In *The Sage handbook of qualitative research,* 3rd ed., ed. N.K. Denzin and Y.S. Lincoln, 443-66. Thousand Oaks, CA: Sage.

Turkle, S. 1984. *Computers and the human spirit: The second self.* New York: Simon and Schuster.

Whitehead, S. 2002. *Men and masculinities.* Cambridge, UK: Polity Press.

Wright, R. 1996. The occupational masculinity of computing. In *Masculinities in organizations,* ed. C. Cheng, 77-96. London: Sage.

5
Negotiating Work and Family in the IT Industry
Ingrid Arnet Connidis and Candace L. Kemp

In this chapter, we examine the negotiation of work and family life in small information technology firms (those with five to twenty employees) in Canada and the United States, paying particular attention to gender relations and the masculine workplace culture of IT. We examine how workers negotiate IT employment and family responsibilities within the different contexts of related policy in the two countries and within the shared context of globalization, individualism, and welfare state restructuring. We address this question: How do gender relations shape negotiating work in the IT industry in tandem with meeting family responsibilities?

The challenges of globalization to balancing family and work life are particularly strong in the IT sector, where technology makes work truly global and especially subject to individual risk. As well, though many traditional professions such as law and medicine, and most entrepreneurial work, involve heavy time commitments, the pace of change in IT work distinguishes it from other forms of employment. Although individuals make decisions to advance their interests (not necessarily self-interests), they do so within a world that is socially constructed to meet capitalist and patriarchal goals. Consequently, many work-family conflicts experienced by individuals are a function of fundamental incompatibilities between the social domains of work and family, as currently arranged. When family-work conflict is viewed in this way, rather than as role conflicts to be resolved by individuals, social policies and social arrangements become the appropriate venues for conflict resolution (see Marshall, Matthews, and Rosenthal 1993). Yet the IT industry stands as a prime example of a new industry operating in a global economy during a time when retrenchment of the welfare state is forcing increasing individualization.

Using quantitative data from the reports of 178 employees in small IT firms in Canada and the United States, and qualitative data from two case studies, we focus on gender as a significant basis of structured social relations that affects labour market involvement (i.e., processes of production), familial responsibility (i.e., processes of reproduction), and the relationship between the two. The gendered demands of both family and work vary according to age and stage in the life course. Following the life-course perspective, the juxtaposition of social and personal time, the interdependence of social network members, the significance of life stage in affecting particular conditions in individual lives, and the drive to negotiate changing circumstances (see Elder 1991; Heinz 2001) is central to considerations of negotiating the balance of work and family in the IT sector.

Individualization, Gender, and the Construction of Work and Family

The emerging global society forms the backdrop for the negotiation of work and family life within the IT industry. The counter-pressures of the pull of a global economy and the push for local autonomy (Giddens 2002) establish paradoxes that are likely to engender ambivalence in family relationships (see Connidis and McMullin 2002a, 2002b) and labour relations. The process of economic globalization involves mobile capital, extensive international trade, enhanced mobility of highly skilled workers and jobs, and growth of multinational companies (Duxbury and Higgins 2003). This has implications not only for the broader political and social order but also for the organization of industries and corporations as well as for how individuals live their everyday lives. The global economic order is an interdependent one that introduces volatility and elements of uncertainty and risk for national governments and economies, corporations, and individuals.

The rise of the welfare state in most Western nations during the twentieth century meant a greater tendency to treat what Mills (1959) termed "personal" or "private troubles" as public issues: that is, a growing assumption of social responsibility for the welfare of individual citizens. Globalization has contributed to the decline of the welfare state; reduced social responsibility requires increased individual responsibility, the basis for what some have termed a "risk society" (Beck 1992, 1999). One form of lowered social responsibility for the government is increased privatization, a term that aptly captures pushing public issues back into the private realm. Because privatization often involves multinational firms, the values of a particular nation or society become more difficult to realize in the private sector.

The ongoing individualization of daily life brought about by globalization and the retrenchment of the welfare state (Beck 1999; Beck and Beck-Gernsheim 2002; Beck-Gernsheim 2002) means that, more and more, the requirements of institutions are directed at individuals rather than families. Referred to as "institutionalized individualism" (Beck-Gernsheim 2002), this trend encourages individuals to separate their lives from family interests and to assume risk and responsibility for their own actions. As discussed in Chapter 1, globalization fosters an economy based increasingly on part-time, self-employed, and contractually limited jobs in which "risk is being redistributed, shifting from the state and the market, on to individuals" (Beck 1999, 12).

Despite some discussion of the consequences of globalization for the interface between paid work and family (e.g., Blair-Loy and Jacobs 2003), considerably more attention is focused on work than on family relations (e.g., Caragata 2003; Denis 2003; Pyle and Ward 2003). Discussions that do relate the two topics to one another tend to be broad, noting global trends such as population aging, declines in birth rates and marriage, increases in co-habitation and divorce rates, and a general theme of the family in decline (see, e.g., Beck-Gernsheim 2002; Bengtson and Lowenstein 2002; Giddens 2002). These trends, along with the greater labour force involvement of women, lead Castells (2004) to conclude that the patriarchal family is in crisis and unlikely to recover. Similarly, Giddens (2002) argues that the move away from the traditional family has been a move toward "emotional democracy" in couple relationships and between parents and children that rests substantially on the emancipation of women.

In their application of the process of individualization to couple relationships, Lampard and Peggs (2007) review the increased risk that goes with the freedom to choose a partner, the increasing selfishness rather than selflessness that motivates finding a partner, and the relative change in the life courses of men and women in which women's experience has changed more than men's. For men, the ongoing obligation to engage in paid work combines with the process of individualized relationships as primarily one of emotional dependence. As a result, men are more anchored in expected and standard ways of doing things in the workplace that may spill over into their couple relationships. For women, the process of individualization creates a tension between "living their own life," including labour force participation, and "being there for others" (Beck and Beck-Gernsheim 1995, cited in Lampard and Peggs 2007). Thus, men and women experience individualism in relationships differently, challenging the assertion that globalization represents a consistent threat to patriarchy. Instead, shifts in men's and women's lives represent a tension between hanging on to patriarchal traditions and emancipating women and children. To the extent that this emancipation is facilitated by public policy initiatives, a turn toward greater individualism is a threat to such change.

Discussions of individualism in the context of partner relationships do not address the broader question of reproducing patriarchy in other spheres of social life – particularly paid labour – and its consequences for family relations. The gendered experience of individualization in relationships may be the basis for different approaches to negotiating careers in IT by married men and women. The traditional expectations of men in the workplace may be mirrored in traditional approaches to the division of labour at home that support their efforts in the market. Such an approach is not likely to be an effective strategy among women in IT given that their involvement in paid labour contradicts traditional assumptions of women's commitment to reproductive labour and that success in paid labour would be thwarted by a traditional gendered division of domestic labour.

Historical analysis shows that Canadian parents spent more time on child care in the 1990s than did parents in the 1970s (Comparative Public Policy Research Laboratory 2004), primarily at the expense of parents' leisure and personal time. According to Daly (1996, 2002), changing cultural expectations and practices pertaining to work and family reflect contradictions in values. In general, women are expected to maintain high levels of commitment to their careers while simultaneously making family a priority. Meanwhile, expectations for men include being committed to family but also being the primary provider. Yet, though many fathers are spending more time with their children and desire more time at home with them (Peterson and Steinmetz 2000), their employers do not facilitate such aspirations (Gornick and Meyers 2003). The contradictions and conflicts created by changing configurations of work and family life that are left largely to individual solutions mean an ever-escalating level of negotiation and planning to manage daily activities (Beck and Beck-Gernsheim 2002).

Gender equality is more evident at early career stages, when the playing field is more level in terms of family obligations (no children) and training (parallel experience in terms of education and recent work). The organization of work and the characteristics of the workplace, including the gender composition and parental status of co-workers, can facilitate or constrain decisions to have children among women who are university graduates (Ranson 1998). Women who perceive their occupations and workplaces as family-friendly are more likely to have children.

For those who have children, the demands of family across the life course are likely to have a greater impact on middle-aged ("older") workers, particularly women, who find it increasingly difficult to look after school-age and adolescent children (Polatnick 2002) and remain successful participants in the labour force. This stage of the life course may also include re-entry into the labour force as a full-time worker following a period of reduced or no paid labour and, consequently, falling behind developments in the field (Demaiter 2004). When fast-paced change characterizes work, as is true of IT work, catching up is especially difficult.

The IT sector is not particularly attractive to women because of the traditional masculine workplace culture that dominates both IT education and work (Dryburgh 1999; Ranson 2003; see Chapters 3 and 4 in this volume). Attempts to explain women's underrepresentation in the IT industry rest heavily on the content of the work, particularly in the higher echelons, in which background training in math, computer programming, engineering, and related fields is seen as essential, putting women at a disadvantage. But this is only part of the story. The organization of IT work is based on what Kanter (1977, 22) has called a "masculine ethic," in which it is assumed that employees have few outside obligations competing with work.

In her qualitative study of married, thirty to forty-four-year-old fathers employed in the high-tech industry, Cooper (2000) suggests that unique definitions of masculinity are central to the negotiation of work and family life. Masculinity in the high-tech sector corresponds with the needs of the technology industry – being competitive and on the cutting edge – and the organization of labour in the new economy – short-term, often contractual employment. Traditional definitions of masculinity rely on athletic ability and appearance; in the IT industry, masculinity is associated with technical skill, brilliance, stamina (working long hours), commitment, and virility (see also Chapter 4 in this volume). Cooper argues that the masculine identity becomes a mode of achieving company goals, a form of control in high-tech workplaces that ultimately spills over into family life. These men's experiences indicate that, under normal conditions, their IT work must come before family. Only in the event of a personal crisis does family take precedence. These contradictions in the IT industry do not add up to a friendly work environment for women or family-oriented men.

At the same time, at least in principle, IT work is often flexible, with greater opportunities for taking advantage of technology, including the opportunity to work at home or outside the office (Demaiter 2004; McGee 2000). Among IT employers who offer their employees flexible work arrangements, many view such flexibility as contributing positively to the bottom line and creating more loyal and contented employees (Gordon 2001). The flexibility of IT occupations is considered by some in the industry to be well suited to women who wish to negotiate work and family (e.g., McGee 2000; Thompson 1982). However, the portability of work also means that work can more easily intrude on family time and resources (Salaff 2000; Webster 2000). Beck-Gernsheim (2002, xi) suggests that attempts to make work practices more flexible are tolerable for those who are young, single, and healthy, but children as well as couples "suffer when work stretches further and further round the clock and around the globe."

The ambiguity of temporal and spatial boundaries designating work from non-work (Duxbury and Higgins 2003) applies to IT-related occupations that demand long hours, are highly competitive, and rely heavily on technology and communication. Women in the IT community are concerned about "round-the-clock demands" of their jobs, and substantial numbers contemplate quitting their jobs as a result (Gordon 2001). Employees who opt for more flexible work arrangements in firms that offer them are often penalized (McGee 2000), and taking advantage of such work arrangements may be more difficult as one's IT career advances.

Gender is a clear marker of contrasting experience as life-course transitions accumulate. The arrival and rearing of children implicate women more than men and interrupt their accumulation of current experience and upgrading of skills in the workplace. Thus, the life-course trajectories of both family and work become increasingly dissimilar over time (by age) and between men and women (by gender). Further, there is far greater variability in experience among women than among men, so that older women are not as representative of all women who entered the labour force at younger ages as are older men of all men. This is probably especially true in relatively new careers such as those in IT.

Methods

We now consider the experiences of 178 IT workers in small firms in the United States and Canada (see Chapter 2 for a detailed description of the study). We have selected twenty-one small firms with five to twenty employees in order not to make firm size an issue. Although we do not have a representative sample of IT workers, we do have a unique opportunity to consider issues related to balancing work and family from the perspective of men and women working in IT firms of similar size in two countries. More importantly, intensive data provided by multiple members from the same firm allow for a case study analysis that reveals different perspectives on a parallel work experience.

For general information on the 178 participants, we combined data obtained from an in-person interview (completed by 178 of the respondents) and online survey (completed by 97 of the Canadian respondents and 36 of the US respondents). For a more intensive analysis of balancing work and family, we selected two firms, one from the United States and one from Canada. We chose these firms because they are similar in size and type of IT business, which facilitates comparison. Further, the men and women from these firms represent a range of experiences in balancing family and career responsibilities. Our case study firms employ both mothers and fathers, allowing us to analyze intensively the experiences of mothers, fathers, and workers without parental responsibilities in similar firms. Our method is a version of an instrumental case study (Stake 2005), in which an intensive analysis of two cases provides insight into the dynamics of balancing work and family in the IT sector, with a particular focus on gender.

Based on information provided in the interviews and online surveys, we selected the Canadian firm Integrative Solutions (Firm 101) and the US firm Advanced Designs (Firm 502). The firms share the following characteristics: they are small software development companies ($n = 11$ and 8, respectively), both have been in business for over five years, they are located in cities of similar size, and both employ individuals of variable ages and family statuses. The firms differ from each other as well. Advanced Designs employs fewer women but has more parents with young children. Also, despite the different policy contexts of the two countries, this firm's flexible work practices make it potentially more family friendly compared with Integrative Solutions. There was not a US firm with as high a proportion of mothers as was true for the Canadian firms, so the US firm has fewer mothers and a smaller proportion of mothers than the Canadian firm.

Our case study analysis began with intensive readings of the transcripts and the survey data relevant to work-life balance for each employee in both firms. We then wrote a work-family profile for each individual, attaching all relevant qualitative data. Our analysis paid particular attention to similarities and differences between employees in each firm and then turned to compare patterns across firms. As we documented individual and firm patterns, we focused on how factors such as gender, location in the life course, work practices, and policies influenced experiences.

Results

We begin by discussing the data for all 178 IT workers. Descriptive data regarding variables that are relevant to capturing variations in demands for balancing work and family are presented in Table 5.1. In both countries, and similar to national averages, women are less than one-quarter of the sample, 24 percent in Canada and 20 percent in the United States. Over three-quarters of the participants in both countries are under the age of forty-five, making a spouse and children the most likely family responsibilities in this sample. Sixty-eight percent of the 129 small IT firm workers in Canada and almost 79 percent of the 49 IT workers in the United States are married or co-habiting. The balance are mainly single (never married), though nearly 10 percent of the Canadian respondents are divorced or separated. Very similar proportions in both countries – 54.7 percent in Canada and 54 percent in the United States – have children.

In the lower half of Table 5.1, the data for each country are presented by gender. In Canada, more men than women are in software development, and more women than men are in consulting or business. Differences between men and women in the United States are muted, perhaps due to small numbers. Similar percentages of men and women are under the age of forty-five in both countries, with slightly fewer women in this age group. In the US sample, similar percentages of women (77.8) and men (78.9) are married, but in the Canadian sample there are marked gender differences in marital status, with almost 83 percent of the women married compared with 67 percent of the men. Yet, in the Canadian sample, similar percentages of women (56.1) and men (54.4) are parents. This means that, even though women are more likely to be married, they are less likely to have children. In other words, a considerably higher proportion of married men than married women in these IT firms have children. This suggests that the combination of IT work with marriage is more of a barrier to having children among women than among men. The same patterns do not play out in the US data, but with such small numbers (e.g., only ten women) it is difficult to make much of these descriptive data. Even the Canadian data are only suggestive, given that they do not comprise a random sample. However, when coupled with

Table 5.1

Percentage of distributions of small IT firm workers for Canada and the United States

	Canada (n = 129)	United States (n = 49)
# Firms	15.0	6.0
% Women	24.0	20.0
% <45 years old	75.8	76.6
Marital status		
% Married/cohabiting	68.0	78.7
% Separated/divorced	9.4	4.3
% Single	22.7	17.0
% Parents	54.7	54.0

By gender	Women (n = 31)	Men (n = 98)	Women (n = 10)	Men (n = 39)
Firm type				
Software/web development	56.1	78.8	80.0	74.4
Systems analysis/support	4.9	7.3	20.0	25.6
Consulting/business	39.0	13.9	0.0	0.0
% <45 years old	73.2	76.9	70.0	78.4
Marital status				
% Married/cohabiting	82.5	67.4	77.8	78.9
% Separated/divorced	5.0	8.9	0.0	5.3
% Single	12.5	23.7	22.2	15.8
% Parents	56.1	54.4	60.0	53.8

the reports of respondents concerning the division of household labour, there is suggestive evidence that men and women take quite different approaches to balancing marriage/partnering with IT work.

In Table 5.2, we show responses from the online survey to a question asking partnered respondents how they divide household tasks with their spouses or partners, by gender, for Canada and the United States combined. Data regarding division of labour were obtained in response to an item on the online survey: "In your home, the household tasks (e.g., cleaning, cutting lawns, dinner preparation, etc.) that you and your partner do (i.e., do not include things that you pay others to do) are taken care of ..." with response categories ranging from "primarily by me" to "primarily by my spouse/partner." Eighty-four of the 127 married respondents completed the survey, and 76 of them answered this question.

Table 5.2

Division of household tasks and child care: Online survey data for small firms in Canada and the United States

	Female	Male	Total
Division of household tasks	(*n* = 20)	(*n* = 56)	(*n* = 76)
Primarily by me	2	3	5
More by me than by my partner	3	4	7
Equally by me and my partner	15	26	41
More by my partner than by me	–	18	18
Primarily by my current partner	–	5	5
Division of child care	(*n* = 10)	(*n* = 34)	(*n* = 44)
Primarily by me	2	2	4
More by me than by my partner	3	1	4
Equally by me and my partner	4	19	23
More by my partner than by me	1	7	8
Primarily by my current partner	–	3	3
Other	–	2	2

Marked patterns emerge, with 15 of 20 women (75 percent) reporting that they share domestic labour equally compared with 26 of 56 men (46 percent). Twenty-three men report a disproportionate division of labour in which their partners do more than they do. None of the female participants make the same claim. Five of 20 women (25 percent) versus 7 of 56 men (12.5 percent) report that they do more of the household tasks. Similar trends apply to Canada and the United States when the data are observed for each country (not shown). These findings correspond with other studies on the division of domestic labour among full-time, partnered adults and suggest that a primary strategy used by partnered women in IT work is to negotiate an equitable division of labour in the home. This would promote a revised gender contract in which both paid and unpaid labour are considered the domains of both men and women. Partnered men in IT work often take an opposite tack. A strategy used by many of them for meeting the demands of IT work is to have a partner who assumes more than her fair share of household labour. Given the predominance of men in IT work, this counter-pressure means, first, that the net effect of the demands of IT work regarding gender relations is likely to be the reinforcement of traditional gender relations in the home. Second, it means that, for the partnered women in IT, even though they are relatively fortunate in having partners who share the division of labour more equitably, they (along with any men who do so) are competing with a dominant model in which men can concentrate on their paid labour, knowing that their partners are taking care of the home front.

Somewhat different patterns emerge regarding the division of child care. Of 97 parents, 44 (10 women and 34 men) answered an online survey item about how parenting responsibilities are shared in their households (see the bottom of Table 5.2). Again, results must be used with caution, but, like other studies on the topic, they suggest that women are more likely to carry out a disproportionate share of child care. Half of the mothers but not quite one-tenth of the fathers say that they do more or most of the child care. As well, 10 of 34 men (30 percent) and only 1 of 20 women (10 percent) say that their current partners provide more or most of the child care. Unlike the division of household tasks, 19 men (56 percent) and 4 women (40 percent) report that child care is shared equally. Thus, a substantial minority of the men rely on their partners to assume more of the responsibilities of child care, and over half of them believe that they share child care equally. Conversely, 5 of the 10 women assume more child care responsibility than their partners, and a substantial minority share it equally. This suggests that, for men, engagement in IT work does not mean forfeiting sharing parental responsibility or being able to assume that a parent will be there to provide child care. For a substantial portion of the women, the reality of the second shift continues in relation to child care, and the possibility of relying on a partner to do the lion's share of parenting applies to relatively few mothers. Once again, it appears that having children is a catalyst for more traditional gender relations at home, even among those engaged in paid labour with a comparatively egalitarian division of household tasks.

When analyzed separately (data not shown), the division of child care is more similar to that of household tasks among the Canadian participants (*n* = 14 women and 36 men); 11 women (78 percent) compared with 17 men (47 percent) report equal sharing of child care, and 14 men (39 percent) versus none of the women report that their partners provide more of the child care than they do. In the Canadian case at least, women may be using the strategy of finding egalitarian partners in order to engage in IT work. Numbers for the United States are small (*n* = 3 women and 9 men), making the impact of one or two cases on the results dramatic. All three women reported doing more of the child care than their partners, while 5 of the 9 men reported equal sharing of parenting duties. It is impossible to say whether this represents national differences.

Table 5.3

Parental status configurations for small firms in Canada (*n* = 15) and the United States (*n* = 6)

Country	Childless women	Childless men	Mothers	Fathers	Total
Canada	14	45	17	53	129
United States	4	18	6	20	48
Total	18	63	23	73	177

In Table 5.3, firm-level data show the breakdown of participants in the study according to gender and parental status. These data show the preponderance of men in most of the firms and the isolating experience of motherhood in the sense that most mothers are in the minority within their own firms. Although a number of firms include fathers, this is un-likely to represent a truly shared experience of parenting among male and female co-workers given the gendered division of labour in many of the men's families. This indicates an important contextual feature of parenting in the IT industry: women are generally in the minority, mothers even more so.

We now turn to our case studies to consider these patterns and their consequences in greater depth. We begin by presenting our Canadian case, Integrative Solutions, before turning to its American counterpart, Advanced Designs. Pseudonyms are used throughout.

Integrative Solutions
Integrative Solutions is located in Ottawa, Ontario, and serves an inter-national clientele. The firm currently employs eleven individuals, includ-ing management. Reflecting wider IT trends, the majority of employees are men whose occupations include president/chief executive officer, IT manager, and programmer. Meanwhile, of the four women employed by Integrative Solutions, Jennifer (1101055) is an IT manager. The remaining women occupy administrative, sales, and marketing roles.

Further reflecting industry demographics, most employees are in their twenties and thirties. Three have never been married, one is divorced, and none has children. Seven employees are married. Of these individuals, four are parents, including the president/CEO of the company, George (1101029), and his wife, Judy (1101107) (the office administrator), both of whom are in their early fifties with three adolescent children; Larry (1101133), the chief technical officer (CTO), also in his fifties with four adult children; and thirty-something Nancy (1101094), who is in sales and is the mother of three children under the age of seven.

As is true in other firms, employee accounts of balancing work and family life vary by location in the life course and by work responsibilities. From the perspectives of those who have children or anticipate having them, there are challenges associated with successfully negotiating a career and family life in the IT industry. Accounts of those without such responsibilities further reinforce this observation. This firm also highlights how gender differences grow increasingly evident over time and how IT work tends to reproduce traditional arrangements.

Work Practices, Family Consequences
As with most firms, personnel at Integrative Solutions speak of long hours, commitment to the product, and working to deadlines. Like the majority of CEOs, George reports putting in the most hours per week, typically sixty-five or more. This is something both he and his wife have come to expect:

> If I took five days and came here at nine and left at five, I think my wife would die of a heart attack. For me, we're typically here about 8:30 [a.m.]. We get up at 6:30. Get the kids off to school ... If I can get out of here at by 8:30 [p.m.], it's kind of been a good day.

Reflecting on George's career, Judy says that having young children did not influence his commitment to IT work. She took time off work to raise their family. However, she speculates that his long hours have come at a cost: "I think George would like to have been there more ... I think George would have preferred to have more time with them." George expresses an interest in spending more time with his family but thinks he cannot reduce his workload.

Of course, George is not alone in his commitment to the company. Referring to IT employment and his own hours, Larry says, "it's fairly intense, and one would have to make a fairly significant personal commitment to the project and getting it done on time." Further, he states that "it's not unusual for me to put in at least a couple of hours at night after I leave here. It's not unusual for me to work on the side on Sunday." Thus, while technology permits Larry and other IT workers to continue working after office hours, it also interrupts time that might otherwise be spent with family. Because of the long hours and unpredictability, Larry believes that IT employment is not good for those with young families.

Jennifer, the lone female IT manager, typically works a fifty-hour week but says that "it's not unusual" for her to work seventy-five-hour weeks for up to two-week periods: "You try not to let that be typical, but in our industry it is absolutely, every day there's things that throw you off, or new problems arise that you have to deal with, and that breaks you away from the tasks that you're working on." Without children, Jennifer is, for the most part, "managing" and has "always met a deadline." She is free to work long hours without needing to worry about child care.

Not only project deadlines keep individuals working long hours in IT. With few exceptions, individuals in technical jobs, including those at Integrative Solutions, agree that the rapid pace of technology means additional pressures. According to Brett (1101068), a never-married, childless programmer in his late thirties,

> The industry is just moving too quickly. If you're not staying caught up, I mean, by the time somebody gets to be an expert on something, there's some newer technology ... You've got to start over and enhance on that again, so, yeah, you really have to keep caught up.

Although this expectation is pervasive, few small firms have formal outlets for skill maintenance, and few encourage such activity on company time (see also Chapter 7). Larry speaks of successful IT employees as those who "invest in keeping themselves current." Thus, beyond the hours invested in projects, those in technical positions must find the time and resources on their own to ensure ongoing skill development. Given the long hours and need for such development, it is not surprising that, of the employees at Integrative Solutions who completed surveys, only those without children report being content with their hours and view work and family life as complementary domains.

Parenthood at Integrative Solutions

George, Judy, and Nancy – all parents – report a desire to work fewer hours in order to have time for themselves and for family. Nancy, the only employee with young children, also identifies child-care responsibilities as a primary reason. Generally, she works nine-hour days, but unlike George and those with technical roles, Nancy is not routinely expected to work overtime. Yet, should the need for overtime arise, she has child-care arrangements in place.

Although Nancy reports that child care is primarily her responsibility (rather than her spouse's), in many ways her home-life arrangements are atypical. In fact, she is not required to negotiate child care on a daily basis:

> I am very lucky that my husband is very supportive. He has a flexible schedule, which means he can pick my daughter up from school, [and] I've got continuity of care with the children. I have a nanny. So that even, even if a kid's too sick to go to school, it doesn't mean I have to miss work.

The presence of a supportive husband and the means to employ a nanny are key resources with which Nancy negotiates work and family life. Having a nanny means Nancy does not "have to do anything" except get herself ready in the morning. Her husband has dinner "waiting on the table" when she gets home, and her child-care responsibilities begin when he goes to bed in the evening.

In many ways, these arrangements put Nancy on par with her male counterparts. However, she says of her current work-family situation, "my family comes first. This is what pays the bills ... Family issues always tear me, always, always. So, like, if I were a man, it wouldn't be as big an issue. I'm sure [my male counterpart] does not have any of the same issues I do." Like the husbands and fathers at Integrative Solutions, Nancy need not worry about the logistics of child care or household responsibilities on a daily basis. Yet she feels that, unlike the men she works with, she is torn about her commitment to work. She feels guilty and worries "a great deal" about juggling IT work and family life.

Parental Leave and Hiring Considerations

To date, Nancy is the only employee at Integrative Solutions who has been eligible for and taken the year of parental leave to which she is entitled by Canadian law.[1] Rather than hire a temporary replacement, George assumed responsibility for Nancy's duties during her absence. This arrangement was possible because of her position and his willingness to assume her responsibilities. For George, as for CEOs of other small IT firms, accommodating a leave, especially in a technical position, is a consideration in the hiring process:

> They don't want you to be prejudiced against women, but when you're building a small company it's really hard to bring in young women and know that in a couple of years you can lose them. And yet some of the really best people are [women] in that age group.

Recently married, Jennifer – the IT manager – is in this demographic. George says it "scares" him "to death" that she may take a year or more off to have children. Yet he hired her because he thought she was the "best person for the job."

Contemplating whether to have children, Jennifer believes that negotiating her career and parenthood will be different for her than for her male co-workers:

> That would mean my time off. So you never know who's gonna replace my job ... There's guys in the office. You know, getting married and having kids, that shouldn't really affect them ... unless they were to take part of the maternity leave with their wife, 'cause they're allowed to do that now. I don't know about these guys, though. I'd expect they'd be the breadwinners.

Unlike her male colleagues and despite her preference for equal responsibility, Jennifer will likely face a greater burden of responsibility for child care than her spouse. This is because she currently has primary responsibility for household chores and because her husband has an occupation that keeps him away from home for long periods of time.

Of the remaining employees without children, two never-married employees in their twenties, Sally (1101003) and Brett, are uncertain about having children. Also in his twenties, Ben (1101016), the lone divorced employee, would like to have children. Indicating a shift away from traditional roles, his preference is to share child-care responsibility equally with his partner. It remains to be seen if this software engineer's preference will be supported by his employer or by work demands.

Accommodating Family Life, Policy, and Practice

Employer flexibility in terms of when, how, and where work gets done can help employees to reconcile their work and family lives, particularly if an unexpected situation (e.g., illness, child's day off school, etc.) should arise. Employees at Integrative Solutions agree that their supervisor shows some flexibility when they face demands from family responsibilities. Yet, unlike workers in many small firms in our study, individuals in this company report having very little flexibility or autonomy in terms of when, where, and how work gets done. Only the CEO and his wife report having flexibility when it comes to setting work hours. The office is the primary work location for everyone at Integrative Solutions, with only two employees (both programmers) reporting the possibility of working outside the office. The rest say that they are not able to do so. Although not a particularly flexible work environment, Integrative Solutions offers its employees sick leave. As a result, employees who become sick or require a day off from time to time can do so with pay for up to six days per year. According to Judy, "if you needed other time off, then it would cut into your vacation."

Despite having these policies in place, typical of many IT workers in small firms, most at Integrative Solutions are unaware of their entitlements. In some cases, this lack of awareness includes managers. For example, Jennifer does not currently manage anyone with children, but when presented with the scenario of having an employee with a sick child at home she replied thus:

> If it did happen, obviously there would be certain amounts of forgiveness – maybe one or two days. I can't see it being more than that, because then it becomes a nuisance to us. I think a couple of days is, I think, enough time for them to come up with other answers to their problems.

Thus, while policies might be in place, they might not be enforced, particularly if one's immediate supervisor views the situation as a private problem.

Vacation time can also help employees to negotiate their family lives. In Canada, the government regulation stipulates a basic vacation entitlement of two paid weeks per full year of full-time employment; longer-tenured employees often receive additional weeks, particularly in larger firms. Despite these legal entitlements, in small IT firms, taking vacation is often difficult to accomplish. Judy comments that "people are supposed to take holidays, but we've been extremely busy ... Larry gets four weeks a year, and he's taking like two weeks, and he says ... banking [holidays] is crazy because he never takes them again because we're too busy." As we will explore shortly, the policy context for sick days and vacation time differs for our US case study, but the long hours and project deadlines have similar outcomes in both cases.

Advanced Designs
Advanced Designs is a high-tech software development company located in the southern United States. It employs eight individuals, including Jerry (5502008), the president/CEO, and a husband-and-wife team, James (5502021) and Sandra (5502047), who act as the chief technical officer (CTO) and chief financial officer (CFO), respectively. The remaining workers – all men – are employed as programmers and software engineers. Those who work at Advanced Designs range in age from mid-twenties

to early forties. All are married except Jon (5502073), who is in his thirties and childless. Both in their twenties, Andrew (5502260) and Jeff (5502099) are also childless. The remaining individuals are parents in their late thirties and early forties, including Jerry, who has three young children; James and Sandra, who have two young children; Matthew (5502086), who has six children ranging from toddler to adult ages; and Kevin (5502034), who has adult children.

Akin to our Canadian case, this group's experiences of balancing IT work and family life speak to the challenges associated with doing so in IT, to the reproduction of traditional gender roles, and to the consequences of prioritizing work over family and vice versa. The relative absence of women and those with primary responsibility for child care, particularly mothers, is telling and reflects leadership preferences and work practices at Advanced Designs as well as structural arrangements. Sandra is an original founder. In the past, she was the CEO but currently works one day a week, mostly at home, and functions in an advisory capacity rather than as a day-to-day worker. This change was prompted by the challenges Sandra and James faced in terms of running the firm, managing their relationship, and meeting their child-care responsibilities. In keeping with traditional gender roles, it was Sandra who made career adjustments.

Hiring Practices, Preferences, and Parenthood in IT

Advanced Designs has employed no other women besides Sandra. Similar to his Canadian CEO counterpart, Jerry views hiring a woman, particularly an engineer, as risky business. From his perspective, when "she's right at the peak of what she'll be doing career-wise," there is "a good chance that she's gonna go out and take six weeks or more for maternity leave." Then, he suggests, she "has a 30 percent chance to come back." Unlike his Canadian counterpart, Jerry has yet to hire a woman and does not face the same government regulations pertaining to parental leave.

Regardless of gender and age, however, Jerry argues that having children dramatically decreases one's productivity levels in IT; in his words, "when they don't have kids, you can get eighty hours a week out of them." James agrees and says that one can "build a pretty amazing little machine" when employees are not married, childless, and have "very few interests outside of work."

Despite being a father, James thinks that most high-tech start-ups, including Advanced Designs, are "not family friendly." He claims that, as a company, they "want to help people raise their kids," but long hours and deadlines can be "very stressful" on families. "If you have a family

[and] choose to work here ... you can expect this kind of environment, or you can go to a big company like IBM, which might be a little more family friendly."

As a father, husband, and CTO, James struggles with balancing work and family life. When Sandra gave up her position, she assumed primary responsibility for their children. James sacrificed parental involvement for the company. Similar to the Canadian CEO, the demands of his career, including a sixty-hour work week, have affected his relationships with his children:

> It's also been very difficult, just in terms of getting to know my children. There's been – I think I did a pretty good job during the years when [Sandra] was a CEO. So I got a – formed a very solid relationship with my daughter. But while Jerry has been CEO, I haven't had quite the same luck with my son. So I, I still feel I haven't got quite enough time to get to know him.

Both Sandra and James worry "a great deal" about juggling IT work and family life and report conflict between the two domains. Ideally, James would like to reduce his hours. Thus far, it has not happened.

Jerry, meanwhile, purports to illustrate his own hypothesis regarding productivity and parenthood: "Me, my kids go to bed at 8 p.m. If I'm not home by 7:30, I don't see my kids ... So I'll go home. Now, sometimes, I'll come back, and sometimes I just won't, but because I have kids I don't work as hard as I used to." Regardless, he reports regularly working sixty-five hours per week, the most of anyone in the firm. His ability to work these hours and be a father is related to the fact that his wife has primary responsibility for the household and their children. Similar to James, he reports that his long hours affect his relationships with others, but unlike James, Jerry is content with the length of his work week.

The experiences of those in non-management positions further reinforce the routine demand for long hours and overtime. According to Jon, "it's such a small place that, if you have to stay two, three days late or even sleep in the office to get this product out, they kinda, you know, implicitly expect that. But they would compensate you [with time off]." Jon reports working an average of fifty hours per week but claims it is often more. In the future, he expects to marry and have children. He would prefer that child care be the primary responsibility of his wife. Meanwhile, his married co-worker, Andrew, works fifty-five hours per week and says that IT "requires long hours, so a lot of people tend to work in IT until they have families." Despite this, Andrew intends to have children and continue working in IT. Unlike Jon, however, should he become a father, he would prefer to share child-care responsibilities equally with his wife. Currently, Andrew does not worry about juggling IT work and family life but ideally would prefer to work at least ten hours per week less in order to spend more time with his wife. Should he choose to prioritize family over work, he will find himself part of a minority of men in IT. Yet he will not be entirely without a role model in his firm.

Commitment to Family

Advanced Designs also employs Matthew, who is atypical in that he is a man in IT who has made the decision to put his family before his career. Unlike his colleagues with children, he reports sharing responsibility for household tasks and child care "equally" with his spouse. Nevertheless, after the birth of their first child, his wife quit her job and remains "a full-time mom." For Matthew, family has "always been a real priority." He wants "to do well" at work and "succeed," but he puts his "wife and children as higher priorities." Such prioritizing has not been without career consequences:

> I have tried to balance the demand to work more by saying no as much as I could and still kind of maintain my job. And that may have affected me some in terms of the speed with which I advanced or I didn't advance compared to other people ... Part of me could think, "ah, you know, I missed those opportunities." But ultimately I'm content to be just more of a worker bee generally and to be able to go home and spend time with my family ... Sometimes I feel like maybe a little guilty, but I think, "well, you know, if I was single and didn't have any kids, I would probably ... work more hours."

As Matthew suggests, his priorities have had consequences for his career: missed job opportunities and advancement. Nevertheless, unlike James, he thinks that Advanced Designs is "very family friendly." This difference of opinion is likely because Matthew is less invested in his career and the company has established firm boundaries and says no. Although work occasionally interferes with family life, requiring him to do "some overtime" or "spend the night working," Matthew suggests that "there's a lot of [leeway] to adjust your work if you need to, for your family." Thus, while long hours and overtime create challenges to balancing work and family life, flexibility in terms of when, where, and how IT work gets done can help individuals to meet family demands.

Flexibility, Informality, and Family Friendliness

Unlike our Canadian case, everyone at Advanced Designs reports having flexible working hours and the possibility of working remotely. They also all "strongly agree" that their supervisor shows flexibility regarding family demands. Kevin, who has a stay-at-home spouse and children who no longer live at home, speaks of flexibility at Advanced Designs, hinting at its advantages and disadvantages. He claims his wife "would prefer a more normal set of work hours," but if he "needed to be someplace, somewhere for some reason, it's certainly possible." Further, he explains, "there is really no mandate as to what hours you have to be here. I think everybody understands the things that need to get done and when they need to get done by."

With the exception of Matthew, most fathers at Advanced Designs routinely put in long hours, particularly with looming deadlines. Those without children typically remain at the office longer. Leaving the office does not mean they are free of work; technology such as instant messenger means that they are typically available around the clock. According to Jon, "the young guys tend to stay [at the office] later." He continues, "what's very helpful is instant messenger. So when Jerry goes home and the kids are in bed, which is fairly quick, well, if I'm working, he's always on instant messenger. If I need anything, he's there." Although technology facilitates flexibility, it can also mean an extended work day and the bleeding of work life into home life.

The flexibility of work practices in terms of where and when work gets done at Advanced Designs, combined with the firm's small size, leads personnel to describe the policies governing sick days, parental leave, and vacation as "very informal." In part, this informality is due to the policy context in the United States, where, unlike Canada, there are few federal or state regulations governing vacation and maternity or parental leave, especially in small companies. With the exception of short-term disability for maternity leave, few rules regulate leave for new parents, and policies vary by state. Employers are under no obligation to provide paid leave for this purpose or for vacation. As previously suggested, with the absence of mothers at Advanced Designs, maternity leave has not been a pressing issue. James and Sandra are the only ones who report taking parental leave, but how their respective absences were negotiated is not discussed. James's absence was less than a month, while Sandra's was three months. Their work patterns suggest that they continued to be involved in the firm remotely during their leaves rather than being fully absent from work. Should a request for parental leave arise in this firm, how it would be accommodated is unclear.

In terms of other family-related benefits, Matthew explains, "a lot of the benefit policies, especially family time off or sick time or even vacation time, is not real rigorously tracked. Everybody just kind of trusts everybody." Informality regarding vacation and sick days contributes to flexibility but can also mean these days go unused. For example, though Matthew makes a point of taking vacation, he says, "a lot of people don't." Regardless of government legislation, this seems to be the case in many small IT firms, where the pressure to compete, meet tight deadlines, and deliver is typical. Failure to take vacation time is related to career mobility. As with other occupations, prioritizing work above all is often considered necessary for advancement in a particular firm and in the IT industry.

Conclusion

In this chapter, we examined how the negotiation of work and family life in small Canadian and American IT firms is structured by gender. Our analysis confirms our assertion that individuals exercise choice in their lives and do so within a capitalist system organized along gender lines. As is borne out in our analysis, structural arrangements make it difficult for women and those with greater family responsibilities to successfully negotiate family life and a career in IT, particularly one in a highly technical position.

As we suggested at the outset, the context of globalization heightens economic competition, which, in turn, intensifies the challenges faced by individuals attempting to reconcile work and family life in the local economy. In IT, intense competition has given way to the notion of ideal workers as those who are committed to the firm's vision and its product and have few interests outside work. In other words, they are considered what Hochschild (2001) refers to as "zero-drag" workers. Although some firms reject this ideal and the long hours and commitment that characterize it, the overwhelming majority of firms in our study, including those studied in this chapter, do not. Indeed, the CEOs of both case study firms reveal prejudices against hiring young women, particularly in technical positions, and their preference is for workers with few outside interests.

As our case studies illustrate, management's preference for workers with few competing responsibilities resonates with the organization of IT work. Workers at Integrative Solutions and Advanced Designs describe IT work as involving long hours, overtime, deadlines (regardless of how unreasonable or imminent), and the need for ongoing skill development and training. Our case studies further show that these conditions typically require *individual and family* adjustments rather than changes in the workplace or work practices. An individualist approach to handling competing responsibilities is evident in employees' lack of knowledge about their firm's human relations policies, a limited understanding that extends to management. More often than not, work-family balance is cast as a private trouble rather than the responsibility of the firm or industry. Personal adjustment is viewed as necessary to realize continued success and advancement in the industry. Moreover, because this expectation holds regardless of gender or family responsibility, it is not surprising that the majority of parents in our case studies do not view work and family life as complementary domains and worry about juggling work and family responsibilities.

The requirement of individual and family adjustment means prioritizing work over family. For those who are willing and able (by virtue of accommodating family arrangements), this action may come at the expense of family relationships (e.g., George, Jerry, and James). Yet not everyone is willing or able to place work before family. Although having qualitatively different (and highly gendered) experiences, Matthew and Sandra illustrate that choosing family over work has consequences for career advancement. By setting boundaries between work and family life, Matthew has not advanced in the same manner as his peers. Meanwhile, Sandra gave up her position as CEO and altered the course of her career in support of her children and her husband's career.

Our analysis sheds light on the gendered ways in which IT employment affects the compatibility of combining paid and unpaid labour. Our survey and case study data reveal that, among men, the conditions of IT employment are more likely to reproduce traditional gender relations at home as a primary strategy for balancing work and family demands. This possibility supports men who would like to have both an IT career and a family. Among women in IT, the opposite seems to be true. To make it in an industry such as IT, an optimal strategy for women with partners is to have an egalitarian division of labour at home. In relation to child care, one way of doing this is to negotiate family arrangements that place women on par with their male counterparts by combining more egalitarian relationships with paid help (e.g., Nancy's supportive husband and use of a nanny). A final option is to find an IT firm that is particularly sensitive to the concerns of its employees' family lives. The relative scarcity of such options appears to make having children among women in IT somewhat less compatible with sustaining an IT career than is true among men in IT.

Although decisions about parenthood tend to have more profound impacts on women's lives, the organization of IT work may also inform the decisions that men make about partners and fatherhood. If IT work is seen to be incompatible with active fatherhood, then a partner who is not committed to full-time work may be more desirable than one who is. Indeed, the fathers in our case study all illustrate this, as do the survey data. The same type of preference could apply to women (e.g., Nancy), though there is still an underlying assumption that men will engage in full-time and long-term paid labour. Ironically, the changing nature of work in the new global economy may engender old ways of relating between partners.

Given the predominance of men in IT, the growth of this sector may undermine advances in gender equality in both the workplace and the home, along with claims of the significance of unpaid domestic labour, including parenting, relative to paid labour. The aspirations and preferences of employees without children show both an acceptance and a rejection of traditional gender roles. The desire to share responsibility for child care equally within a partnership is promising for men and women who wish to be involved in family life and have a career in the industry. Yet it remains unclear how such preferences might be accommodated by employers and, hence, translate into practice.

Despite the overrepresentation of men and the firm's preference for highly dedicated employees, accounts of flexibility at Advanced Designs offer some promise for those attempting to negotiate IT work and family life. The freedom to determine when and where work gets done can help individuals to reconcile the needs of both domains. Such flexibility led the majority of Advanced Designs employees to refer to the company as family friendly. Nevertheless, as Jerry and James illustrate and as others have cautioned (e.g., Salaff 2000; Webster 2000), having the flexibility to work remotely and at any time of day can lengthen the work day and heighten rather than reduce the intrusion of IT work into family life.

Our analysis shows a gendered response to balancing work and family in the IT sector. As some of the fathers in our sample show, however, the challenges of combining active parenting with IT work do not apply only to women. The ongoing gendering of family life is a key reason why balancing work and family remains predominantly the responsibility of women. Our survey and case study data illustrate that this tendency is reinforced in industries such as IT, where the workplace culture is masculine and the pressure to stay current in a global market is ever present. Although most professional and entrepreneurial work has always required extensive time commitments that conflict with active involvement in family life, a key difference in IT is that the pressure is not confined to an early period of one's career (such as medical residency or articling in law) or to the start-up phases of a business that can build on itself once established. The rate of change of IT work and the competition of a global economy minimize the benefits of seniority and experience. As George's experience shows, aside from moving into management, getting older and wiser does not have as direct payoffs in the IT sector as is true in other work domains (see Chapters 6 and 7).

Does IT work provide an opportunity to carry out current approaches to being partners and parents? If the IT industry remains highly competitive, particularly in relation to hiring, there may be an effort to offer family supports to attract the best and the brightest, including women. However, if women are not drawn to IT work, and there are enough men happy to pursue traditional paths regarding family in which parenting is accepted as a woman's enclave, there is reduced incentive to offer family supports. This can create a vicious cycle in which the IT sector is not attractive to women or to men who wish to be actively involved in parenting, minimizing what could be internal pressure to make IT family friendly (e.g., through family-leave policies), effectively reinforcing a traditional male labour force in IT. Such a tendency may be compounded by globalization when outsourcing occurs in sites where more traditional family values predominate, reducing the pressure to offer family-friendly policies at home. When coupled with declines in public support and the increased individualism fostered by globalization, there is reduced incentive for social change.

As our discussion and analysis have shown, IT work is structured by gender, and generally a successful IT career tends not to be compatible with assuming substantial family responsibilities. IT work is also structured by age; youth dominates the applied side of IT work, and the pressure to stay current makes management a desirable avenue for older workers (see Chapters 6 and 7). However, age crosscuts gender: being a young woman is also viewed as a risk from an employer's perspective because young women might have children.

What are the prospects for the future? The view of globalization as a universal and unstoppable force (see, e.g., Friedman 2000) provides a pessimistic picture of the prospects for gender and age equality in the quest to balance IT work and family life. If the key message is that all societies must do whatever it takes to compete in a global economy, then public and private initiatives in support of better work-family balance are likely to be seen as interfering with the bottom line. Such a view will be reinforced if more traditional views of gender and family permeate particular industries. Alternatively, globalization may create pressures to work harder at instilling local beliefs and values in work policy and practice (following Foer 2004; Giddens 2002).

The extent to which familial commitments interfere with paid work is shaped in part by the extent to which governments and workplaces support those who meet them. Policies that allow for flexible hours, parental leave, care leave (when family members are ill), and on-site child care are an important beginning. For example, Britain has committed state funds toward the development of work-based programs designed to encourage more flexible working practices. These programs have been aimed primarily at negotiating work and parenthood, with little attention paid to the care of older family members (Evandrou and Glaser 2003). Our case studies suggest important differences between the United States and Canada based on the context set by legislation. In the Canadian case, government regulations require some support for maternal and parental leave; in the United States, they do not.

Studying the presence of family-related policies is not enough. Even if such policies exist, issues of accessibility must be examined. Restrictive stipulations, gender bias, and narrow definitions of family limit employees' access to and use of family-related policies (Medjuck, Keefe, and Fancey 1998). In addition, if the quality of the policies and programs is low, then options for negotiating work and family, especially care, are likely to reinforce gender inequality at home and in the workplace (Morgan and Zippel 2003). In some workplaces, supervisors may not agree with the policies in place and effectively "punish" those who take advantage of them (Duxbury and Higgins 1994). In our case studies, we see that managers (e.g., Jennifer) are not always aware of policies, raising questions about the extent to which they are actually practised and highlighting an individualistic approach to balancing work and family. Given the informality of workplace policies in small firms, employees are not always aware of their entitlements. Moreover, even when they are aware of them, the commitment to meeting deadlines and the difficulty of truly getting away from work mean that employees do not necessarily take advantage of policies that could help them to balance IT work and family life (e.g., taking vacation or time owed). Thus, the workplace culture as reflected in actual operations rather than policies on paper must be studied. We are also encouraged to consider new approaches to meeting the demands of work and family in the private and public sectors of nations operating in a global village.

Note

1 After working 600 consecutive hours in the past fifty-two weeks, employed birth or adoptive mothers are entitled to take up to fifteen weeks of maternity leave. Birth or adoptive parents are also entitled to take up to thirty-two weeks of leave and are paid a percentage of their income through the government's Employment Insurance program. Individual employers can supplement the government benefits if they so choose. Employees are guaranteed their jobs when they return.

References

Beck, U. 1992. *Risk society: Towards a new modernity.* London: Polity Press.
–. 1999. *World risk society.* Cambridge, UK: Sage.
Beck, U., and E. Beck-Gernsheim. 1995. *The normal chaos of love.* Trans. M. Ritter and J. Wiebel. Cambridge, UK: Polity Press.
–. 2002. *Individualization: Institutionalized individualism and its social and political consequences.* Trans. P. Camiller. London: Sage.
Beck-Gernsheim, E. 2002. *Reinventing the family: In search of new lifestyles.* Trans. P. Camiller. Cambridge, UK: Polity Press.
Bengtson, V., and A. Lowenstein, eds. 2002. *International perspectives on families, aging, and social support.* Thousand Oaks, CA: Sage.
Blair-Loy, M., and J.A. Jacobs. 2003. Globalization, work hours, and the care deficit among stockbrokers. *Gender and Society* 17: 230-49.
Caragata, L. 2003. Neoconservative realities: The social and economic marginalization of Canadian women. *International Sociology* 18: 559-80.
Castells, M. 2004. *The power of identity.* 2nd ed. Vol. 2 of *The information age: Economy, society, and culture.* Oxford: Blackwell Publishing.
Comparative Public Policy Research Laboratory. 2004. *Parents' time investment into children.* University of Calgary, Department of Sociology, Research Brief Series 3. http://www.soci.ucalgary.ca/.
Connidis, I.A., and J.A. McMullin. 2002a. Ambivalence, family ties, and doing sociology. *Journal of Marriage and the Family* 64: 594-601.
–. 2002b. Sociological ambivalence and family ties: A critical perspective. *Journal of Marriage and the Family* 64: 558-67.
Cooper, M. 2000. Being the "go-to guy": Fatherhood, masculinity, and the organization of work in Silicon Valley. *Qualitative Sociology* 23: 379-405.
Daly, K. 1996. *Families and time: Keeping pace in a hurried culture.* Thousand Oaks, CA: Sage.
–. 2002. Time, gender, and the negotiation of family schedules. *Symbolic Interaction* 25: 323-42.
Demaiter, E. 2004. Women's experiences in the information technology sector: Opportunities and barriers. Paper presented at the Canadian Sociology and Anthropology Association Annual Meeting, Winnipeg.
Denis, A.B. 2003. Globalization, women, and (in)equality in the south: Constraint and resistance in Barbados. *International Sociology* 18: 491-512.
Dryburgh, H. 1999. Work hard, play hard: Women and professionalization in engineering adapting to the culture. *Gender and Society* 13: 664-82.
Duxbury, L., and C. Higgins. 1994. Families in the economy. In *Canada's changing families: Challenges to public policy,* ed. M. Baker, 29-40. Ottawa: Vanier Institute.

–. 2003. *Work-life conflict in the new millennium: A status report.* Ottawa: Health Canada.

Elder, G. Jr. 1991. Lives and social change. In *Theoretical advances in life course research: Status passage and the life course,* ed. W. Heinz, 58-85. Weinham: Deutscher Studies Verlag.

Evandrou, M., and K. Glaser. 2003. Combining work and family life: The pension penalty of caring. *Ageing and Society* 23: 583-601.

Foer, F. 2004. *How soccer explains the world.* Toronto: HarperCollins.

Friedman, T.L. 2000. *The Lexus and the olive tree: Understanding globalization.* New York: Anchor Books.

Giddens, A. 2002. *Runaway world: How globalisation is reshaping our lives.* London: Profile Books.

Gordon, D.T. 2001. Balancing act. *CIO* 15: 58.

Gornick, J.C., and M.K. Meyers. 2003. *Families that work: Policies for reconciling parenthood and employment.* New York: Russell Sage Foundation.

Heinz, W. 2001. Work and the life course: A cosmopolitan-local perspective. In *Restructuring work and the life course,* ed. V.W. Marshall, W.R. Heinz, H. Kruger, and A. Verma, 3-22. Toronto: University of Toronto Press.

Hochschild, A.R. 2001. *The time bind: When work becomes home and home becomes work.* 2nd ed. New York: Metropolitan Books.

Kanter, R.M. 1977. *Men and women of the corporation.* New York: Basic Books.

Lampard, R., and K. Peggs. 2007. Identity and repartnering after separation. New York: Palgrave Macmillan.

Marshall, V.W., S.H. Matthews, and C.J. Rosenthal. 1993. Elusiveness of family life: A challenge for the sociology of aging. In *Annual review of gerontology and geriatrics,* ed. G.L. Maddox and M. Powell Lawton, vol. 13, 39-72. New York: Springer.

McGee, M.K. 2000. Women in technology: Women at work. *Information Week,* 28 February, 63-68.

Medjuck, S., J.M. Keefe, and P.J. Fancey. 1998. Available but not accessible: An examination of the use of workplace policies for caregivers of elderly kin. *Journal of Family Issues* 19: 274-99.

Mills, C.W. 1959. *The sociological imagination.* New York: Oxford University Press.

Morgan, K.J., and K. Zippel. 2003. Paid to care: The origins and effects of care leave policies in Western Europe. *Social Politics: International Studies in Gender, State, and Society* 10: 49-85.

Peterson, G.W., and S.K. Steinmetz. 2000. The diversity of fatherhood: Change, constancy, and contradiction. *Marriage and Family Review* 29: 315-22.

Polatnick, M.R. 2002. Too old for child care? Too young for self-care? Negotiating after-school arrangements for middle school. *Journal of Family Issues* 23: 728-47.

Pyle, J.L., and K.B. Ward. 2003. Recasting our understanding of gender and work during global restructuring. *International Sociology* 18: 461-89.

Ranson, G. 1998. Education, work, and family decision making: Finding the "right time" to have a baby. *Canadian Review of Sociology and Anthropology* 35: 517-33.

–. 2003. Beyond "gender differences": A Canadian study of women's and men's careers in engineering. *Gender, Work, and Organization* 10: 22-41.

Salaff, J.A. 2000. Where home is the office: The new form of flexible work. In *The Internet in everyday life,* ed. B. Wellman and C. Haythornthwaite, 464-95. Oxford: Blackwell.

Stake, R.E. 2005. Qualitative case studies. In *Handbook of qualitative research,* 3rd ed., ed. N.K. Denzin and E.S. Lincoln, 443-66. Thousand Oaks, CA: Sage.

Thompson, J. 1982. DP management doors open for committed women. *CIPS Review* July-August: 8-9.

Webster, J. 2000. Today's second sex and tomorrow's first? Women and work in the European information society. In *The information society in Europe: Work and life in an age of globalization,* ed. K. Ducatel, J. Webster, and W. Herrmann, 119-40. New York: Rowman and Littlefield.

Part 3:
Age Regimes and Projects

In this section of the book, the focus turns to how age influences the structure and nature of paid work in small firms. Within the context of the gendered workplace cultures established in Part 2, the chapters in Part 3 show that age emerges as an element of inequality within the small IT firms in this study.

Chapter 6 shows that IT workers and managers in Canadian and American firms invoke generational discourse to describe perceived age-based differences in skill, innovation, and adaptability. In Australia and England, the concept of generation was rarely used, but more nuanced articulations of the relationship between age and ability were drawn on and linked to life-course changes, personal agency, or structural workplace issues.

In Chapter 7, age discrimination is considered in greater detail, and the issue of relative age is considered. This chapter shows that older workers are considered old at quite young ages within the IT firms in our study. It also shows that ageist attitudes about the inability of older workers to adapt to new technologies, their lack of ability and desire to train, and their inability or refusal to work long hours were commonly expressed among workers in these small IT firms.

6

Generational and Age Discourse in IT Firms

Julie McMullin, Emily Jovic, and Tammy Duerden Comeau

This chapter examines generational and age-based discourse and how it influences workplace cultures within information technology firms. It builds on a previous paper (McMullin, Duerden Comeau, and Jovic 2007) in which we developed a set of objective generational locations, based on computing technologies in use when birth cohorts came of age. We assessed whether and how people within these locations invoked generational discourse in their discussions of IT employment. In particular, we considered whether developments in computer technology provided a basis for generational formation and identity and whether and how the concept of generation was used as a way of describing disadvantages for some workers. Using Canadian data, this paper showed that members in different generational locations reported varying levels of affinity with computing technology. All generations talked about the importance of "growing up" with technology. Those who lacked this early exposure were believed to be at a disadvantage in the paid work environment because they did not possess a natural affinity for computers. In this chapter, we examine whether there are international variations in this regard.

Technology in general and computing technologies in particular infiltrate almost every aspect of social life. Businesses invest in them to improve competitiveness and productivity and, in some cases, control over employees. Workers also need to master certain technologies to gain employment or to remain employed. Yet technology is also an "indispensable medium" that may be used for the expression, transformation, and dissemination of culture (Castells 2000, 14). The spread of computing technology has led researchers to explore how technology is integrated into existing cultural fields and how it could facilitate the creation of new ones (Consalvo 2006; Edmunds and Turner 2005; Kubicek and Wagner 2002).

This dual character of technology, as both a productive and a cultural resource, is an important consideration in studies of work because technological exposure or expertise gained in the cultural realm (e.g., playing video games or tinkering with computer equipment) can translate into valuable workplace skills and knowledge. With the proliferation of paid employment requiring advanced computer skills, and with the rise in gaming and Internet media, which are often embraced by youth, the link between generations and the cultural and productive aspects of computing technology is in need of further study.

The Concept of Generation

In "The Problem of Generations," Karl Mannheim (1952) generalizes Marx's conception of class to demonstrate the sociological significance of generations. Theoretically, this is our starting point. Mannheim argued that a generation represents a unique type of social location based on the dynamic interplay between being born in a particular year and the sociopolitical events that occur throughout the life course of the birth cohort, particularly as that cohort comes of age. Hence, all individuals, whether they acknowledge it, belong to a particular generational location within a given society.

Just as class consciousness does not necessarily accompany class position, so too Mannheim recognizes that generational consciousness does not arise because one is born in a particular year. Two components comprise actual generations in this regard: the objective consideration of generational location, and the subjective experience of historical consciousness. Whereas membership in a historical community is the widest criterion of generational location, actual generations form only when "a concrete bond is created between members of a generation by their being exposed to the social and intellectual symptoms of a process of dynamic de-stabilization" (Mannheim 1952, 303). So, just as Marx makes the distinction between a class in itself and a class for itself, so too Mannheim acknowledges that, under certain social conditions, generations could share a collective awareness and become politically motivated.

Generations and Culture

Recent research has examined the concept of generation through the lens of culture. For example, Eyerman and Turner (1998) draw on Bourdieu's concept of *habitus* to theorize how cohorts build generational solidarity through shared cultural symbols such as music and fashion. Following Bourdieu, generations can gain and control access to cultural capital and resources (Turner 1998). Eyerman and Turner (1998, 93) define "generation" as "a cohort of persons passing through time that come to share a common habitus, hexis and culture, a function of which is to provide them with a collective memory that serves to integrate the cohort over a finite period of time." As Gilleard (2004, 114) points out, "generational style or consciousness can be treated ... as generational 'habitus' – dispositions that generate and structure individual practices and which emerge and are defined by the forces operating in a particular generational field."

Besides music and fashion, computing technology is a marker of culture through which generations may be formed. For example, Kubicek and Wagner (2002) explore how technological advancements influenced the development of "technological generations" of community electronic networks. Computing technology enthusiasts in each era (i.e., mainframe 1970s, personal computing 1980s, Internet 1990s, wireless communications 2000s) utilized the latest technology to build and disseminate their public countercultural electronic networks. According to Kubicek and Wagner (2002, 305), "the first mainframes, then the first PCs, online services and web capabilities, can be interpreted as Mannheimian 'collective events' that influenced the respective actor groups." Within the framework of community networks, technology and actors stay linked, and "old" actors do not make the leap to new technologies; instead, new technologies are taken up and disseminated by "new" actors. Given popular associations between youth and computing expertise, young people who are not exposed to computing technology or who lack expertise may be disadvantaged (Facer and Furlong 2001).

Timing is an important factor in forging shared generational bonds and crafting a collective cultural milieu (Corsten 1999). Like Mannheim, Pilcher (1994) notes that the formation of generational consciousness tends to occur in relation to events and exposures experienced in youth, when people are "coming of age." This period of life, typically early adolescence to early twenties, is thought to be crucial to the development of generational attachments because of the volume of contact with like-aged individuals and the centrality of identity formation during this phase (Cavalli 2004; Corsten 1999). Although generational consciousness is not frozen in adolescence, experiences and exposures during this time influence the development of socio-interpretive maps and reactions to social phenomena across the life course (Vincent 2005).

McMillan and Morrison (2006, 89) find significant variance in computing expertise in their youthful sample: "While the young participants in this study grew up with the internet, within their age cohort vast differences and skill levels are evident." They examine how Internet use constitutes a "coming of age ritual" for many youth in their teens when the World Wide Web was launched in 1993. Respondents locate themselves generationally as "boundary spanners" between older and younger family members; more computer savvy than parents and grandparents but "relative dinosaurs" compared with younger siblings (80). The authors conclude that "technology so defines this generation of young adults that not using it means running the risk of being left out" (91). Indeed, a lack of technological skills at any age presents this possibility, particularly in the realm of employment.

Generations at Work

Recently, management gurus and academics, concerned about workplace relations among Baby Boomers and Generation X,[1] have examined whether there are differences in work values, work ethic, and managerial strategies across these generations (e.g., Appelbaum, Serena, and Shapiro 2004; Burke 2004; Smola and Sutton 2002). These studies often explore the degree to which popular generational stereotypes are present in the workplace. According to Appelbaum and his colleagues (2004), existing generational myths indicate that Baby Boomers and older generations are "less adaptable and harder to train" than Gen-Xers and younger generations. Gen-Xers are also characterized as less committed than their predecessors, though they are said to be the first "techno-literate" generation in the workforce (Losyk 1997, 41). Although researchers have found evidence of generational differences in work values, the supposed productivity declines and the untrainability of older workers are more myth than reality (Appelbaum, Serena, and Shapiro 2004). Still, workers may draw on popular understandings of generations to make sense of their working lives and experiences in the workplace.

These studies provide interesting assessments of differences between generations that have been enshrined in popular culture, but in doing so their existence is perhaps unduly reified. Prevailing conceptions of the Baby Boomers and Generation X encompass many birth years. For instance, the Baby Boom group (born approximately from 1946 to 1964) originated from a demographic assessment of fertility trends, which was then extended to include aspects of social and cultural sameness. Although this categorization may make sense in some instances, uncritically assuming that a like-minded group of people exists by virtue of being born within a twenty-year span is problematic. Doing so risks overlooking theoretically informed subgroups within generations, thereby under- or overstating generationally based differences. Other research takes a more refined approach to the concept of generation in relation to paid work. Down and Reveley (2004), for instance, found that workers mobilized the concept of generation in their formation of entrepreneurial identities in business with the older generation portrayed as "old farts" and the younger generation portrayed as entrepreneurial "young guns." Younger entrepreneurs drew on the notion of "growing up together" in old economy firms amid "outmoded" business practices and managers and set themselves in contrast to this. The embracing of technology by the new generation was an important part of the generational distinction. In short, Down and Reveley show that popular cultural dialogue linking younger generations with "technoliteracy" emerges in the realm of paid work too.

With these theoretical ideas about generations, technology, and work in mind, we are interested in assessing whether cultural and paid work experiences lead IT workers to identify as generations of computer users, whether doing so puts particular generations at a perceived advantage or disadvantage in paid work environments, and whether there are international variations in this respect. The demographic composition of the information technology field is, on average, younger, and workers are considered old at relatively young ages, indicating that age and related issues need to be investigated as a potential basis for inequality in IT firms. We consider the sorts of generational or age-based discourse mobilized by workers and how their interactions and interpretations in this regard may contribute to naturalizing differences based on age within firms and an uneven distribution of privileges and opportunities in IT.

Method

This analysis employs data from 399 in-depth interviews with IT workers in Australia ($n = 91$), Canada ($n = 141$), England ($n = 61$), and the United States ($n = 106$). In the WANE study, respondents were generally asked directly about age relations in their firms and in IT more generally; however, questions about generations in the workplace were not posed. Any such dialogue was emergent, suggesting that some respondents were drawing on terms such as "generation" to convey their perceptions and experiences. The analytic strategy in this chapter presupposes that discourse is critical in making sense of our social world and that attending to people's interpretations of their experiences can generate insights into social relations (Gubrium and Holstein 1997) – such as those entailed in the structure and organization of work.

A qualitative data analysis software package, Nvivo, facilitated the cross-national analysis, and we worked collaboratively throughout the process. The WANE interview transcripts had already been submitted for organizational coding (Lofland and Lofland 1995; see Chapter 2), and two of these categories were selected for further analysis: (1) "Age," containing data regarding age and age relations; (2) "Education and Pathways to IT," which held material about origins of interest in IT as well as school and leisure experiences with technology. This material was combined with that from a series of textual searches designed to catch any dialogue that might have been missed in the organizational coding. The concept of generation was raised directly by several respondents, and a search for related terms, such as "growing up/grew up," "Baby Boomer," and "Generation X," yielded additional interview segments. Within the pathways category, computer gaming had emerged as significant in the collective memory of many workers, and a textual search for passages containing "games" and "gaming" was also conducted.

Consistent with the literature, analytical codes relating to generational and life-course bonds, inequality, diversity, and conflict were apparent in the data. Two themes that emerged originally in the Canadian interviews (McMullin, Duerden Comeau, and Jovic 2007) were applied to the data from Australia, England, and the United States: (1) *generational affinity* (e.g., growing up with technology), (2) *discourses of difference* in technical aptitude (skills, adaptability, and innovation). The qualitative data were recoded in accordance with these two themes and organized by region. Each author read the recoded material from all four regions to verify the classification and check for similarities, discrepancies, and emergent themes. The scheme from the Canadian data was found to fit the international data, and additional codes were not required. Respondents from Canada and the United States tended to employ stronger and more explicit generational references than those from Australia and England especially.

Results

Generational Discourse: Growing Up with Technology

For Canadian and American respondents, particularly the younger men, generational discourse was prominent. One way in which it emerged was through discussions of technological affinity and growing up with computers. In response to queries about entry into the field and interest in IT, many respondents discussed growing up with computers and invoked generational discourse to set their experiences apart from those of both older and upcoming generations of workers. For instance, two programmers describe their early experiences in parallel terms:

> I grew up with computers ... I guess it's our generation, our age. We had computers in the home from the time we were able to punch on a keyboard. (1103029, man, late twenties, Canada)

> I think younger people, people from straight out of high school up until their early thirties I'd say, were part of the first generation that grew up with a keyboard under their fingers at all times, and so it's more natural ... I think it's a huge advantage for younger workers ... The kids who are growing up with what will become the newest technology will have an advantage. (5511162, man, mid-twenties, United States)

In the eyes of many Canadian and US respondents, having grown up with certain forms of technology – for example, personal computers and gaming consoles – confers an advantage that older generations do not (and cannot) have. Although older IT generations are viewed as having to learn, unlearn, and relearn computer skills, many believe that younger generations innately know new technologies. Hence, the timing and extent of exposure to technology are viewed as relevant to one's level of technological expertise and ability to adapt to new or changing technology.

Growing up with technology was also seen by some to account for the youth of the IT field in general. Again, perceptions of Canadian and American respondents are very similar, suggesting that early experiences with technology may draw younger people to the industry and that this is a natural inclination and normal progression. Again, two young programmers explain their generational positioning and advantage relative to other groups of workers:

> I think definitely the IT industry is populated by younger people, you know, because, when you grow up using computers, it's only natural that you look for a job that uses computers. So I definitely think generationally younger people are more inclined to work in IT. (5511110, man, mid-twenties, United States)

> I know my generation is pretty big into the technology now. I think a major reason that the IT workforce is younger than, I don't know,

different workforces is just that the younger generations have just had a lot more exposure to the technology than some of the older guys have. And I guess we just pick it up easier just because we've had so much experience using it ... The younger guys have had more experience, and they've kind of grown up with it, whereas the older generations kind of had to integrate it into their existing skills. (1112055, man, late teens, Canada)

Besides attributing workforce youthfulness to generational contact with certain types of computing technology, these responses link early exposure and skill development, noting that younger generations "pick up" computing skills naturally, spontaneously, and more easily than older ones.

Explicit generational discourse about growing up with technology and computers is virtually absent in the conversations with the oldest group of Canadian and American IT workers (fifty-one and older) as well as with most women and Australian and English respondents of any age. Instead, these groups tend to express more practical (e.g., good career prospects) or "by chance" reasoning for their selection into IT work:

I never set out to be a programmer, it was just the way it turned out, and I was quite fortunate I enjoy it and it's well paid. (4404162, woman, early thirties, England)

So I didn't go into IT because I love IT ... I didn't go there because that's my life pursuit or something. Ah, I went into IT because it's a job I could do. (2203133, man, mid-forties, Australia)

[I got into the industry] kind of by accident, I think. I saw the job opening on the career services website, and I just decided to apply. (5511019, woman, mid-twenties, United States)

Even when they discuss growing up with technology more directly, there is some distance and a notable lack of any strong affinity for technology itself. Instead, the tone tends to be more casual and at times flippant and even disinterested:

I mean, I was interested in gaining some things like that [programming skills] before, not specific ... but that, that was where, where I was coming from. And I've grown up sort of pretty much with computers, so I've grown up with it all. (4407027, man, early twenties, England)

I didn't really like playing on sort of computers until I was about, I think I was about sixteen or so. (4404734, man, mid-twenties, England)

I wasn't much good at anything else ... Well, I had a computer from the time I was probably, ah, below ten, probably around ten, say, and always liked what they could do. That interested me for a little while. (2207149, man, mid-twenties, Australia)

As well, many Australian respondents spoke about family influence and encouragement as a significant part of the impetus to enter the field more so than personal or generational affiliations with technology:

I've got my father to thank for giving me a bit of an interest in it ... He got me a little VIC-20 personal computer when I was eight, and I just got hooked on it from there. So it was very much encouragement from my parents. (2202029, man, early thirties, Australia)

I changed my major to multimedia, so I decide[d] to work in IT industry ... My uncle is also in the company, which is ... the microchip things, so he encouraged me. (2204185, woman, mid-twenties, Australia)

This variation in level of affinity speaks to Mannheim's (1952) distinction between objective and subjective generational locations. Objectively, computer technology generations are formed through the dynamic interplay between being born in a particular period and the technological advances that occur throughout the life course of the cohort. Generational consciousness, on the other hand, is formed through subjective experiences as one type of technology gives way to another over time and place. The data suggest that many Canadian and American respondents formed a sort of generational consciousness based on technological innovations introduced in the home and at school when they were growing up. On the other hand, many women, older respondents, and those from Australia and England seem to lack the same sort of generational affinity and consciousness when it comes to computing technology.

Discourses of Difference

The respondents in this study also spoke of differences in skill, adaptability, and innovation, which have implications for inequality in the workplace and lead to material consequences in the lives of IT workers. Again, there were variations in how these issues were broached, particularly between Canada and the United States, where generational discourse was often raised to frame "natural" differences between workers, and Australia and England, whose respondents relied on age-based distinctions and more tempered structural or life-course explanations.

Canada and the United States: Generational Advantage/Disadvantage
As with pathways into IT, Canadian and American participants continue to draw on generational discourse when discussing perceptions of difference in skills, adaptability, and innovation. Technological skill and capacity to learn are believed to be naturally linked to youth and early exposure to computing technology. Hence, those who come to IT later in life and generations that missed growing up with certain technologies are perceived to be disadvantaged from the outset. As this programmer from the United States explains,

> It might be a generational thing. Because I was [the] generation, well, born a little bit before but essentially growing up when the first personal computers came out. So technology was a little more comfortable to my generation than it was to someone who was twenty years older than me at the time ... growing up in times before we even had vacuum tube computers. (5509032, man, mid-thirties, United States)

Similarly, a Canadian engineer says that,

> Ever since Windows, it's been a thing where kids have played with it and then grown up with it. So it seems like more a natural course ... I mean, unless you've grown up in the Windows generation, you probably aren't into IT ... So I think that might be something that keeps somebody who's forty from getting into IT now. (1112068, man, early thirties, Canada)

In short, the perception is that those who did not grow up with computers not only lack overall comfort and familiarity but also are essentially unable to catch up to younger generations. Such opinions reflect a larger, cultural construction of generations, and the attribution of such deficiencies to those in older generations can impede entry into or acceptance in the field for workers who actually are not that old.

The belief that younger people, especially children, learn better and more easily infiltrates the discourse around generations and skill. Within this context, there is a naturalized equation between youth and technological expertise that is perceived to leave those even a few years older at a disadvantage. As the following quotations illustrate, children and younger workers are assumed to learn with little effort or consciousness:

The older generation of people, say, like my father's age or ... even my sister's age, they didn't really grow up with computers as far as working with them ... Now that they're older ... they're using computers, but they have to learn how to use 'em, like I just kinda grew up with a computer. (5507123, man, late twenties, United States)

Technically, in the IT world, if you're a young person and you've heard of it [a form of technology], that means you do know it 'cause you can learn it ... I mean, someone who's grown up on the computer all day or someone who has never seen any computer until they're thirty; it's a huge difference just because of the educational development stages of a younger person compared to an older person. (1106042, man, late teens, Canada)

The flipside is that adults and older workers must really exert themselves to learn new skills, and even then their efforts may be insufficient. As a result, some respondents think that older IT workers actively resist new forms of technology, having developed a "loyalty" to older ones. Resistance to change and generational allegiance to particular technologies are sometimes interpreted in the workplace as a refusal to adapt. According to one manager, "the older generation of IT people were not interested in the new technology at all, showed no interest ... a lot of push back from the older IT generation, 'get that toy off my desk' kind of thing" (1112146, man, late thirties, Canada). A younger technician expresses a similar idea: "I think that, since it's just so new, older workers just don't want to transition to the new technology or move on with different things. They don't like change" (5504112, woman, late twenties, United States).

In addition to technical skills, innovation is highly valued in IT and is often discussed relative to generations. Not only is there a strong opinion that younger generations are innately connected with new technology, but some also believe that technological innovation is generational:

I have a feeling that IT's going to be a generational thing. Like we probably won't see a lot of new advances in IT until we kind of reach a generational break ... The students about to start university they'll come out, and there'll be some sort of breakthrough, and it will be a completely new generation in IT. (1114058, man, late twenties, Canada)

Although many respondents talk about a generational advantage for younger IT workers, there are discrepancies about how young this generation is. For all but the oldest workers, the disadvantaged generation is perceived to be the one just slightly older than theirs. In other words, the generation just ahead of one's own is the one believed to be disadvantaged due to a lack of early exposure to technology and a diminished ability to learn and innovate.

Australia and England: Age and Life-Course Considerations
While many Canadian and American workers invoke generational discourse to frame differences in skill, adaptability, and innovation, English and Australian ones do not. In these regions, respondents are less inclined to use the concept of generation to discuss variations in technological skill, adaptability, and other characteristics. They typically do not mention growing up with technology or the advantages "naturally" associated with younger generations in the same way as Canadians and Americans. Instead, their discourses of difference are more evident on the basis of age and life stage.

As with generational discourse, technical skill is still linked to youth; however, here the association is often more indirect, discussed euphemistically in terms of age-based variations in interest, enthusiasm, and desire rather than the sudden onset of inability to learn or keep up. There was more discussion of personal choice, with workers preferring to forgo the constant burden of keeping up with changes in skill. This sentiment is expressed in the following quotations:

> I think it's about how you feel. It's not about age, it's about energy, I think, so when people run out of energy for one reason or another they're too old. (2202120, man, late twenties, Australia)

> So it depends on the nature of the person, doesn't it? If people want to, if people are interested in the technology, they can probably absorb it. It's a question of whether they want to, I think. (4402068, man, early fifties, England)

An uncritical link between youth and enthusiasm is sometimes an offshoot of this line of thinking. Although it may be "about how you feel," the younger workers are typically viewed as "fresh" and "bright-eyed" – in short, more enthusiastic. They often attribute this to themselves as well: "I think perhaps as being a bit younger I'm slightly more enthusiastic, if you like, to want to go and fix stuff" (4404591, woman, early twenties, England). Youthful exuberance is a common cultural perception; however, it can become problematic when enthusiasm is conflated with ability. A few respondents express this view, suggesting that boundless enthusiasm can mask a lack of substance and unnecessarily devalue experience. IT managers from Australia and England express similar opinions in this regard:

Just because you're enthusiastic doesn't mean you know what you're doing, and as you get older you get less enthusiastic about [things] all the time, and so that equates with being less knowledgeable. (2207474, man, early forties, Australia)

It's a sad state of affairs when people just sort of look at the – it's almost like a veneer – the youthful, exuberant sort of things. There are quite a lot of young companies starting up that, yes, they've got the sort of the, the flash marketing, but there doesn't seem to be any sort of substance to what they're actually providing ... So, yeah, it's very glossy, but has it got the content? And the experience doesn't seem to count for as much as maybe it should. (4401042, man, late thirties, England)

Among Australian respondents in particular, talk about innovation and creativity draws out more naturalized differences between younger and older workers, to the point where genuine innovation is believed to peak at a young age and decline sharply thereafter. The following quotations reflect the link between innovation and age:

If you're going to do innovative programs, you have a "use-by" date, and I would suggest that that's grown considerably to what it was, but I doubt very much whether you're really going to get people at the cutting edge above forty. And I would suggest that real innovation is going to happen below thirty. (2203003, man, mid-fifties, Australia)

The way I see it, when you get, as you grow older, you start losing innovation, and in IT industry innovation is the key ... Young people are more innovative, so if you're a designer or developer say in your early twenties you could probably stay in there for about a maximum of ten years. Yes, and you'd have to move into [an]other sector of the industry where people are older. (2205016, man, mid-twenties, Australia)

As with any blanket statement about any group, the consequences of such perceptions can be significant. As workers age, then, it appears that they must be prepared to move on, whether they wish to or not, to roles or sectors less reliant on innovation, such as management, or to other industries entirely.

Australian respondents also tend to draw on life-course considerations as they attempt to explain IT career trajectories and variations in skill. Rather than age-based assumptions about aptitude, for some it is the relative lack of other obligations that enables younger workers to latch more easily onto new skills and technology: "It would be younger people who are less, who've got a, like, less financial commitment, less family commitments, who just [can] be nomads and go around from place to place" (2209002, man, early twenties, Australia). Put simply, undistracted by family and other responsibilities, they are perceived to have both the time and the inclination. At the same time, younger workers often anticipate changing obligations with respect to family and an eventual shift in priorities in their own lives. By extension, this would compel the choice, explicit or otherwise, to diminish the time and resources spent on learning and updating skills:

> Once you're thirty-five, you have a family, it would be pretty hard to learn new technology and learn code, unless you're a designer or at a higher level, then you don't have to use things. (2201029, man, mid-twenties, Australia)

> I think the older you get, it doesn't necessarily make you any more stupid or any less open to new ideas. Um, maybe they've got a different set of priorities ... When I have kids, I don't want to be studying and doing all this ... I want to have a life, which is fair enough. (2206081, man, early thirties, Australia)

Thus, for these respondents, rather than age per se, changing life-course commitments over time may contribute to a decline in interest and intensity when it comes to learning new IT skills. Because of the rapidly changing skill requirements, however, this may engender a shift in career trajectory – likely out of the core technical stream at least and perhaps out of IT altogether.

In England, respondents often preferred to frame discussions of age and technical skill in terms of structural barriers in the workplace. Affiliations of age and skill are not seen to be necessarily natural or generational. Youth is still linked to greater innovation, adaptability, and skill, but respondents look to career paths that veer away from technical jobs – often a function of seniority and pay scales as much as anything else

– as a primary explanation. As this analyst says, "I mean, there are a few older programmers in here, but generally you, as you kind of progress your career, you do get, uh, tramlined into management rather than keeping your technical skills up to speed with the new people who are coming in" (4404812, man, late thirties, England).

Thus, the organization of IT work itself can constrain exposure to new technology and acquisition of skills for workers as they age, particularly in project-driven scenarios. Job content thus influences the need to keep current for some workers as well as the sorts of possibilities available to update skills and knowledge. The following quotation from a manager is illustrative of this general idea:

> It does kind of get a bit boring after a while. I do wonder if that's why you get the young workforce. If you think about programmers, they'll come in, and they'll be using a certain technology ... and they'll be working on those projects, and then .Net comes out, but the only people that can actually get their hands on that are the younger ones that are just starting and not building the projects. So these guys who have now got the experience, the guys don't actually get onto those projects, they tend to be left on the wayside a bit and put onto mainte-nance jobs. (4404006, man, early forties, England)

Finally, there was also evidence of well-worn age stereotypes in the English and Australian samples (see Chapter 7 for a more detailed an-alysis). For example, a relatively young manager attributes a lack of in-terest in change, and therefore in improvement, to the older workers in her firm:

> If you're looking for someone to really improve things or change things or take it to the next level, ... I would not [be] relying on the older guys because they're more happy to be comfortable. I mean, you see it here, like the older guys don't really want to change, and then they're very happy with the way [the firm] runs and their job. Whereas the younger people, you know, we could do it better, and we could make it like this. (2208149, woman, mid-twenties, Australia)

A manager from England echoes the view that older workers in general are less adaptive, less flexible, and less able to learn than younger work-ers – though he indicates that there are rare exceptions to this "rule," and those are the people he is seeking:

There's the old saying, isn't there, that you can't teach old dogs new tricks. It's a horrible thing to say, but I'm looking for the old dog who will learn new tricks. Not somebody who's going to come in and only do what they've done for twenty years for some other company and not be open to new ideas. Someone who's as malleable to the environment and adaptive and flexible in their ways of working as a younger person. (4405188, man, early thirties, England)

Thus, common stereotypes of inertia and resistance to change are attributed to older workers in general, with little regard for variation. As with American and Canadian respondents, English and Australian respondents confer certain advantages on younger IT workers; however, there is a greater tendency to pinpoint particular ages (e.g., thirty, thirty-five, forty) at which disadvantage begins. Perhaps because of this, there seems to be some recognition of potential age bias in the assumptions expressed about younger and older workers. Comments were sometimes prefaced with qualifiers: "I don't want to appear discriminating [to] older people or anything ... " (2205016, man, mid-twenties, Australia); "I'm not at all ageist ... " (4405188, man, early thirties, England)

Conclusion

In this chapter, we extended a previous examination of technology and generational identity (McMullin, Duerden Comeau, and Jovic 2007) by considering age-based attributions in the workplace and by assessing whether and how they vary across four countries. Our data show that respondents draw on various discourses to talk about age and technological skill; however, there is some international variation in how differences are discussed. Discourse drawing on the concept of generation was most common in the United States and Canada, where respondents often mobilized it to account for innate differences in technological skill. Generational discourse was less prevalent in Australia and especially in England. Instead, skill attributions tended to invoke age stereotypes and structural or personal circumstances. Age stereotypes linking youth and innovation were common in Australia, as were life-course considerations such as changing family commitments. English respondents tended to address these issues in more nuanced ways, acknowledging an association between youth and skill yet leaning toward more structural and agentic bases for their affiliation.

How can we account for these variations? We speculate that popular and media discourse on intergenerational inequities, technological cultures, and generational differences in the workplace may be more prevalent in North America than in Australia and England. Although age and generational differences in work values, productivity levels, and trainability have been largely debunked (e.g., Appelbaum, Serena, and Shapiro 2004), some of the IT workers in our sample continue to draw on popular understandings of generations to interpret their experiences. The degree to which this phenomenon varies across countries and sub-groups suggests that the creation of generational affiliations with tech-nology is uneven. Nonetheless, for select groups, early exposure to computers and associated technologies may have helped to produce a shared generational solidarity that then carries over into workplaces, particularly where the demographic composition may encourage it.

According to Eyerman and Turner (1998), generational cohorts some-times engage in forms of "strategic closure" of material resources and cultural capital. Theorizing on age-based inequality has often focused on labour market disadvantages faced by younger people. Yet our data show that mechanisms of closure may be used to exclude older groups. Among our respondents, the matter-of-factness with which youth and technological expertise are linked suggests that technological closure by the younger generations is not strategic. Nonetheless, shared views about generational advantage and disadvantage in relation to computing have a bearing on work relations and conceptualizations of older and younger IT workers that disadvantage older workers. The pervasiveness of this view points to biases in terms of age and ability to learn. As McDaniel says,

> The internalization of beliefs about age and technologies, about gen-erations who are trainable or not, has the effect of rendering human generations obsolescent in ways similar to generations of technologies ... Technology, socially interpreted, deflects responsibility to the indi-vidual, and yet individual agency is usurped because one cannot deage, or readily switch into a more technically literate generation. (2002, 584)

Respondents prioritized "generation" over other bases of difference; hence, the articulation of affinities and inequalities through generation is significant. The fact that some respondents discussed growing up with technology in generational terms would be a matter of intellectual interest only if such discourse had not spilled into the realms of skill as-sessment and work structure. Yet our data show that IT workers invoke generational discourse when discussing perceptions of difference in skill, innovation, and adaptability. It is not a stretch to suggest that such perceptions carry over into interactions among staff and organizational processes such as recruitment or job description. Hence, those who come to IT later in life, and groups that missed growing up with certain technologies, may well be at a disadvantage, indicating the presence of age-based inequality regimes within IT firms. Besides skill differences, older generations of workers were also faulted for their perceived refusal to adapt to new technologies and the dictates of new economy business. These findings speak to the salience of generational bonds and timing as mechanisms of social inequality. Reliance on generational discourse to articulate degrees of technical expertise demonstrates that employment relations in IT are shaped by more than objective computing capabilities.

Given the dissemination of computing technologies in many workplaces, our findings have implications beyond the boundaries of IT work. Whether and how generational affinities to technology shape work environments, organizational processes, and concepts of skill in other industries remain to be seen. Sociological studies of the concept of generation need to consider further how generational bonds influence social capital and proffer links between productive and cultural realms in relation to social inequality. Invoking the concept of generation in explanations of technical skill may create additional challenges in transcending age bias and discrimination. Although legal and policy measures to deal with age discrimination are already in place in many regions, generational attributions are more nebulous, appearing "natural" and therefore potentially more difficult to target. For older IT workers, age bias and discrimination may be difficult to transcend given the apparent rigidity of links between age, technology, and skill. Again, it is the perception of these linkages more than their actual fixity that fuels existing stereotypes about age and technological aptitude. The pace of change in IT has been accelerating, which means that progressively younger workers may be linked to old and aging technologies. The displacement of technological marginalization to the generation "just before" one's own suggests that generational advantage in computing technology is a moving target.

Note

1 There has been recent media focus on the group following Generation X, sometimes labelled the "Millennials" or "Generation Y" (e.g., Huntley 2006; Tulgan 2009). At the time of the research, this cohort had not yet infiltrated the workforce in significant numbers and therefore is not considered here. Nonetheless, related literature tends to be similar in content and form to the Generation X/ Baby Boomer comparisons.

References

Appelbaum, S.H., M. Serena, and B.T. Shapiro. 2004. Generation X and the Boomers: An analysis of realities and myths. *Management Research News* 28, 1: 1-33.

Burke, M.E. 2004. *Generational differences survey report*. Alexandria, VA: Society for Human Resource Management Research.

Castells, M. 2000. Materials for an exploratory theory of the network society. *British Journal of Sociology* 51, 1: 5-24.

Cavalli, A. 2004. Generations and value orientations. *Social Compass* 51, 2: 155-68.

Consalvo, M. 2006. Console video games and global corporations: Creating a hybrid culture. *New Media and Society* 8, 1: 117-37.

Corsten, M. 1999. The time of generations. *Time and Society* 8, 2: 249-72.

Down, S., and J. Reveley. 2004. Generational encounters and the social formation of entrepreneurial identity: "Young guns" and "old farts." *Organization* 11, 2: 233-50.

Edmunds, J., and B.S. Turner. 2005. Global generations: Social change in the twentieth century. *British Journal of Sociology* 56, 4: 559-77.

Eyerman, R., and B.S. Turner. 1998. Outline of a theory of generations. *European Journal of Social Theory* 1, 1: 91-106.

Facer, K., and R. Furlong. 2001. Beyond the myth of the cyberkid: Young people at the margins of the information revolution. *Journal of Youth Studies* 4, 4: 451-69.

Gilleard, C. 2004. Cohorts and generations in the study of social change. *Social Theory and Health* 2, 1: 106-19.

Gubrium, J.F., and J.A. Holstein. 1997. *The new language of qualitative method*. New York: Oxford University Press.

Huntley, R. 2006. *The world according to Y: Inside the new adult generation*. Crows Nest, Australia: Allen and Unwin.

Kubicek, H., and R.M. Wagner. 2002. Community networks in a generational perspective. *Information, Communication, and Technologies* 5, 3: 291-320.

Lofland, J., and L. Lofland. 1995. *Analyzing social settings: A guide to qualitative observation and analysis*. Belmont, CA: Wadsworth.

Losyk, B. 1997. Generation X: What they think and what they plan to do. *The Futurist* 31, 2: 39-44.

Mannheim, K. 1952. *Ideology and utopia: An introduction to the sociology of knowledge*. New York: Harcourt, Brace.

McDaniel, S. 2002. Information and communication technologies: Bugs in the generational ointment. *Canadian Journal of Sociology* 27, 4: 535-44.

McMillan, S.J., and M. Morrison. 2006. Coming of age with the Internet: A qualitative exploration of how the Internet has become an integral part of young people's lives. *New Media and Society* 8, 1: 73-95.

McMullin, J.A., T. Duerden Comeau, and E. Jovic. 2007. Generational affinities and discourses of difference: A case study of highly skilled information technology workers. *British Journal of Sociology* 58, 2: 297-316.

Pilcher, J. 1994. Mannheim's sociology of generations: An undervalued legacy. *British Journal of Sociology* 45, 3: 481-95.

Smola, K.W., and C.D. Sutton. 2002. Generational differences: Revisiting generational work values for the new millennium. *Journal of Organizational Behaviour* 23: 363-82.

Tulgan, B. 2009. *Not everyone gets a trophy: How to manage Generation Y.* Toronto: John Wiley and Sons.

Turner, B.S. 1998. Ageing and generational conflicts: A reply to Sarah Irwin. *British Journal of Sociology* 49, 2: 299-304.

Vincent, J.A. 2005. Understanding generations: Political economy and culture in an ageing society. *British Journal of Sociology* 56, 4: 579-99.

7
Aging and Age Discrimination in IT Firms
Julie McMullin and Tammy Duerden Comeau

Segrave (2001, 4), in his social history of age discrimination, recounts the following comment from a *New York Times* editor circa 1907: "Employers, naturally, look to the young. A man or woman of advanced years is too apt to be given to old-fashioned ways of doing things, and open to suspicion of having the unforgivable fault, in modern business, of slowness." It seems that this view remains significantly unaltered. Today ageist stereotypes suggest that older workers are "less productive, have less relevant skills, are resistant to change and new technology, are less trainable, and more prone to absenteeism and ill health" (Duncan 2003, 104; see also Henkens 2005; Segrave 2001; and Shah and Kleiner 2005). These beliefs persist despite studies that have shown the willingness and capability of older workers to learn new technologies and acquire new skills (Cutler 2005). And they are resilient in light of the evidence that shows only minimal cognitive decline during normal working ages, which is rarely so great as to fall below levels required for satisfactory performance (Charness and Bosman 1992; Earles and Salthouse 1995).

Despite having a long-standing history, ageism remains a relatively understudied dimension of labour market inequality. This is particularly problematic when considered within the context of population and workforce aging and the concerns about macrolevel productivity declines that are predicted to result from this demographic trend (England 2002; Guillemette 2003; OECD 1998). As Rix (2006) points out, employers seem to be far from ready to facilitate employment in later life. The extent of this challenge is acknowledged by a recent twenty-one-country OECD report on employment policies and older workers (OECD 2006). According to the study, older workers are highly vulnerable in the labour market, and their prospects for re-employment after facing job loss are significantly lower than they are for younger workers. In the United States, age discrimination constitutes a mounting concern, with as many as 60 percent of respondents in a recent survey reporting that they have either witnessed or experienced workplace age discrimination (OECD 2006, 65). Similar data are unavailable in Canada; hence, the OECD report on Canadian older workers recommends assessing the degree to which older workers themselves feel discriminated against and stresses the need to ameliorate employer attitudes and practices (OECD 2005, 97).

The age at which one is an "older worker" depends largely on context, and older workers have been defined in varying ways (e.g., age forty in US Age Discrimination in Employment Act). The inherent subjectivity of age and understandings of "older" is acknowledged by the OECD even though it uses age fifty as the chronological marker for the older worker. The importance of context is further acknowledged in the Ontario Human Rights Commission's Policy on Discrimination (2002, 4), in which it notes that,

> While older workers are generally those over age 45, if the average age in a workplace is 25, a 37 year old job applicant may be turned away because of a perception that she is unable to fit in with the workplace culture. Therefore in some situations ... it may be necessary to think not in terms of absolute, but rather relative age.

Although relative age is likely an important dimension of ageism, we are unaware of any research that has assessed ageism in industries, occupational groups, or workplaces where the average age of an employee is less than forty-five. Hence, in this chapter, we examine ageism among information technology workers, a group that is predominantly young, male, white, and well educated. This demographic profile of IT workers has been remarkably stable and invariant in Canada (Wolfson 2006) and is similar in the United States, Australia, and the United Kingdom (McMullin 2004).

Besides its demographic profile, IT work is of interest because it is characterized by the fast-paced and continuous need to reskill and update knowledge (Kotamraju 2002). Studies of older workers and new workplace technologies have tended to examine the computer-learning capabilities of *non-technological workers* and the potential for technology either to replace or to enhance older workers' performance (Charness 2006; Cutler 2005; Gunderson 2003). Alternatively, IT workers in this study are highly skilled and computer literate. Given the wide dispersion and increasing acceleration of new computing technologies into work settings in general, and the well-documented trend of workforce aging, there is good reason to examine the occurrence of ageism in the context of IT work itself. Exploring the nature of being older in the field of computing technology is highly relevant in a context where techno-logical aptitude is strongly associated with youth. Further, the pace of technical change in the field and the constant requirement to upgrade and learn new skills mean that IT workers comprise a population who must relentlessly learn and reskill (Kotamraju 2002). This in itself makes an inquiry into the nature of age-based inequality projects in IT relevant as a way to gauge the extent of ageism in a form of work demanding qualities typically thought to be lacking in older workers.

Ageism in the Context of Paid Work

Ageism is complicated and encompasses a number of distinct though potentially interrelated elements (Bytheway 2005; MacNicol 2006; McMullin and Marshall 2001; Palmore 1999). As many scholars have pointed out, ageism more broadly applies to negative attributions and/ or discrimination on the basis of age at any time from birth to death; however, most discussions of ageism refer to prejudice and discrimina-tion in relation to those designated as old or older, on the basis of either age chronology or age-identity attributions (Bytheway 2005). Here is Butler's (1975, 35) classic definition of ageism:

> A process of systematic stereotyping of and discrimination against people because they are old, just as racism and sexism accomplish this for skin color and gender. Old people are categorized as senile, rigid in thought and manner, old-fashioned in morality and skills ... Ageism allows the younger generations to see older people as different from themselves, thus they subtly cease to identify with their elders as human beings.

Hence, individuals categorize others on the basis of age markers and formulate ideas about what it means to be older or younger. And, as recent research by Kathleen Riach (2007) suggests, these ideas become entrenched as taken-for-granted assumptions that may, in turn, influ-ence behaviour.

Within the context of paid work, several studies have examined at-titudes toward older workers. These attitudinal measures address issues of trainability, adaptability, productivity, and age relations in the work-place. Taylor and Walker (1998) asked employers a series of questions addressing these issues with the options of "agree/disagree slightly or strongly" and "not sure." Combining the categories of "strongly" and "slightly," their results show that 43 percent of respondents agreed that "older workers are hard to train," 38 percent agreed that "older workers dislike taking orders from younger workers," 40 percent did not think that "older workers are interested in technological change," 40 percent agreed that "older workers cannot adapt to new technology," and 36 percent agreed that "older workers are too cautious."

Similarly, Marshall's (1996) study adapted Taylor and Walker's (1994) attitudinal scale to assess attitudes toward older workers in three case studies of medium to large firms. Marshall (1996, 5) found that "attitudes were more favourable than not" toward older workers, that older workers often mentored and taught younger workers, and that older workers could adapt to organizational change (though less so to technological change). Indeed, among managers in Marshall's (1996) study, 30-35 percent agreed that older workers "cannot adapt to new technology," 17-31 percent agreed that older workers "do not want to receive training," and 27-43 percent agreed that older workers are "harder to train." Clearly, managers' attitudes varied across the cases, though in each, managerial attitudes toward older workers were more favourable than those of employees. More recently, Gray and McGregor's (2003) analysis of attitudinal data from 1,003 New Zealand employers found that 55 percent agreed that "older workers have problems with technology," 33 percent agreed that they are "less willing to train," and 39 percent agreed that they have "trouble working longer hours." At the same time, several studies have shown that older workers are often considered more reliable and in some cases equally productive workers (Duncan 2003; Henkens 2005). Taylor and Walker (1998, 651) found that older workers are seen to be more reliable than younger workers (75 percent) and "very productive workers" (63 percent). Yet the segment of respondents who express negative attitudes toward older workers is by no means inconsequential. Indeed, if a segment of this size expressed negative attitudes of this sort toward groups based on gender or race/ethnicity, interpretations of their favourability might differ.

Still, holding negative attitudes toward older workers is not likely a sufficient condition for discriminatory behaviour, and on this score the evidence is inconclusive. This is, at least in part, because age discrimination remains notoriously difficult to study and to prove, especially in the area of hiring, where decisions are often made behind closed doors with explanations for hiring younger workers given in terms of cost factors and the currency of skills (Gunderson 2003; MacNicol 2006). Some studies have found linkages between age-biased behaviour and ageist stereotypes (Chiu et al. 2001; Henkens 2005; Reed, Doty, and May

2005; Rupp, Vodanovich, and Crede 2006; Taylor and Walker 1998), which may result in tangible and material effects on people's lives and livelihoods (Koeber and Wright 2001; McMullin 2004). For instance, McMullin and Marshall's (2001, 121) study of garment workers shows that ageist stereotypes are retrospectively drawn on to enact more covert types of age discrimination in which "seemingly neutral age strategies of cost reduction become systems of inequality in which age is implicated and older workers are placed at a heightened disadvantage relative to younger workers." Rupp and her colleagues (2006) found that managers who expressed more ageist attitudes were also more likely to support personnel decisions that were age biased.

Although Taylor and Walker (1998) found that adaptability to new technology was less relevant than trainability and other measures in explaining ageist practices, more recent studies have found attitudes toward technological adaptation to be indicative of ageist behaviour (Chiu et al. 2001; Henkens 2005). Henkens (2005) found that managers' negative views of older workers' technological adaptability were associated with a lack of support for later retirement. Views of older workers' technological adaptation were identified as an "Achilles' heel" in ageist attitudes over a decade ago among managers and workers in largely non-technological industries (Lyon and Pollard 1997, 253; Marshall 1996). Despite the persistence of negative views of older workers' ability to adapt to technological change, scholars have suggested that perceptions of older workers are generally "favourable." Yet in demographically young fields such as IT, where technological adaptation is crucial and ongoing, views of the ability of older workers to adapt to new technologies may become a more critical factor in employment practices.

Employers want to hire the most productive, least costly workers, which makes perfect sense if the goal of an organization is to maximize profits. However, determining which workers are the most productive is not an exact science, and employers sometimes make such decisions based on information about average characteristics of the group or groups to which an individual belongs. This is referred to as "statistical discrimination," whereby "discrimination and segregation in job assignment represents rational reactions of employers to different average productivity levels between easily identifiable classes of job applicants" (Tomaskovic-Devey and Skaggs 1999, 423). For instance, employers may not hire a younger woman because, on average, younger women cost more to employ than younger men, largely because of high turnover rates due to childbirth. The individual woman in this example may be unable or may not want to have children, yet she is not hired for the job simply because she is a member of a group. Applying the model of statistical discrimination to older workers, employers may not hire older workers because, on average, they are less productive than younger workers (Posner 1995; Sterns, Sterns, and Hollis 1996). Any particular older worker may have certain characteristics that would counter the average productivity claim, but through the process of statistical discrimination such an older worker would remain unemployed.

Paula England coined the term "error discrimination," linked to statistical discrimination, to refer to "the situation where employers underestimate the relative average productivity of a group and, based upon this mistaken belief, are unwilling to hire group members or will hire them for a lower wage" (1992, 60). Here the process of discrimination is similar to that of statistical discrimination, but employers rely on assumptions rather than evidence about the productivity of a group. For instance, in the case of gender, there is little evidence supporting the view that women are less productive than men (Tomaskovic-Devey and Skaggs 1999). Yet some research shows that employers use gender-based productivity differences in their employment decisions (England 1992). Applying the model of error discrimination to older workers, assumptions about older workers' lower productivity or inability to adapt to technological change may make employers less likely to hire them or, if hired, to provide training or career advancement opportunities.

Although a substantial body of research has examined race- and sex-based statistical and error discrimination, the same cannot be said for age. Hence, this chapter considers age-based statistical and error discrimination in highly skilled IT employment. To begin, we examine the age at which highly skilled IT workers within our sample begin to be classified by employers as older and assess their attitudes toward older workers. Next we examine how several of these attitudes are discussed in relation to hiring decisions within the IT industry.

Method and Analysis

The analysis is based on 399 semi-structured qualitative interviews with IT workers in Australia (n = 91), Canada (n = 141), England (n = 61), and the United States (n = 106). Respondents were asked about their attitudes toward older workers and their assessments of older workers in a quantitative web survey. The attitudinal questions were adapted from those developed by Taylor and Walker (1994) on attitudes toward older workers. Respondents to these questions in our total sample equalled 409 (Australia = 70, Canada = 95, England = 118, United States = 126), and their demographic profile closely matched that of our qualitative respondents (see Chapter 2). Frequencies from these quantitative questions were then assessed in light of our corresponding qualitative data.

A qualitative data analysis software package, Nvivo, facilitated the data analysis, which proceeded in two phases: the organizational coding of interview transcripts (Lofland and Lofland 1995), and then age-specific analytical coding of interview passages attending specifically to ageist attitudes identified in our survey data. One organizational category from the first phase, "age," was selected for further analytical coding and intersected with five relevant thematic categories: "industry landscape, recruitment, skill, employment turnover, and human resource policy." In our qualitative data, ageist attitudes addressing the inability of older workers to adapt to new technologies were predominant, along with negative implications for older workers' ability and desire to train and work longer hours. Therefore, our broader organizational codes were collapsed into four analytical codes addressing (1) older workers' adaptation to new technologies, (2) older workers' desire and ability to train, (3) older workers' ability to work long hours, and (4) ageism expressed in relation to hiring practices. As our analysis progressed, it became clear that ageist discourse was expressed primarily in relation to technological adaptation, training issues, and working hours/time constraints; therefore, hiring implications are discussed concurrently with these attitudinal measures in our qualitative results section.

Results

Quantitative Data
The attitudes of our respondents toward older workers largely mirrored those of previous studies. Respondents saw older workers as productive and reliable employees who were largely able to adapt to organizational change. Overall, 96 percent of respondents agreed with the statement that "older workers are productive employees," and 85 percent agreed that "older workers can adapt to organizational change." Eighty percent of respondents thought that older workers serve as mentors for younger workers, 75 percent agreed that older workers are "highly respected," and half thought that older workers are more reliable than younger workers. Nearly one-quarter of our sample (23 percent) agreed with the statement that older workers do not want to receive training. Among our Canadian respondents, as many as 35 percent agreed with this statement, while only 13 percent of Australian respondents agreed that older workers do not want to receive training. Twenty-two percent of respondents agreed that older workers have trouble working longer

hours, though among our Canadian respondents as many as 33 percent agreed with this statement.

In contrast, ageist attitudes were evident in regard to issues of techno-logical adaptation and learning, as just over a third of all respondents respectively agreed with the statements that "older workers cannot adapt to new technology" (32 percent) and that "older workers are harder to train than younger workers" (30 percent). Among Australian respond-ents, as many as 42 percent agreed that "older workers cannot adapt to new technology." Again, these numbers are similar to those found by Taylor and Walker (1998): 40 percent of their respondents agreed that older workers "cannot adapt to new technology," 43 percent agreed that they are "harder to train," and one-quarter agreed that they "do not want to receive training." Similarly, 36 percent of our respondents and 38 percent of respondents in Taylor and Walker's study (1998) agreed that older workers "dislike taking instructions from younger workers." Given that respondents were aware that our study was investigating the implications of workforce aging, agreement with ageist statements seems to be significant. The fact that the average age of our sample is thirty-eight also begs the question of who is older in this context, where less than a third (29 percent) of our sample is forty-five and older.

Who Is an Older Worker?

In a field such as IT, known for its youthful demographic, being an older worker is highly relative. In our qualitative data, respondents in their late twenties and early thirties often positioned themselves as older workers, thereby suggesting the constructed nature of "older" in the IT field. For example, a Canadian IT worker recently transitioned into management and suggested that it was time to "leave the programming and stuff to the young guys" (1102029, man, early thirties). An Australian program-mer defined an older worker in IT as someone with "over five years [of] experience. [That] would be my definition in that term of older ... So you don't have to be particularly old [respondent laughs] to be older in those terms" (2202055, man, late thirties). In this way, getting older in IT happens relatively early.

Evidence of an accelerated age identity in IT work was also apparent in our quantitative data. After answering the attitudinal questions on older workers, our respondents were asked whether, when answering these questions, they were thinking of older workers as "in their twen-ties," "in their thirties," "in their forties," "in their fifties," and so on. Indeed, nearly half of our overall sample (49 percent) thought of older workers as in their forties or younger. In our Canadian data, 14 percent of respondents thought of older workers as in their thirties, and 8 percent thought of older workers as in their twenties. Only 6 percent of our respondents overall thought of older workers as in their sixties. These data suggest that assessments of who is older are important in determining the outlook for workers as they age within a given field. In our sample, nearly half of respondents thought of older workers as under fifty; therefore, ageist attitudes expressed toward older workers' ability to adapt to and train in new technology in a technological field must be considered in this light.

Previous studies have found ageist attitudes toward older workers' ability to train in and adapt to new technologies among non-IT workers (Gray and McGregor 2003; Marshall 1996). Our respondents are employed in a high-tech industry and in most cases perform highly skilled technological work. In this environment, it seems to be particularly critical to assess views on older workers' ability to adapt and train, and whether and how these views affect hiring practices. In the context of an aging population and an increasing reliance on technology in the workplace, IT workers provide an especially relevant barometer of ageism in technological environments since 32 percent of our respondents agreed that older workers cannot adapt to new technology and virtually half viewed older workers as under fifty.

Qualitative Data

Overall, in our qualitative data, the ageist attitudes expressed addressed the inability of older workers to adapt to new technologies, their lack of aptitude and desire to train, and their inability or refusal to endure long hours. In many cases, these issues emerged simultaneously with discourse on hiring preferences and practices. A general age preference for youth in IT hiring for technical positions was acknowledged and evident across each of the countries, though respondents from England tended to offer more nuanced and structurally based explanations for this phenomenon. Indeed, ageist attitudes were less evident among our respondents from England compared with our respondents from Australia, Canada, and the United States.

The impetus of long hours and the need for training or skill upgrading in IT go hand in hand with new technology adaptation. The "marketability" of workers in the industry is directly tied to their ability to remain current. Workers who cannot keep up with change are "left behind" and quickly become "unmarketable" or unhirable in the IT labour market.

Therefore, if older workers who are in their twenties, thirties, and forties are seen to be less able to adapt, then this bodes poorly for those who intend to work in IT in their fifties and beyond. We discuss our qualitative results in the sections below, with respondents' discourse on (1) older workers' ability to adapt to new technologies, (2) older workers' ability/desire to train, and (3) older workers' ability/desire to work long hours. Within each section, discourse on the relation of these attitudes to hiring practices is also discussed.

Older Workers' Ability to Adapt to New Technologies
The nature and pace of computing innovation are structural factors over which workers have little control; however, many IT workers (younger and older) associated both the desire and the ability to adapt to new technologies with youthfulness. Ageist beliefs are evident in the notion that younger people are simply more adept, eager, and able to learn new technologies. The following quotations are representative of many respondents in Australia, Canada, and the United States (employers, management, and workers) who associated ability and the desire to learn new technologies with younger workers:

> As IT workers age, gosh, I hate sounding like this, but I think younger IT workers have a better grasp on current technology, and older IT workers by and large lose the ability or the interest or the inclination to learn about new technology. (5511162, US programmer, man, mid-twenties)

> Well, my observation is this: that, if you're going to do innovative programs, you have a use-by date, for sure, and I would suggest that that's grown considerably to what it was, but I doubt very much whether you're really going to get people at the cutting edge above forty. And I would suggest that real innovation is going to happen below thirty. (2203003, Australian CEO, man, mid-fifties)

> A lot of the older workers were not interested in learning latest technologies, sort of stuck in their ways, I found. So, in many ways, I would say that a lot of the younger people are more interested in learning new stuff ... I guess it must be hard as well because technology changes so quickly. (1107055, Canadian programmer, man, late twenties)

Overwhelmingly, respondents characterized older workers as resistant and less flexible in their approach to technology and learning new tactics. For example, one Canadian CEO (1112146, late thirties) recalled his efforts a decade ago to train older workers on the PC platform and described the response of older workers as "I don't want to accept it, I don't want to know about it, just get it away, I want to do my old stuff, and I don't know why."

This mulish attitude attributed to older workers categorizes them as employees who become "stuck" and therefore have less longevity and usefulness over time. Older workers are viewed as less adaptable, less malleable, and less open to change than younger workers, and for some these attributes are seen as a straightforward consequence of aging:

It's a natural tendency for people to learn a set of skills and sort of calcify. Um, they like to continue using the same hammer that they're comfortable with, ... and that's one reason I like to hire people right out of college. There's no untraining for me to do. (5502021, US programmer, man, early forties)

I think, unfortunately, as you get older, your ability to adapt and change to the new whatever tends to sort of go off a bit. (2211058, Australian programmer, man, late forties)

Although respondents in England seemed to view ageist stereotypes with a more critical lens, there was evidence of ageist attitudes in terms of the ability of older workers to adapt to new technology. An owner at a firm in England intended to bring in "young blood":

I think the biggest concern that I have really is obviously the need to take on, continue to take on, younger people, who bring fresh ideas and new challenges and new enthusiasm ... Otherwise, we can, you know, as you mature you're less naturally inclined to take on new things, you just carry on doing what you've done for the last ten years, the way you've done it for the last ten years ... You're not really interested in change and attempting new things. (4402029, English CEO, man, early fifties)

Many IT owners consider these associations to be "common sense" and take them into consideration in staffing decisions. In terms of differences between older and younger workers, this Australian owner noted that "older people get tired of the learning process, younger people generally are not, they're eager to learn" (2206029, Australian owner, man, mid-fifties).

These categorical judgments on the adaptability of older workers are not supported by objective findings but by anecdotes that in many ways abstract the structural constraints at work. Yet the persistence and proliferation of these associations between older workers and adherence to older technologies are particularly damning in a technological field.

Some workers claim a growing resistance to change for themselves; however, most distance themselves from it and see themselves as exceptions to the "general rule" that older workers are poor at transitioning and keeping pace with technology. For example, this Canadian programmer, in his early forties, suggested that

> The only limitation I find is that, as you get older, you become more rigid, less willing to accept change. In IT, that's not good, right? ... I've seen it, like not me personally, but I've seen it with others, for sure. I had one guy who was willing to lose his job because he wasn't willing to go from the big mainframes to the small microsystems, and he got laid off because of that, right? And my comment to him in one meeting, I got really tired of listening to him, I stood up and said, "Whether it's right or wrong, do you want to be employed?" (1107081, Canadian programmer, man, early forties)

Adaptability and employability were related again and again among respondents. More than one-third of our respondents thought that older workers lose their technological edge over time. Still, there are other, less acknowledged, factors at play in the quest to maintain technical relevance. Although this respondent from England saw himself as currently marketable, he voiced concern over the structural constraints of continually upgrading in this field over time:

> I still think I'm very marketable. But I know in five years' time ... it's going to require that much more work to stay at that same sort of level. And you're always going to get young guys coming in out of college, and they're always going to just have the edge ... They'll still be enthusiastic and bright eyed ... I don't know any design engineers in their fifties, let's put it that way. (4405076, English engineer, man, mid-thirties)

In general, views among both management and workers about hiring suggest that younger workers are preferred, in part because it is assumed that they are both up to date and keen to work with new technologies. In the following quotations, the preference for younger workers and new graduates to work in newer technologies is evident:

I love young blood. I like giving the opportunity for new people to come in and see what we have and go with it ... Age is not a necessary criteria as much as it is aptitude, inquisitiveness, ability to work with other people in a team environment, and a strong interest in growth. But for some of the tools that we have, if younger people are better able to address that, then fine. Age is not a first criterion for working in IT. (1108003, Canadian CEO, man, early sixties)

The most important thing they are looking for is the ability to learn fast, because of the changes that happen constantly, and the trend seems to be, from what I can see, they prefer young people, though I'm not sure it should be that way, but it seems to be that way on the whole in the IT industry. (2201016, Australian manager, woman, age unknown)

So as we grow, I will certainly look to bring in younger, enthusiastic, technically competent people, because I think that will inject a bit of impetus in the technology side. (4402250, English manager, man, early fifties)

Again, these quotations express a clear association between younger workers and the ability to learn and adapt along with the contention that attitude is crucial. This Canadian CEO suggested that attitude among older workers more than age deters him from hiring them:

If I had a fifty year old come in here and he had the personality and the ability to fit in here, I'd hire him. In fact, we've hired or we've interviewed lots of them ... The fact is that the people that have come in here that are that old have been working in IT for pretty much their whole life, or at least the last twenty years, and have those set ways of doing things, and it's almost like this unionized mentality ... This is the way we do things, this is how it's done, and you can see that they're more individualistic in their approach rather than kind of fitting in as a team. (1106003, Canadian CEO, man, late twenties)

This CEO took on new graduates in four of the company's latest hires. Similarly, this Australian manager noted a preference for younger workers for their more malleable nature:

Certainly, with our architects and programmers, we look for younger people more than older people. So we'd look for people that are in their early twenties to mid-twenties ... They're better programmers, they're able to understand what we do, they've got much more open minds ... They're not set in terms of their learning and their way of programming or the methodologies that they've used ... They're still very impressionable, so we're able to actually give them our view. (2203133, Australian IT manager, man, mid-forties)

Ironically, even though workers are encouraged to view their skill development in individualistic terms, the experience that older workers bring tends to be viewed in negative terms as limiting rather than informative. As Sennett (1998, 94) states, "from the institutions' vantage point, the flexibility of the young makes them more malleable in terms of both risk-taking and immediate submission." Even those firms that seek more experienced workers appear to end up hiring workers in their late twenties and early thirties. For example, the following Canadian CEO suggested that his firm must hire experienced workers but not necessarily older workers:

We're looking for a very unique skill set. They need to have been typically ... objective-oriented developers for five years, three years of Agile, you know, you've got to have had two years of .Net, and it's only been around three years. And you're looking for five or more years of Java, right? So it's hard ... They tend to be twenty-eight and up, usually. Sometimes thirty. (1107029, Canadian CEO, man, late fifties)

The constructed nature of age in this field is evident here because workers in their thirties are perceived to be older in many cases. Indeed, one respondent from England was told by a career counsellor at age twenty-eight that he was "perhaps considered too old as a software developer at that point" (4405055, English engineer, man, early thirties). Capturing a workforce that is locked in a "high youth" phase seems to be a priority for IT owners. Indeed, youthfulness was associated not only with adaptability but also with pure learning capacity among our IT respondents.

Trainability: Capability and Desire to Learn
Older workers' ability to stay current and by implication "hirable" is seen by most workers and firms as an individual problem rather than an industry or social issue. Older workers are seen to be past the stage of learning, and well-worn ageist stereotypes are recycled among many respondents. A Canadian manager stated that "it's harder to teach an old dog new tricks ... You can do it, but it's definitely hard" (1117149, Canadian IT manager, man, early thirties). Likewise, a US respondent

described older workers as being unable to adapt, noting that "most old people are set in their ways, ... and they don't want to see anything else" (5504112, US other IT, woman, late twenties). Although the following manager from England suggested that he is not ageist in his hiring, he drew on ageist stereotypes and associations in his descriptions of workers' attributes:

> There's the old saying, isn't there, that you can't teach old dogs new tricks. It's a horrible thing to say, but I'm looking for the old dog who will learn new tricks. Not somebody who's going to come in and only do what they've done for twenty years for some other company and not be open to new ideas. Someone who's as malleable to the environment and adaptive and flexible in their ways of working as a younger person. (4405188, English IT manager, man, early thirties)

Again, the ability to learn is tied to being young. A Canadian CEO recalled his entry into IT and attributed his success and quick rise through the ranks to his "young, fresh mind" and the fact that he had "no preconceptions about how the technology should work" (1102003, man, late twenties). Likewise, mental agility and youth are linked in the following quotations:

> I would say there's a reason why there's not a lot of older developers. They've usually moved into QA and support and management, and that's because they just physically, I mean I've seen that, even one of our owners, he's getting to that stage where he can't keep up ... Your mind has to be very, very active, and you're always constantly thinking ... As you get older, ... it goes slower. (5504008, US IT manager, man, early thirties)

> Just not quick mentally, you just lose it as you get older, number one, and number two, you just couldn't be bothered learning new stuff anymore because you've just seen it all before. (2207474, Australian IT manager, man, early forties)

In part, the difficulties attributed to learning over time refer not only to mental capacity (though that is certainly present) but also to the desire and drive to continue to change and adapt to new work methods. Many construe older workers as both less able and less willing to learn new things:

If you're looking for someone to really improve things or change things or take it to the next level generally, and this is in a sense pretty rude, but I would not be relying on the older guys, because they're more happy to be comfortable. I mean you see it here, like the older guys don't really want to change ... whereas the younger people, we could do it better, and ... you know have got the enthusiasm to move it. (2208149, Australian manager, woman, mid-twenties)

The older you get, the harder it is to learn new things. The less motivated you are to keep up with trends and new techniques, so I think those things are going to make a real problem for programmers [who] aren't willing to learn the new languages, learn the new techniques, or who are unable to for time constraints. (1110029, Canadian IT manager, man, early forties)

The older IT people, whether they're male or female, prefer desk work and management. They get tired of the hands-on ... but they're striving for retirement and doing the least amount of work for the most amount of pay. (5503008, US IT manager, woman, early forties)

Our results suggest that ageist beliefs in regard to learning and technological adaptation are shared and normative among workers and managers and younger and older respondents. These ageist stereotypes about older workers may impede training for some:

I've repeatedly come up against the assumption that they think that I wouldn't want to learn new technology or that I resent having to do technological things. All along I keep going "no, no, that's fine." They just keep going "oh, don't worry, we'll get you help with this." I'm like "no, it's OK, I'll learn it." (5508234, US other IT, woman, age unknown)

In addition, IT workers' descriptions of the process of up-skilling suggest that they have internalized ageist beliefs about their own capacity to learn. These beliefs are illustrated by the following quotations, which are representative of many respondents:

I used to be the best, but I'm just, you know, my brain – the brain is like being an athlete's brain. You don't expect a thirty-five-year-old guy to go out there and run the 200 metres in the Olympics and win. The guy who's gonna win ... is, what, twenty-two, I don't know how old. But he's at his peak now ... Be really hard to do that again in four years and pretty much impossible to do it again in eight years, and it's the same way for this stuff. It's just like being an athlete. (5502008, US CEO, man, early forties)

Ah, well, it's one of those things that I worry about ... I'm forty-five now ... Your synapses are not firing quite the same [respondent laughs] as when you're thirty ... I have a harder time learning things ... I've seen so many incarnations of software and stuff like that it's just like [thump] not another thing that I have to learn. (1114097, Canadian programmer, man, mid-forties)

In IT, these ageist categorizations linking youth and mental capacity seem to be internalized and operationalized at earlier and earlier ages.

Further, these ageist stereotypes about learning, age, and ability are evident in the hiring decisions of IT firms. One US respondent stated that in her firm they "get a little nervous if we interview older ... like fifties ... Our initial reaction is they don't understand IT" (5510032, US other IT, woman, mid-thirties). An Australian respondent said that her company "tends to pick the young ones because they're fresh with their training, they're easy to mould, they're keen, that sort of thing" (2204198, Australian non-IT worker, woman, late forties). Similarly, in describing his hiring practices, a Canadian CEO noted that the ability to work in their particular software framework was of utmost importance; however, in talking with the employees, we found that none in fact had previous experience with the software. In this climate, "no experience" is "good experience." Attitudes of workers within the field further support the tendency to hire younger workers in new technologies. The following quotations express this thinking:

I think when you're younger you just have [the] ability to learn faster, learn quicker, learn newer technologies; as you [get] older, obviously you're going to slow down, right? So I guess it's just natural for IT companies to keep the newer, younger employees around who can get the work done more proficiently. (1112172, Canadian engineer, man, late twenties)

The way I see it, when you get, as you grow older, you start losing innovation, and in [the] IT industry innovation is the key. (2205016, Australian non-IT worker, man, mid-twenties)

> They do discriminate against older professionals ... People are looking for the young graduate or the person who's been working for three years, but they're looking for those people because they think that they've got the new groovy ideas. (2210019, Australian manager, man, early forties)

The general acceptance of the ageist view that younger workers are more technically proficient – "younger" here often referring to workers in their late twenties or perhaps early thirties – means that older workers are far more likely to be further removed from new technologies in their daily work.

Judgments on being an older worker are bounded in some ways by the age of technology itself (McMullin, Duerden Comeau, and Jovic 2007). This tends to leave older IT workers in a situation where they may be engaged in "production programming" or working in a technology of which they are experts with no room to learn something new. One English respondent thought that older workers are often steered to work on "maintenance programming," noting that, in terms of exposure to new technology at work,

> The only people that can actually get their hands on that are the younger ones that are just starting and not building the projects, so these guys who have now got the experience, the guys don't actually get onto those projects, they tend to be a bit left on the wayside a bit and put onto maintenance jobs. (4404006, English IT manager, man, early forties)

Once this technology is phased out, these workers have lost their place in the industry, and without either technical or managerial skills they are highly vulnerable to unemployment:

> Because they would view, I think they view the younger people as ... wrong to say better. I don't know. It is very strange, but there is still a lot of ageism in the workplace. So it would be difficult for me to move to get a better job than I was doing. (4402198, English manager, man, early fifties)

> Technology changes at such a rapid pace that if you don't take the initiative it is quite easy to be left behind. When I say "left behind," your skills are antiquated, and your employability is reduced. (1115048, Canadian analyst, man, mid-thirties)

And so the question is what do we do with people like me who are, you know, over the hill technically ... I mean, if you've got people who are peaking at early twenties or earlier and hitting their stride as far as experience by mid-twenties, what do you do with them from forty to seventy? (5502008, US CEO, man, early forties)

The above quotations illustrate how a number of IT respondents recognize the vulnerability of older workers in the job market. We argue that hiring practices that target young workers make it more likely for older workers to become redundant at the same time that their chances in the labour market are compromised.

Younger workers are hired to work in younger and newer technologies based on the erroneous assumption that they innately know it or can learn it; in this way, older workers may be systematically denied opportunities to work in new technologies. Attempts to attract and hire younger workers may be motivated by financial rationale in part; however, the experience of older workers in the job market suggests that the assumption that older workers demand higher wages also acts as something of an excuse. In fact, new graduates of IT programs who are older do not seem to garner any advantage in the job market even in light of their "new" technological skills. The following quotations outline the experience of age discrimination in searching for jobs among older IT workers. As one recent graduate said,

Even applying for jobs, and you send your resumes out, even see people. Ah, they look at me ... there's an age ... they can't tell you they're not going to hire me because ... you know you're an old guy, you know "you get the hell out of here kind of thing." They won't tell you that because they can't, it's against the law. But there's definitely a bias for age. (1116097, Canadian technician, man, early sixties)

Likewise, a US technician notes,

I think there's definitely age bias. They had a recruiter here ... and when I came in to meet with him for my first interview I brought my resume, a printed copy. And he said, "I've reformatted it so that it wouldn't show your age." I had too much history on it ... He tailored it to get rid of a lot of my early jobs so that the people here who looked at it wouldn't know how old I was. (5505318, US technician, woman, late forties)

Even current skills are not enough to offset the erroneous associations linking older technologies exclusively with "older" workers, particularly for workers who are well past typical definitions of older in the realm of IT. Among our respondents, the investment of time to remain current was seen as a further barrier impeding the quest to maintain relevant skills over time.

Older Workers' Ability to Work Long Hours
Again in relation to time, older workers are viewed as less willing and less able to invest long hours in technological work. Time constraints and other responsibilities tend to be mentioned in conjunction with ageist attitudes toward the learning capacity of older workers. The following quotations are representative of this outlook:

> It seems as though as you start to get older you might actually get weaned out of the programming because you don't have the mental capacity to keep it up from, you know, six-thirty in the morning until ten at night, if you really had to, whereas somebody who's twenty-three or twenty-four they're used to that ... Eventually, you get to be twenty-eight, twenty-nine, thirty, and you start to lose it, you're getting tired, you're thinking about family, you're not thinking about I want to work all the time. (1104172, Canadian IT manager, man, late twenties)

> If I was a manager, I probably can't expect someone past forty-five to really embrace new ideas or ha[ve] the time or the patience to really change. (5511409, US programmer, man, mid-twenties)

> In my mind, the difference between young and old is the younger ones that I have known are generally more enthused, okay, because they are fresher. They are not worn out as much. (2203055, Australian IT manager, man, early thirties)

Here again getting older and losing the endurance to work longer hours may apply even to those in their late twenties. At this relatively younger age, workers "feel old" in IT, and in some cases they do tire of the constant rate of change with relatively little organizational support for retraining and relearning. This in turn feeds the need to work longer and longer hours to meet deadlines and to keep up with technological change.

Indeed, older workers talked about the drudgery of working long hours and learning yet another software tool:

It's demanding in the sense where the long, spontaneous hours that you have to put in, you better be able to do that. I think, if you're older, you can't do that as much. And the young professionals are willing to do that. (5502073, US programmer, man, early thirties)

Yes, it's very detail oriented, and maybe it is a function of getting older, but I can't concentrate on those details for that long a time anymore. I don't want to put in ten to twelve hours a day like I used to ... The stuff I am learning I don't want to learn, I don't care to learn. I mean, yeah, sure, it's another technology, here today gone tomorrow. If I don't learn it now, well, it'll be obsolete next year. (1107003, Canadian analyst, man, mid-forties)

There continues to be the perception that true commitment to technology means enduring long work hours, and workplace environments are structured with this perception in mind. This belief extends to all levels in the industry. One Canadian CEO described how older workers may be systematically excluded from IT environments because they are perceived to have both less ability and less desire to work in a technical capacity:

A lot of the decision making in the high tech, especially the high tech where it's publicly listed, or it's driven by venture capital funding, it's pure money motivated ... And they'll have a board controlling them that has no knowledge of the industry and has no desire for longevity. They're just looking for the exit strategy. And I think in some of those shops where the expectation is that [while] you'll have a low salary you'll get stock options, and you'll be a multimillionaire in five years' time when they go public or when they get bought out. I think the older workers they would get discriminated out of those environments – because they won't be seen as willing and/or able to put in the hours that they perceive as being necessary. (1115006, Canadian CEO, woman, late forties)

Likewise, these respondents noted,

I've had some experience working with older programmers, and I think there's some things about programming specifically that it is just made for young people ... Standard deadlines are always blown. And everything is always behind time, so if you can work twenty-four hours a day that's a big tick. (2205055, Australian programmer, man, late thirties)

I would guess mostly people prefer younger ... employees because they're more flexible, they work harder, and they come cheaper. (5502099, US engineer, man, age unknown)

I think that they've that view that they want to get rid of the old ones, and bring in the new ones, and that's been said ... They think the old ones just aren't good enough in their attitudes, work practices ... I guess they want a workforce that's more motivated and maybe [will] work harder or something. (2209005, Australian manager, woman, late forties)

Here the intersection of financing and ageist views of productivity and technical ability combines to disadvantage and alienate older workers from entrepreneurial ventures. We've seen that IT owners in some cases openly acknowledge that they are seeking younger workers. A Canadian CEO (1112016, man, early sixties) said that his company structured its work environment to appeal to younger workers because "we knew we were going to be hiring younger people, and it was important to them." The battle to stay close to new technologies is exacerbated for older workers given employers' preferences to seek newer and younger workers to work in new technologies as opposed to investing in training their current staff.

Again, the penalty for not upgrading and staying relevant in one's work is potential marginalization and vulnerability in the labour market. These quotations reflect the notion of an age cap in IT longevity:

I wonder if they end up there [in contract work] because there really isn't anywhere else for them to go as an employee in a firm. So whether they're actually wired to be a self-employed contractor or have the discipline to get the contracts and all that stuff I don't know. Because I'm sure there's people like that out there obviously, but I also wonder if sometimes they're that because they're perceived to be irrelevant when they get to be fifty or there's just nowhere for them to go. (1191081, Canadian IT manager, man, mid-forties)

There is a certain amount of rejection in this field, in the computer field, to say that it's a young man's trade ... Once you've got to forty-five, that's it as far as the industry's concerned. If you get another job after that, then you're going to be lucky. And you're going to be struggling to get one, in all seriousness. (4402159, English IT manager, man, late fifties)

Hirability is time limited, skills expire, and IT workers are seen to virtually sour on technology and its ever-changing character over time. Technologically immobile, mentally rigid, and averse to long hours, older IT workers succumb to these ageist attitudes, and the constructed nature of these beliefs is doubly evident when older workers are those in their late twenties and early thirties. In this context, productivity is a loaded term, and in fact "production programming" is a term often applied to the work of older employees who become highly proficient in ancient and "dying" technologies. Adaptability and flexibility and not productivity per se appear to be at the crux of hiring considerations among IT employers. The general persistence of ageist stereotypes and rationales in hiring decisions among IT owners makes older IT workers highly vulnerable to displacement and unemployment in the field.

Conclusion

The relationship between ageism and age discrimination in the workplace is complicated, and, as McMullin and Marshall (2001, 111) point out, "very little is known about the role that age plays in disadvantaging certain groups of people relative to others within labour markets." In considering the ability to learn and adapt to evolving computing technology, we noted that ageism emerged in multiple ways among IT workers. For many respondents, attitudes toward learning over the life course were seen as most decisive in whether IT workers could remain technically relevant as they aged, and in this way ageist attitudes toward the ability and the desire to learn new technologies were common. Yet, overall, the structural constraints that workers face in their efforts to maintain up-to-date technical skills tend to be downplayed, though these constraints are considerable for workers who wish to age in technical work. Employers operate their firms under considerable financial constraints, so hiring younger employees assumed to know new technologies saves on training and theoretically on wages. Yet these structural actions reinforce and legitimate existing ageism, linking younger workers with technically adept skills. The importance of structural constraints in perpetuating age discrimination means that solutions targeted to finances in the form of funded training and other incentives may find more success than ameliorating attitudes alone.

It is telling that these well-worn stereotypes about learning and adapting to technology come from workers who are already highly skilled technically. Previous studies have examined ageist stereotypes and technology in non-technological realms in regard to older workers who perhaps did not have technological backgrounds. In our research, older workers were engaged in high-skill technological work, yet the same stereotypes tended to apply in terms of the abilities of older learners. At the same time, older workers who do manage to maintain their technical skills do not tend to see themselves as proof against ageist stereotypes. Instead, differences among older workers and exceptions to the rule are seen as attitudinally based. Likewise, Reed and his colleagues (2005, 224) found that, contrary to ingrained stereotypes about older workers and change, no relationship existed between attitudes toward change and technical abilities; instead, their research suggests that "age-related decline in computer skills [is] a function of specific beliefs about successful performance." Given that our research suggests an internalization of ageist beliefs in regard to aging and the ability to keep up, action is needed to attempt to ameliorate these stereotypes.

The mechanisms of age discrimination in the field of information technology shed light on the importance of age identity. The accelerated age at which IT workers are considered to be old and seem to consider themselves older in the realm of new economy "knowledge work" is telling. In an environment where adaptability, flexibility, and ability to rapidly learn new skills are paramount, the acceleration of age among an aging population seems to be particularly ominous.

References
Butler, R.N. 1975. *Why survive? Being old in America.* New York: Harper and Row.
Bytheway, B. 2005. Ageism and age categorization. *Journal of Social Issues* 62, 2: 361-74.
Charness, N. 2006. Work, older workers, and technology. *Generations* 30, 2: 25-30.
Charness, N., and E. Bosman. 1992. Age and human factor. In *The handbook of aging and cognition,* ed. F.I.M. Craik and T.A. Salthouse, 495-551. Hillsdale, NJ: Erlbaum.
Chiu, W.C.K., A.W. Chan, E. Snape, and T. Redman. 2001. Age stereotypes and discriminatory attitudes towards older workers: An east-west comparison. *Human Relations* 54, 5: 629-61.
Cutler, S.J. 2005. Ageism and technology. *Generations* 29, 3: 67-72.
Duncan, C. 2003. Assessing anti-ageism routes to older worker re-engagement. *Work, Employment, and Society* 17, 1: 101-20.
Earles, J.L., and T.A. Salthouse. 1995. Interrelations of age, health, and speed. *Journal of Gerontology and Social Psychological Sciences* 50, B.1: 33-41.
England, P. 1992. *Comparable worth: Theories and evidence.* New York: Aldine de Gruyter.
England, R.S. 2002. *The macroeconomic impact of global aging: A new era of economic frailty?* Washington, DC: Center for Strategic and International Studies.

Gray, L., and J. McGregor. 2003. Human resource development and older workers: Stereotypes in New Zealand. *Asia Pacific Journal of Human Resources* 41, 3: 338-53.

Guillemette, Y. 2003. Slowing down with age: The ominous implications of workforce aging for Canadian living standards. *C.D. Howe Institute Commentary* 182: 1-14.

Gunderson, M. 2003. Age discrimination in employment in Canada. *Contemporary Economic Policy* 21, 3: 318-28.

Henkens, K. 2005. Stereotyping older workers and retirement: The managers' point of view. *Canadian Journal on Aging* 24, 4: 353-66.

Koeber, C., and D.W. Wright. 2001. W/age bias in worker displacement: How industrial structure shapes the job loss and earnings decline of older American workers. *Journal of Socio-Economics* 30: 343-52.

Kotamraju, N.P. 2002. Keeping up: Web design skill and the re-invented worker. *Information, Communication, and Society* 5, 1: 1-26.

Lofland, J., and L. Lofland. 1995. *Analyzing social settings: A guide to qualitative observation and analysis.* Belmont, CA: Wadsworth.

Lyon, P., and D. Pollard. 1997. Perceptions of the older employee: Is anything really changing? *Personnel Review* 26, 4: 245-57.

MacNicol, J. 2006. *Age discrimination: An historical and contemporary analysis.* Cambridge, UK: Cambridge University Press.

Marshall, V.W. 1996. Issues of a workforce in a changing society: Cases and comparisons. *CARNET: The Canadian Aging Research Network.* Working Paper. Toronto: University of Toronto Centre for Studies of Aging: 1-202.

McMullin, J.A. 2004. Ageism in information technology employment. Presentation at Inter-Congress Conference of the International Sociological Association – RC-11 Sociology of Older Workers. London, England, September.

McMullin, J.A., T. Duerden Comeau, and E. Jovic. 2007. Generational affinities and discourses of difference: A case study of highly skilled information technology workers. *British Journal of Sociology* 58, 2: 297-316.

McMullin, J.A., and V.W. Marshall. 2001. Ageism, age relations, and garment industry work in Montreal. *The Gerontologist* 41, 1: 111-22.

OECD. 1998. *Maintaining prosperity in an ageing society.* Paris: OECD.

–. 2005. *Ageing and employment policies, Canada.* Paris: OECD.

–. 2006. *Ageing and employment policies: Live longer, work longer.* Paris: OECD.

Ontario Human Rights Commission. 2002. *Policy on discrimination against older persons because of age.* http://www.ohrc.on.ca.

Palmore, E.B. 1999. *Ageism: Negative and positive.* 2nd ed. New York: Springer Publishing Company.

Posner, R.A. 1995. *Aging and old age.* Chicago: University of Chicago Press.

Reed, K., D.H. Doty, and D.R. May. 2005. The impact of aging on self-efficacy and computer skill acquisition. *Journal of Management Issues* 17, 2: 212-28.

Riach, K. 2007. "Othering" older worker identity in recruitment. *Human Relations* 60, 11: 1701-26.

Rix, S.E. 2006. The aging workforce: Will we ever be ready for it? *The Gerontologist* 46, 3: 404-9.

Rupp, D.E., S.J. Vodanovich, and M. Crede. 2006. Age bias in the workplace: The impact of ageism and causal attributions. *Journal of Applied Social Psychology* 36, 6: 1337-64.

Segrave, K. 2001. *Age discrimination by employers.* Jefferson, NC: McFarland.

Sennett, R. 1998. *The corrosion of character: The personal consequences of work in the new capitalism.* New York: W.W. Norton.

Shah, P., and B. Kleiner. 2005. New developments concerning age discrimination in the workplace. *Equal Opportunities International* 24, 5-6: 15-23.

Sterns, A., H. Sterns, and L. Hollis. 1996. The productivity and functional limitations of older adult workers. In *Handbook on employment and the elderly,* ed. W. Crown, 276-303. Westport, CT: Greenwood Press.

Taylor, P., and A. Walker. 1994. The ageing workforce: Employers' attitudes toward older workers. *Work, Employment, and Society* 15, 4: 569-91.

–. 1998. Employers and older workers: Attitudes and employment practices. *Ageing and Society* 18: 641-58.

Tomaskovic-Devey, D., and S. Skaggs. 1999. An establishment-level test of the statistical discrimination hypothesis. *Work and Occupations* 26, 4: 422-45.

Wolfson, W.G. 2006. *Analysis of labour force survey data for the information technology occupations 2000-2005.* Prepared for the Software Human Resource Council. Toronto: WGW Services.

8

Conclusion: Inequality Regimes and New Economy Work

Emily Jovic and Julie McMullin

This book is anchored in interesting and changing times for the world of work against the backdrop of an information revolution (Benner 2002) and vestiges of twentieth-century trends such as globalization, individualization, increasing polarization, and the ascendance of risk and uncertainty for many workers and employers (Beck 1992; Castells 1996). The research (see Chapter 2 for a description of the study and its methodology) was conducted in the wake of the technology sector downturn, a time when memories of immense prosperity were still painfully fresh, and battered new economy survivors were attempting to recover alongside new high-tech upstarts. This concluding chapter was written in the midst of substantial economic instability and rousing political changes – all with important implications for thinking about paid work.

Much social and economic inequality is generated in workplaces through the organization of work, relations of power, domination, and control, and the ways in which individuals interact in that context (Acker 2006a). Further, the precise ways in which inequalities are manifested are "sometimes so fleeting or so minor that they are difficult to see" (Acker 2006a, 452). The goal of this book was to examine age and gender in this regard. More generally, this goal entailed an examination of work organizations, in this case small and mid-sized information technology firms and how they can inhibit or support the establishment of equitable employment relations. We focused on workplace structures and experiences of work, workplace cultures, and employment relations within new economy firms, taking into account that individuals negotiate work within the larger contexts of a global economy, communities, firms, families, and interactions with one another.

The IT sector is an important exemplar of the new economy and its model and content of work (e.g., non-standard forms of work, project orientation, changing products and skills). Obsolescence is a perpetual risk for both firms and workers as industry volatility, competition, and the fast pace of change necessitate rapid shifts and upgrades in skills and knowledge and generate a high rate of turnover within firms. In the WANE study, the average length of employment in one's current firm was just five years, and one-quarter of respondents (26 percent) had logged one year or less with their current firms. There is considerable value placed on innovation and drive within this sector, and extreme competitiveness can generate excessive work demands, particularly in firms focused on growth. It is not a stretch to speculate that the glorification of individual success, seen in the colossal achievements of industry superstars such as Bill Gates or minor players who have succeeded in having their firms bought out, may lead to unique workplace behaviour driven, in part, by the possibility of a financial windfall. For their part, many employees rise to the occasion, logging long hours, responding to tight deadlines with a frenetic pace of work, and demonstrating an almost all-encompassing commitment to their jobs. At the same time, with the omnipresence of technology in the home as well as the office, IT work is often perceived to be more flexible than work in other sectors, opening more possibilities for working at home or rearranging hours.

This book helps to shed light on some of the structural features of privilege and opportunity in IT workplaces but also shows how certain groups of workers may be exposed to greater risk and potential disadvantage within this context. The first chapter provided some background on working in IT and then, drawing on the work of Joan Acker (2006a, 2006b) and R.W. Connell (2002), outlined the concept of *inequality regimes*. Recall that inequality regimes are organizing practices and processes used to achieve organizational goals. They are rooted in intersecting sets of structured social relations and can produce inequalities along various lines. Comprising loosely interrelated *inequality projects*, these regimes produce, maintain, and re-create patterned differences in the rewards and privileges people enjoy.

Although Acker focuses largely on class, gender, and race/ethnicity as the primary bases of inequality, and Connell on gender, we present age as an equally significant foundation, one that is just as thoroughly entrenched in organizations as other structured social relations. Gender and age, along with inequality regimes and projects based on them, are both structural and individual features, and they are particularly salient in IT employment, where the demographic composition is largely (though not completely) young and male.

Inequality Projects and the Exemplary IT Worker

The substantive chapters in this book revealed that workers and managers are involved in the performance of inequality projects and that such projects simultaneously shape experiences of work and contribute to inequality regimes within firms. Part 2 considered gender projects and how they come to shape the work environment and experiences so that IT firms emerge as gender regimes. The three chapters in this section demonstrated various ways in which gender remains a persistent basis for inequality among workers in many IT firms. In particular, our research suggested that there is a certain preference for an "ideal" IT worker that resembles the "unencumbered" worker Acker (2006a) describes or the "zero-drag" worker in Hochschild's (2001) research. This idea was raised in Chapter 1 and extended in Chapter 5 and is based on the image of a man who is wholly dedicated to his work, with no distractions or responsibilities beyond career progression and earning a salary. All workers are expected to conform to this archetype; however, since women tend to have more obligations outside paid employment, work organized around this model helps to maintain gender inequality. The added caveat for the ideal IT worker and perhaps for other knowledge workers is that, besides being available to the company 24/7, IT workers in small firms must also find the time to maintain and upgrade their skills, adding to the difficulty of combining work with anything else. Further, as shown in Chapters 3 through 5, management orientations in combination with industry factors, such as downsizing and job insecurity, contribute to work arrangements that place excessive demands on workers in some firms.

Part 3 focused on age-based inequality projects and regimes, such as those created when generational discourse is mobilized to account for disparities in skill, innovation, and adaptability. Use of the term "generation" by the study participants is closely linked to relative age; the assumption is that there are always older and younger generations and that one is more adept at technological work than the other. In this way, generational and age discourse can be seen as an age project that creates age-based inequality regimes in small IT firms.

An age component is introduced to the "ideal" IT worker. It stems largely from age-based assumptions about propensity to learn and perceived attitudes toward change – important qualities in IT employment. As well, age-graded life-course transitions (e.g., family formation) introduce new responsibilities that may serve as "distractions" for workers. Our work shows that in IT employment youth conveys certain naturalized abilities and inclinations as well as fewer outside distractions – attributes that are certainly favourable in IT.

Ageist discourse and cultural exemplars also shape perceptions of the suitability of workers in certain roles as they age (see Chapter 7). For example, being "too old to code" was a prototypical cultural message discussed by many programmers. In these risky and dynamic work settings, then, gender and age structures are produced in particular historical contexts (right after the IT bubble burst) and firm contexts (quite small), resulting in uneven experiences and outcomes for women and men, older and younger workers, and employees and owners/managers.

Intersections of gender and age are complex, highly variable, and often difficult to specify analytically with appropriate breadth and depth; however, the younger unattached man represents the archetypal IT worker in academic and popular imaginations, and inequality regimes within firms tend to favour him accordingly. Since young men dominate numerically within firms and in the overall composition of many occupations in the IT sector, gender- and age-based inequality regimes and projects may be more difficult to discern simply because they are less visible and fewer individuals are affected. Workers are "doing" gender and age in everyday interactions in ways that reconstruct relations in the workplace. Thus, the organizing processes that create and re-create inequalities can be subtle and, as a result, difficult for workers to identify, challenge, or change. They lead to deep structures of inequality (Sewell 1992), with resultant, taken-for-granted assumptions about what it means to be an IT worker of a particular sex and age.

Inequality regimes are often implicitly legitimized, and in some cases explicitly so, by female and male, older and younger, workers alike. Extenuating economic circumstances can lend additional validation to certain work practices or management decisions. For example, downsizing (or fear of it) may lead workers to take on excessive workloads or perform tasks outside work time. Similarly, a "love" of programming or other work tasks and the frequent crossover of technology into the realms of hobby and leisure may draw attention away from employer deficiencies in terms of training support.

Masculinity Projects, Gender Regimes

Chapters 3, 4, and 5 examined the reciprocal influence of gender projects and the organization of IT firms and work arrangements. In these analyses, individuals were seen to bring personal attitudes and identities into the workplace that shape everyday interactions as processes of "doing gender" (West and Zimmerman 1987) as well as the structure of work. These processes draw on existing gendered cultural constructions and metaphorically transfer them to the realm of work by, for example, viewing one's work group as a "brotherhood" (see Chapter 3) or characterizing the company CEO as a "father figure" (see Chapter 5).

The chapters in Part 2 also showed that organizational responses to outside economic forces and industry trends and conventions produce a range of gendered practices and arrangements, which in turn influence workers' experiences and outlooks. The result is an array of gender regimes that emerge out of the personal projects of workers, managers, and owners. Individuals use their social understanding and personal attitudes to frame these regimes and projects. Because workplaces are sites where power and control are embedded in social relations, there is the potential to foster opportunity or privilege for some and disadvantage for others.

There is some evidence of inequality based on gender in many of the IT firms studied. The paucity of women in IT in general is a documented demographic fact in the field; however, we looked more closely at the implications of this gender segregation for firms and workers. Work experiences are mediated by this context, and women are often required to navigate additional challenges as a result. In Chapter 3, Ranson and Dryburgh noted that, at the level of the workplace, where there may be just one or two women in a given firm, the impact can be particularly significant.

Lacking a critical mass of female workers means that IT workplaces are often masculine in composition and culture and that the organizational logic is more likely to favour male workers. For example, many small firms possess an entrepreneurial bent, and as Duerden Comeau and Kemp pointed out in Chapter 4, such ventures are traditionally associated with risk taking and competitive masculine pursuits such as war or sport. As a result, essentialist notions of gender or gendered stereotypes are sometimes mobilized to explain the absence of women in IT or to defend the status quo in terms of work organization. This does not mean that such workplaces are necessarily unfriendly to all women; however, under such circumstances, how work is organized can produce gendered inequalities that appear natural.

Gender segregation of jobs in IT firms tends to further reinforce gendered expectations of workers. In the WANE interviews, women held nearly two-thirds (63 percent) of the non-technical jobs in firms, including administrative support, HR personnel, and sales/marketing positions. Comparatively speaking, 24 percent of female respondents and just 6 percent of male respondents were in these roles. Complementary patterns were evident for the highly technical occupations of programmer, engineer, and technician, where 81 percent of these jobs were held by men. Nearly half of the male respondents (47 percent) were in these technical positions, compared with just over one-quarter (27 percent) of the female respondents. Finally, for upper management, CEOs, owners, and presidents were overwhelmingly male (90 percent); not quite 4 percent of women were in upper management, compared with 12 percent of men. And, as Ranson and Dryburgh discussed, the mere presence of women, even in leadership positions, does not automatically undermine masculinity or negate gender stereotyping in firms.

The gender regimes identified in Chapter 3 emerge through intersections of demographic composition and gender segregation with workplace cultures and everyday interactions among individuals. Although outright discrimination is not acceptable in the larger social context, certain inequality regimes can foster exclusion on the basis of gender. For example, the masculinist gender regime is legitimated on the basis of "fit," which euphemistically taps acceptance of the prevailing workplace culture as well as a degree of demographic similarity. Under these circumstances, many women fit in gender-stereotypical support roles, while others are well aware of their outsider status. Those who are "tokens" in male-dominated occupations seem to prefer to align themselves with their male co-workers and the dominant workplace culture, discursively minimizing the space between them. Sometimes this entails acting as a "conceptual man" (Ranson 2005) and embracing prevailing ideals; it can also mean taking an outwardly dismissive attitude toward other women and traits perceived to be stereotypically feminine.

Fit also serves as a key criterion for recruitment and retention processes in many firms and thus contributes to the maintenance and reinforcement of existing structures. For example, hiring through social networks is prevalent, and seeking like-minded (and usually demographically similar) potential employees is often an offshoot of this practice. Thus, it is no surprise that some resultant workplace cultures, particularly those involving sports, games, or fun, may appeal to a relatively narrow demographic. Non-participants are likely to be excluded from the camaraderie and bonding generated from informal interactions. The solidarities that form between workers under such conditions further highlight differences for those who are left out and can create a less friendly environment for others. It can be difficult to incorporate new people into these tight-knit groups – a concern in a field where high turnover is the norm. Further, membership in these workplace groups is not necessarily sustainable as lives and careers progress.

Workers themselves also mobilize personal gendered resources and contribute to gender regimes. In Chapter 4, Duerden Comeau and Kemp emphasized how multiple masculine workplace cultures intersect and influence organizational logic. In the often volatile and insecure world of IT employment, and in firms comprised mostly of men, interactions influence work practices, and ideals and forms of masculinity are ordered hierarchically. For example, absolute commitment to work may be an offshoot arrangement of intense competition in one firm, while the personal orientation of an owner-manager may shape flexibility options and family friendliness in another. In any case, particular arrangements of work tend to favour certain kinds of workers, often those whose life circumstances mimic those of management or those who can be compelled to fit in prescribed roles.

In addition to demographic composition, management practices, and personal attitudes, cultural exemplars of "ideal" workers shape work experiences. Many firms have recruitment processes, job designs, and work arrangements based on a model of a worker who can handle and even embrace the excessive and unpredictable work demands common in IT. This is largely because he (or she but mostly he) is not distracted by any outside obligations or competing interests. The situation is exacerbated by communication technologies that render work possible any time, any place. As a result, workers are differentially exposed to risks with respect to career success and work-life balance. Choosing family over work, or vice versa, has consequences.

Women, who continue to take on the brunt of family, house, and care work, face additional challenges in maintaining work-life balance, for they may be competing against those who have few such obligations. Conversely, those who prioritize work over other aspects of life may come to regret it. "Encumbered" men (i.e., those who wish to participate more in family life or outside interests or at least reduce the status quo) can also face difficulties. They are confronted with pressure to perform and get the job done in spite of life circumstances and other responsibilities. Women are often slotted into peripheral roles in IT, and while not ideal, these roles do provide a socially sanctioned option for attending to family obligations and personal interests that is largely unavailable to men.

As Connidis and Kemp indicated in Chapter 5, deviations from ideal worker expectations are often perceived to be personal refusals to conform to work requirements rather than problems with how work is arranged. Thus, work-life balance issues are framed as private troubles, and responsibility for arriving at solutions generally falls to individuals and their families. The informality and ad hoc management in small firms mean that workers may not always be aware of their entitlements and how firms might assist in creating solutions. Or, if they are informed, a workaholic culture and a competitive environment can render them reluctant to "take advantage" of what is perceived as management "generosity" unless absolutely necessary.

Workers in small IT firms often wear many hats in terms of their responsibilities and duties, and handling requests for flexibility can be more risky for a firm that is just getting by. Large organizations tend to have bureaucratic capacities in place to support policies such as sick days or parental leave; however, it can be difficult for smaller firms even to meet their legal obligations, let alone extend benefits. Although personnel may be cross-trained in roles, small teams and the lack of a career ladder mean that there simply are not personnel available to take on extra responsibilities should a worker take an extended leave. From a statistical perspective at least, small business owners may be wary of such risks, relying on fit and similar measures when hiring.

Acker notes an "almost unshakable fusion" of gendered identities and workplace organizing practices (2006a, 457). Nonetheless, gender-based projects and regimes, while sometimes seemingly enduring, are not fixed; they are constantly in flux and therefore contribute to the evolution of workplace cultures. In the WANE study, there were examples of firms with structures that changed over time in response to workers' life-course transitions as well as those that managed to accomplish more inclusive and equitable practices. These cases demonstrate that it is not necessary to base work arrangements on gender structures and differentiation.

Generation Projects, Age Regimes

In Chapters 6 and 7, age as an understudied basis for inequality in the workplace was articulated and explored. As discussed in Chapter 1, age presents additional challenges in the identification and interpretation of inequality: what or who is old or young is relative, depending on contextual issues such as industry and occupational group as well as broader cultural factors. There is no universal cut point for determining older or younger. Moreover, the benefits and disadvantages associated with age do not accrue uniformly for one group or the other; the balance of power also shifts with context. That said, in IT, age-based stereotypes and generational assumptions influence the assessment of skills and ability by management and workers. Maturity and experience are typically assets in the labour market; however, older workers are perceived to be outdated in terms of knowledge and skills. This has real consequences for IT personnel, especially those who may wish to have longer careers in the field.

In some ways, age emerges in our work as one of the few remaining acceptable "-isms," and in most circumstances "old" carries negative connotations in IT workplaces. Inequalities are often legitimated through arguments that naturalize the inequality (Acker 2006a), and this is accomplished easily with age given the lay expertise that most people can summon with respect to growing older. There is a strange manner of egalitarianism insofar as everybody is aging and, presumably, vulnerable to its effects, inconveniences, or benefits, sooner or later. In the realm of social interaction, people of all ages frequently claim age-linked maladies and symptoms for themselves – ironically, sarcastically, mockingly, and genuinely. For example, "I must be getting old" is a common rejoinder to absentmindedness and memory gaffes as well as physical ailments (see also McMullin and Shuey 2006). Yet internalized ageist attitudes toward one's own capacities are unlikely to be challenged in the same way as those based on gender or race/ethnicity.

Strong age stereotypes were reported consistently by respondents in all study countries. However, in Canada and the United States, the use of generational discourse steers attention away from age, effectively masking generational projects and age-based inequality regimes within IT firms as issues of fit. There is a robust cultural and structural favouring of youth in IT; yet, individually, younger workers report unfavourable treatment on the basis of age more frequently. Co-opting of the term "generation" in IT circles to distinguish newer versions of technology and software means that anything older than the latest release tends to be synonymous with "out of date" – and this goes as much for people as it does for mp3 players (McMullin, Duerden Comeau, and Jovic 2007). And, as Chapter 7 showed, being out of date confers disadvantages on older workers, especially in hiring processes.

The pervasiveness and general cultural acceptance of age stereotypes render age less likely to be recognized as a basis for inequality projects and regimes within organizations. Indeed, as Duerden Comeau and McMullin indicated in Chapter 7, age discrimination is notoriously difficult to substantiate. However, the structure of IT work is premised on age-based assumptions related to learning and working. Respondents repeatedly associated the field's most valued qualities – innovation, competitive drive, velocity, adaptability, risk taking, technical aptitude, and so on – with youth, leaving antonyms and less valued features, such as reliability and experience, implicitly linked with older age. With the exception of the oldest echelon, workers of all ages attribute a stronger "natural" affinity for technology to those younger than themselves. At the same time, many workers tend to see themselves as "exceptions" to any age-graded rules when it comes to their personal adaptability and longer-term prospects in IT.

Under these circumstances, older workers are presumed to be unable to catch up to younger generations, who have had a head start and an inborn aptitude for all things technical. Younger workers are believed to be easier to train and more capable of learning new things – on their personal time, using their own resources to boot. They are also presumed to have greater stamina, be able to work longer and harder, and to adapt, innovate, and meet the demands of new economy firms. Organizations have adapted accordingly, for example, by offering buffers to extreme work requirements in the forms of fun, sport, and leisure that are integrated into the workplace. Even if particular firms do not offer such perks, cultural representations of IT workplaces remain youthful, with denim, jukeboxes, pool tables, pranks, and pizza lunches.

Given the notion of an unencumbered, zero-drag worker (Acker 2006a; Hochschild 2001), age and the accumulation of life-course transitions are presumed to negatively impact both the capacity and the desire to learn. In a field where knowledge and skill sets are fleeting at best, staying current is a requirement. Over time, there may be changes in ability and orientation to learning and working for some individuals; however, they are neither inevitable nor universal and are often only loosely coupled with aging. Nonetheless, IT career trajectories within small to mid-sized firms seem to be structured around these assumptions. For example, there is a general lack of technical ladders, allowing only limited opportunities for workers to age in IT. As with solutions to the "private" troubles of balancing work and other aspects of life, adapting and staying current are also individual problems requiring personal solutions. Raised in Chapter 6, the particular company niche and project models of work organization in IT can make it more difficult for workers to gain exposure to new technologies and cutting-edge knowledge and skills.

Employment careers in general are structured such that there is an expectation of "progress" in terms of expertise, responsibility, and remuneration, regardless of whether this expectation is representative of careers in IT. These circumstances create heightened risks when it comes to keeping current and finding a new job, particularly for workers as they age. To advance their careers, IT workers are left with five options: (1) keeping up with the pace and demands regardless of the circumstances and tolls, (2) taking on maintenance jobs that use old (and therefore outdated) technologies, (3) moving into a management stream or consulting (which is not for everybody), (4) starting up a firm (which is not feasible for many), and (5) leaving the IT sector. In each instance, workers face risks – of burning out, of obsolescence, of career plateaus, of financial difficulties. Shifting orientations to working and living, such as wanting (or needing) to spend more time with family, can lead to marginalization in workplaces that place high value on work demands.

Fluidity is one of the interesting elements of inequality regimes, and there can be significant changes in firms and organizational structures corresponding to age-graded transitions in the life courses of managers and owners. As a result, age regimes may be subject to change over shorter periods of time.

New Projects, Shifting Regimes?

It is important to situate the findings of this book in the larger social and organizational contexts within which small and mid-sized firms conduct their business. Entrepreneurial sensibilities, such as risk taking, affinity for competition, or disdain for bureaucratic rules, shape the structure of work in many smaller organizations. Small IT firms are also potentially more vulnerable to industry volatility, and there can be heightened instability and insecurity within these organizations. They often operate within extremely narrow margins, in terms of time and capital, that directly influence issues such as workload, wages, and benefits and perks for workers. There are additional challenges for supporting career progression, for example, through skills upgrading and training.

Organization size itself likely influences how structured social relations are reflected and reproduced (Acker 2006b,107). Size has an impact on the relative demographic composition and steepness of organizational hierarchies. Firm size can also temper or amplify the influence of individuals on workplace culture partly because the lines of communication between upper management and workers are thin in these organizations. Presumably, all of these issues become more salient in small firms, where bureaucratic structures are less likely and there are more opportunities for workers to share similar life-course transitions and personal experiences. Ad hoc management practices, the effects of strong personalities, and the lives and circumstances of workers outside the firm can contribute to greater variation in structures and processes within small organizations. Daily interactions can influence overarching regimes, and relations within small firms can mimic family ties – the effect of which opens up possibilities for balanced and accommodating workplaces (as argued in Chapter 5) as much as structures that are more exclusionary or detrimental to workers; however, even the best intentions can be overshadowed by extraneous factors such as misread market trends or competition from low-cost providers overseas.

A key function of work organizations of any size is to persuade workers to tacitly accept systems of inequality in the pursuit of organizational goals. As the foregoing chapters show, in IT this is accomplished along several dimensions of organizational control (Acker 2006a). Direct measures such as wages are used in conjunction with indirect ones such as selective recruitment to assemble an amenable workforce. However, internal control, elements that workers can assume as part of their personal identities or outlooks, seems to be more significant in the reproduction of gender and age regimes in IT firms. There is a belief in the legitimacy of work demands in some firms, and many workers take pleasure and satisfaction in their work, further validating the organizational logic. External industry factors also contribute to legitimacy. For example, job insecurity may generate fear, which acts as an internalized control on behaviour.

Transforming inequality regimes is a difficult process that, according to Acker (2006a), is usually bound to fail. The reasoning is simple: "Opportunity hoarding" is a mechanism through which power is maintained (Tilly 1998). Material well-being aside, for those in positions of power, increasing equality can also mean assaults on personal identity, dignity, and masculinity, all elements that individuals in power will strive to protect. Nonetheless, Acker (2006a, 2006b) suggests that a combination of high visibility, or awareness of inequalities, and low legitimacy of the bases of inequality (insofar as they are not masked by class processes or essentialist notions of superiority) holds the most promise for changing inequality regimes.

Civil rights legislation, such as the Charter of Rights and Freedoms in Canada,[1] anti-discrimination laws, and diversity initiatives serve to limit certain discriminatory practices and render them illegitimate. So, in the case of gender regimes, explicit discrimination on the basis of gender already lacks legitimacy. Establishing a critical mass of women in IT firms, particularly in technical stream occupations, could help to make gender regimes and inequalities more visible. For age-based regimes, the situation is trickier. Age discrimination remains at least somewhat legitimate: markers for old and young are highly relative, either group can face disadvantages, and ageist beliefs can be easily masked by generational discourse.

Gender and age inequality regimes can be difficult to target because they emerge out of interactions and draw on shared understandings of generations, family, and the like. Individuals categorize others on the basis of age and gender markers and formulate ideas about what it means to be older or younger, male or female. Such ideas become entrenched as taken-for-granted assumptions that influence behaviour, such as hiring decisions. People tend to use concepts uncritically as discursive tools to make sense of the social world and their working lives. However, there are embedded meanings in these structures. Generational affinity can mask ageist assumptions about ability, as Chapter 6 demonstrated; similarly, traditional notions of motherhood and fatherhood shape perceptions of flexibility in the workplace and who should take advantage of accommodations.

According to Acker (2006a, 455), successfully changing inequality regimes requires focusing on a limited set of inequality-producing mechanisms. The social context for change needs to be ripe; past changes have most often occurred through a social movement (e.g., the feminist movement) that gained legislative support (e.g., equal opportunity legislation). Not incidentally, these types of social change often involve coercion or a threat of loss. In small firms, where the hierarchy is not as steep, management orientation to change likely depends on what owners and managers stand to gain (or at least not lose). There is a laundry list of obstacles to change, the fundamental contradiction between organizational goals in capitalist systems (i.e., reducing costs and increasing profits) and diminishing inequality being an obvious one. Competitive pressures entail getting the most out of workers for the least, hardly a situation that supports the reduction of inequality. Recent economic circumstances and the heightening of uncertainty and risk also become excuses of sorts – threats of downsizing, offshoring, and competition for good jobs keep workers in line with the prevailing system. They are vulnerable: "Fear of loss of livelihood controls those who might challenge inequality" (Acker 2006a, 459).

Interventions that target specific policies or practices rarely address underlying processes contributing to inequality in the first place, such as the unencumbered/zero-drag model of the ideal worker. This represents another obstacle to change. As Chapter 5 showed, inequality is often cast as personal failures requiring individual solutions rather than systemic change. Finally, another problem with changing inequality regimes within firms is the possibility of simply changing their basis by moving or externalizing work practices. For example, in some of the firms studied, jobs (and inequality) were exported to low-wage countries where more extreme, detrimental regimes based on class, gender, or race/ethnicity may be possible and acceptable.

Gender and age are clear markers of contrasting experiences as life-course transitions accumulate. Some of the firms described in this book demonstrate how workplace culture can evolve over time and how such transformations can be responsive to the life-course transitions of workers, effectively reducing some forms of inequality. Changes in the life circumstances of individuals in small firms can spur changes in organizational logic. Similarly, the efforts and personal agency of workers themselves, particularly the degree to which they resist conformity, can be a source of change.

Note

1 "15. (1) Every individual is equal before and under the law and has the right to the equal protection and equal benefit of the law without discrimination and, in particular, without discrimination based on race, national or ethnic origin, colour, religion, sex, age or mental or physical disability" (Canada, Department of Justice, 2008).

References

Acker, J. 2006a. Inequality regimes: gender, class, and race in organizations. *Gender and Society* 20, 4: 441-64.

–. 2006b. *Class questions: Feminist answers.* Toronto: Rowman and Littlefield.

Beck, U. 1992. *Risk society: Towards a new modernity.* London: Polity Press.

Benner, C. 2002. *Work in the new economy: Flexible labour markets in Silicon Valley.* Malden, MA: Blackwell Publishing.

Canada. Department of Justice. 2008. *Canadian Charter of Rights and Freedoms.* http://laws.justice.gc.ca/en/charter/.

Castells, M. 1996. *The rise of the network society.* Cambridge, UK: Blackwell.

Connell, R.W. 2002. *Gender.* Malden, MA: Polity Press.

Hochschild, A.R. 2001. *The time bind: When work becomes home and home becomes work.* 2nd ed. New York: Metropolitan Books.

McMullin, J.A., T. Duerden Comeau, and E. Jovic. 2007. Generational affinities and discourses of difference: A case study of highly skilled information technology workers. *British Journal of Sociology* 58, 2: 297-316.

McMullin, J.A., and K. Shuey. 2006. Ageing, disability, and workplace accommodations. *Ageing and Society* 26: 1-17.

Ranson, G. 2005. No longer "one of the boys": Negotiations with motherhood, as prospect or reality, among women in engineering. *Canadian Review of Sociology and Anthropology* 42: 145-66.

Sewell, W.H.J. Jr. 1992. A theory of structure: Duality, agency, and transformation. *American Journal of Sociology* 98: 1-29.

Tilly, C. 1998. *Durable inequality.* Berkeley: University of California Press.

West, C., and D. Zimmerman. 1987. Doing gender. *Gender and Society* 1, 2: 125-51.

Contributors

Ingrid Arnet Connidis is a professor of sociology in the Department of Sociology at the University of Western Ontario. Her work in the areas of family ties across the life course, adult-sibling relationships, gay and lesbian family relationships, intergenerational relations, aging and policy implications, and conceptual and methodological issues in research on aging and family, has been published in a variety of books and journals including the *Journal of Gerontology, Social Sciences, Journal of Marriage and Family, Canadian Journal on Aging, The Gerontologist,* and *Research on Aging.* Her book *Family Ties and Aging, 2nd edition,* was recently published by Pine Forge Press/Sage (2010).

Heather Dryburgh is a sociologist currently managing the Microdata Access Division at Statistics Canada. She joined Statistics Canada after completing undergraduate and Masters degrees at the University of Western Ontario and her PhD in Sociology at McMaster University. She has researched and published in the areas of technology and society, education and work, and social inequality with a focus on gender and immigration.

Tammy Duerden Comeau completed her Masters and PhD degrees at the University of Western Ontario. While writing and researching the chapters in this book, she was post-doctoral researcher on the (WANE) project in the Sociology Department at Western. More recently, she has shifted careers within the educational field and is now an occasional teacher with the Grand Erie District School Board in Brantford, Ontario. She is currently enjoying maternity/parental leave with her family.

Emily Jovic worked as a graduate research assistant on the WANE project and recently completed a PhD in sociology at the University of Western Ontario. She is currently a post-doctoral researcher at UWO, working in the areas of aging, the life course, work, and learning. She has published articles in these areas, most recently in the *British Journal of Sociology.*

Candace L. Kemp completed a PhD at McMaster University and is currently an assistant professor in the Gerontology Institute and the Department of Sociology at Georgia State University in Atlanta, Georgia. Her research agenda explores aging and family life, social and intimate relationships, formal long-term care settings, and planning for later life. Her recent work appears in journals such as *The Gerontologist, Ageing and Society,* and the *Journal of Family Issues.*

Julie Ann McMullin is a professor in the Department of Sociology at the University of Western Ontario. She received her BA and MA from the University of Western Ontario and her PhD from the University of Toronto. Her recent work examines social inequality in paid work, especially in relation to older workers and in families. She was the principal investigator of the *Workforce Aging in the New Economy* project (WANE). Her edited book (with Victor W. Marshall), *Ageing and Working in the New Economy: Careers and Changing Structures in Small and Medium Size Information Technology Firms* (2010), was recently published by Edward Elgar Press and a second edition of her book, *Understanding Social Inequality: Class, Age, Gender, Ethnicity, and Race in Canada* (2010), was published by Oxford University Press.

Gillian Ranson is an associate professor in the Department of Sociology at the University of Calgary. Her research interests are in the interrelated areas of gender, families, and paid employment. Her work on the WANE project built on her earlier research on gender in engineering. She has recently completed a study of couples with dependent children whose division of earning and caring work contravened conventional gender stereotypes. This study resulted in a book *(Against the Grain: Couples, Gender and the Reframing of Parenting)* published by University of Toronto Press Higher Education in 2010. She is currently conducting a study of men who take parental leave from their regular jobs to become sole caregivers to babies.

Index

Note: "t" after a number indicates a table

Acker, Joan, 11-12, 160, 161, 166, 170, 171

age: and adaptation to new technologies, 115, 142; and association of pay with performance, 10; in balanced gender regimes, 13; brotherhood masculinity and, 13-14; and changes in priorities, 126; coming of, 115; and disadvantage, 155; and exemplary worker, 161; and fringe benefits, 10; and gender differences, 86; generational discourse and, 167; hiring practices and, 141, 154; and hours of work, 10; identity, 156; and inequality, 11; and innovation, 9, 125-26; intersection with gender, 162; of IT firms, 56; of IT workers, 5, 9; and job security, 10; and labour force participation, 11; and learning capacity, 122-23, 143, 168; and life-course trajectories, 86; in masculinist gender regimes, 13, 41, 42, 64-65, 70; neutrality, 8; occupational roles by, 31; of participants, 28; and pay satisfaction, 10; and permanent employment, 10; and productivity, 116; in professional sports, 9; and redundancy, 15; stereotyping of, 11, 127-28 (*see also* ageism); structure within occupation/industrial groups, 9; structuring of

IT work by, 105; and supervision of others, 10; and technological skills, 122, 124-25; of technology, 150; and training, 116, 168; and unemployment, 11, 15; and unencumbered workers, 15; workplace cultures and, 72, 73. *See also* older workers; relative age; younger workers

age discrimination, 11; ageism and, 155; and hiring practices, 14-15, 136; and inequality, 137; and search for jobs, 151; substantiation of, 167

age projects, age discourse and, 161; defined, 12; generational discourse and, 161

age regimes, 166-69; defined, 12; targeting of, 171; transformation of, 169, 170

ageism, adaptation to new technologies and, 137, 139; and age discrimination, 155; age-biased behaviour and, 136-37; and computing technology, 14-15; cultural acceptance of, 167; defined, 135; effect on older workers, 155, 156, 157; generational discourse and, 170; in hiring, 147, 149-50; internalization of, 156, 167; and learning capacity, 146-47, 148-49, 152, 155; and occupational roles, 162;

organization/structure of work and, 167-68; relative age and, 134; and skills, 166; and training, 148-49; as understudied, 133

Appelbaum, S.H., 116

Australia, age and innovation in, 9; age of IT employees in, 5; age and pay satisfaction in, 10; age of WANE participants in, 28; ageism in, 141, 143, 147, 148; benignly maternalistic gender regimes in, 52-53; benignly paternalistic gender regimes in, 48-49; contract workers in, 30; difference discourses in, 124, 125-26; fringe benefits in, 10; gender of IT employees in, 5; generational discourse in, 120, 121, 122; hiring and age in, 145-46, 149, 150, 154; hours of work in, 10; hours of work and age in, 152, 153; job security in, 8, 10; length of tenure in, 37; masculinist gender regimes in, 42-43; numbers of employees in small and mid-sized IT firms, 19, 37; numbers of women in IT, 36; older workers' adaptation to new technology in, 140, 148; participation rate in, 25, 25(t); pay in, 8, 10; permanent employment in, 10; relative age in, 140; sampling strategies in, 21; training of older workers in, 139; visible minorities in, 28; women's positive perceptions of work in, 8

authoritarianism: defined, 60; in masculinist gender regimes, 65

Baby Boomers, 116-17

balanced gender regimes, 53-55; age in, 13; defined, 13; employee benefits in, 54-55; family friendliness in, 54; gender stereotypes in, 54; parental leave in, 54; salaries in, 54; women in, 13, 55; work-life balance in, 13, 54; workplace culture in, 54; workplace flexibility in, 13

Beck, Ulrich, 4, 6-7

benefits. *See* fringe benefits

benignly maternalistic gender regimes, 51-53; defined, 13; home-based work in, 52; hours of work in, 52; human resource policies in, 53; job tenure in, 53; psychological well-being in, 52; remuneration in, 53; training in, 53; women in, 51-53, 56; workplace cultures in, 48, 53

benignly paternalistic gender regimes, 44-51; and death in family, 47; defined, 13; employer-employee relationships in, 51; family friendliness of, 50; hours of work in, 49; leadership in, 13, 47; and parental leave, 47; size of firms in, 45; skill versus education hierarchy in, 50; women in, 45-47, 48-51, 56; and work-life balance, 50; workplace culture in, 45, 46

Bird, S.R., 42

Bourdieu, Pierre, 114-15

brotherhood, familial masculinities and, 77-78; in masculinist gender regimes, 68, 69, 72; workplace culture as, 78, 163

brotherhood masculinities, 13-14, 65; characteristics of, 63; entrepreneurial masculinity and, 77; life-course transitions and, 78; and younger men, 78; youthfulness and, 72

bureaucratic masculinity: craftsman-like masculinity versus, 14, 74, 76; in masculinist gender regimes, 74; strategic, 63

Butler, R.N., 135

Calasanti, T., 61

Canada, age discrimination in search for jobs in, 151; age and hiring in, 149; age and hours of work in, 152, 153; age of IT employees in, 5; age and pay satisfaction in, 10; age of WANE participants in, 28; ageism in, 141, 144, 146, 148; balanced gender regimes in, 53-54; benignly paternalistic gender regimes in, 44-47; child care in, 84, 91; computing education in, 36; contract workers in, 30; demographic profile of IT workers in, 134; employability of older workers in, 150, 154; fringe benefits in, 10; gender differences in occupational roles in, 88, 89(t); gender of IT employees in, 5; generational discourse in, 118-20, 121-22, 122-24, 167; hiring of experienced workers in, 146; hiring of younger workers in, 145; hours of work in, 10; hours of work and age in, 140, 152, 153; hours of work and women in, 7-8; human resource policies in, 101; ICT employment in, 6; interviews conducted in, 23; job security in, 8; mean age of IT workers in, 28; new economy in, 3; numbers of employees in small and mid-sized IT firms, 19, 37; older workers' adaptation to new technology in, 140; older workers and hours of work in, 140; parental leave in, 106; participation rate in, 24, 25(t); permanent employment in, 10; relative age in, 140, 141; sampling strategies in, 20; training of older workers in, 139, 149; unfavourable treatment of younger workers in, 10; visible minorities in, 28; wages/salaries in, 8, 10, 36

Castells, M., 83

child care, equal responsibility for, 91, 100, 104; gender differences in, 90(t), 91, 96; gendered division of labour in, 103; and illnesses of children, 97; men and, 99-100; spending on, 84; women and, 94-95, 98, 99-100

Collinson, D., 60

Comeau, Tammy Duerden. *See* Duerden Comeau, Tammy

compensation. *See* wages/salaries

competition/competitiveness: in global economy, 56, 102; in masculinist gender regimes, 42, 43; masculinity and, 61; and work demands, 160

computer services: design and related services industry, 6, 15n3

computing technology. *See* technology

Connell, R.W., 13, 38, 60, 61, 160

Connidis, Ingrid Arnet, 14, 165

Cooper, M., 61, 85-86

craftsman-like masculinity, 78-79; about, 14; and bureaucracy, 14; bureaucratic masculinity versus, 76; characteristics of, 63; in masculinist gender regimes, 74; and skill, 14

culture: and acceptance of ageism, 167; generations and, 114-16; and stereotypes about IT workplaces, 42; technology and, 113-14, 115; workplace (*see* workplace culture[s])

Daly, K., 84

discrimination, civil rights legislation and, 170; error, 138; statistical, 137-38. *See also* age discrimination

domestic labour, gender relations and, 11; gendered division of, 84, 89-91, 96, 103. *See also* child care

Down, S., 117

Dryburgh, Heather, 13, 59, 60, 61, 62, 69, 163, 164

Duerden Comeau, Tammy, 13-15, 163, 165, 167

earnings. *See* wages/salaries

education: computer, 36; and income, 37; of IT workers, 36, 37; skills versus, 50; of women, 56; of workers in masculinist gender regimes, 43. *See also* learning capacity; training

Elder, G.H. Jr., 5

England. *See* United Kingdom

England, Paula, 138

entrepreneurial masculinity: about, 13; characteristics of, 60-61, 63; and familial/sibling masculinities, 77

entrepreneurialism: and generations, 117; in masculinist gender regimes, 67-68, 70, 74; masculinity and, 163; older workers and, 154; and risk

taking, 163; and small and mid-sized IT firms, 169; and work-life balance, 69; as workplace culture, 63
error discrimination, 138
exemplary workers, 102; characteristics of, 15; inequality projects and, 161-62; unencumbered workers as, 162, 165
experience: and demand for IT workers, 36; and different types of firms, 56; enthusiasm versus, 125; global economy and, 105; and hiring, 146; life-course transitions and, 96; older workers and, 140, 146, 166, 167; rate of change in IT and, 105; relative age and, 151; among younger workers, 120, 149
Eyerman, R., 114-15, 129

familial masculinities: and brotherhood, 77-78; characteristics of, 64; and entrepreneurial masculinity, 77; in masculinist gender regimes, 68, 69, 70, 71, 74
family/-ies, accessibility to human resource policies for, 106; benignly paternalistic gender regimes and, 47; death in, 47; globalization and, 83; life-course transitions and demands of, 85; masculinist gender regimes and, 41-42, 71; and skills updating, 126. *See also* child care; domestic labour; parenthood; work-family balance
family-friendly workplaces: and balanced gender regimes, 54; and benignly paternalistic gender regimes, 50; flexible working arrangements and, 100, 101-2 (*see also* flexible working arrangements); hours of work and, 98-99; and masculinist gender regimes, 42, 44; masculinity and, 86; and parenthood, 85, 103. *See also* work-family balance
fatherhood. *See* parenthood
Fine, Gary Alan, 12
flexible working arrangements: in balanced gender regimes, 13, 54;

life-course transitions and, 76, 77; in masculinist gender regimes, 42, 66, 68-69, 71, 73, 76; and parenthood, 171; penalization for use of, 86; and work-family balance, 86, 96-97, 100, 101-2, 104, 165. *See also* home-based work
Fraser, J.A., 9
fraternal masculinity. *See* brotherhood masculinities
fringe benefits, age and, 10; in balanced gender regimes, 54-55; health care delivery and, 10; informality regarding, 101-2; in large versus small firms, 166

gender, 35; concentration within professions, 35; and inequalities, 55, 161; intersection with age, 162; and life choices, 102; neutrality, 7; occupational roles by, 31; and paid versus unpaid labour, 103; of sample in WANE study, 28; segregation, 163, 164; social constructionist perspective, 57; stereotypes, 41, 54; traditional roles, 98, 104; and treatment in jobs, 7; and unencumbered workers, 15; wage gap, 36; workplace cultures and, 72, 73
gender differences, age and, 9, 86; in career-parenthood negotiations, 96; in child care, 90(t), 91, 96; in experience of individualized relationships, 84; hours of work and, 104; in life-course transitions, 86; in marital status, 88, 89(t); in occupational roles, 88; in parenthood, 84-85, 86, 88, 89(t), 92; in productivity, 138; in social contexts of risk/uncertainty, 35; in work-family balance, 99, 103; in work-life balance, 84
gender equality: at early versus later stages of career, 84-85; growth of IT sector and, 104; organization of work and, 163
gender projects: defined, 12; individualism as, 14; in IT industry, 12-13;

life-course stages and, 14; marriage and, 14; as not fixed, 166; parenthood and, 14; small IT firms as, 14

gender regimes: balanced (*see* balanced gender regimes); benignly maternalistic (*see* benignly maternalistic gender regimes); benignly paternalistic (*see* benignly paternalistic gender regimes); as changing, 59, 166; defined, 12, 38; IT firms classified as, 39(t); in IT industry, 12-13; masculinist (*see* masculinist gender regimes); nature of work and, 56; structure of work and, 162-63; targeting of, 171; transformation of, 170; workers contributing to, 165; workplaces as, 38

gender relations: and domestic labour, 11; and glass ceiling, 11; inequality projects and, 12; and power relations, 11; social inequality and, 11; and wage gap, 11; and work-family balance, 103

gendered division of labour. *See* child care: gendered division of labour; domestic labour: gendered division of

generational consciousness, 114, 121

generational discourse: and age, 167; and age projects, 161; and ageism, 170; and computing technology, 14; of difference, 121-28; and "fit," 167; of older workers, 120-21; of women, 120, 121; and workplace cultures, 14; of younger workers, 118-20

generations: and adeptness at technological work, 161; advantages versus disadvantages among, 122-24; Baby Boomers versus Generation X, 116-17; class and, 114; and culture, 114-16; defined, 115; differences between, 116-17; entrepreneurialism and, 117; and generational locations, 114, 121; historical consciousness and, 114; and innovation, 123; relative age and, 123-24, 161; as social locations, 114; solidarity

among, 114-15; subgroups within, 117; of technology, 167

Giddens, A., 83

Gilleard, C., 115

globalization/global economy, characteristics of, 3-4, 82; and competition, 56, 102; and decline of welfare state, 82; and entrepreneurial masculinity, 60; and family relations, 83; and family/work-life balance, 81; and individualism, 14; of IT industry, 4; and knowledge economies, 3; local autonomy versus, 82; nature of work within, 83; and paid workers, 3; and patriarchy, 84; and polarization, 3-4; and work-family balance, 105-6

Gray, L., 136

habitus, 114-15

Hearn, J., 60

hegemonic masculinities, 61, 78

Henkens, K., 137

hierarchies/hierarchical relations: and management orientation to change, 171; in masculinist gender regimes, 68, 165; masculinities and, 61; organizational size and, 169; paternalism and, 50; of skill and education, 50

hiring, age and, 14-15, 136, 141, 154; ageism in, 147, 149-50; of experienced workers, 146; individualism and, 146; learning capacity and, 149-50; in masculinist gender regimes, 41; parental leave and, 95-96; and productivity, 137-38; through social networks, 164; of young women, 95-96, 102; of younger workers, 144-46, 154, 155

Hochschild, A.R., 102, 161

home-based work: in balanced gender regimes, 54; benignly maternalistic gender regimes and, 52; and hours of work, 101. *See also* flexible working arrangements

hours of work, age and, 10; in benignly maternalistic gender regimes,

49, 52; and commitment to technology, 153; and family friendliness, 98-99; gender differences in, 104; home-based work and, 101; and learning capacity, 152-53; in masculinist gender regimes, 42, 65, 75-76; of men, 7-8; older workers and, 136, 139-40, 152-55; pace of technology and, 94; and parenthood, 93-94, 101; and productivity, 98; women and, 7-8, 36, 94, 98; and work-family balance, 93-94, 100
human resource policies, 53, 74-75, 101-2, 103, 166. *See also* fringe benefits

income. *See* wages/salaries
individualism/individualization: and couple relationships, 83-84; and currency with technology, 168; as gender project, 14; globalization and, 14; and hirability, 146; institutionalized, 83; and skill development, 146; social responsibility and, 82; welfare state retrenchment and, 81; work organization and, 102-3; and work-life balance, 165
inequality projects, 11-12, 160; age projects and, 12; and age relations, 12; exemplary workers and, 161-62; gender projects and, 12; and gender relations, 12
inequality regimes, 11-15, 160, 161; age regimes and, 12; defined, 11-12; gender regimes and, 12; legitimization of, 162; organization of work and, 170; transformation of, 170, 171-72; and workplace culture, 12
inequality/-ies: age discrimination and, 137; age relations and, 11; difference discourses and, 121; factors generating, 159; fluidity of, 169; gender and, 55, 161; gender relations and, 11; legitimization of, 167; organization of work and, 162; relative age and, 15, 166; underlying processes of, 171-72

information and communication technologies (ICT), 6, 15n3
innovation, age and, 125-26; value placed on, 160
Internet, 116
IT firms, age of, 56; archival data collection, 22-23; bias in selection of, 19-20; as cases, 18; criteria for selection in WANE study, 18-19; cross-company comparisons, 18; cross-national comparisons, 18; demographic profiles of, 92-93, 97-98; as gender regimes, 38-55, 39(t); geographical location of, 19; heterogeneity of, 19; interviews with, 23-25; longevity of, 27-28; numbers of women in, 38; observational notes of, 22; prototypes/stereotypes of, 59; self-administered web surveys, 23-24; size of, and social relations within, 169. *See also* small and mid-sized IT firms
IT sector, age of workers in, 9, 14, 119-20; bust in, 6; characteristics of, 4; demographic composition of, 117, 160; downturn in, 6, 37, 159; economic bust, 36-37, 55; gender projects in, 12-13; gender regimes in, 13; globalization of, 4; growth of, and gender equality, 104; individual success in, 160; layoffs in, 6; as male-dominated, 7; masculinity in, 85-86; and new economy, 159-60; outsourcing in, 37, 171-72; pace of change in, 81, 105, 134-35; relative age in, 14, 140-41; risk and, 7; volatility within, 170; women and, 85
IT workers, career advancement and, 168-69; demographic profile, 134; education of, 36, 37; experience and, 36; gendered stereotypes about, 41; marketability of, 141-42; mean age, 28; migration of, 36, 37; numbers, 19; relative age, 146; risk and, 7; supply and demand, 36; unemployment rates, 36. *See also* exemplary

workers; men; older workers; unencumbered workers; women;
younger workers

job security, age and, 10; and demands on workers, 161, 170; downturn and, 6, 37; globalization and,
4; new economy and, 35; size of
firm and, 169; of women, 8. *See also*
unemployment
job tenure, average length of, 160; in
benignly maternalistic gender regimes, 53; and changing workplace
cultures, 69; in masculinist gender
regimes, 69-70; masculinities and,
59; older workers and, 143, 154; of
sample in WANE study, 30, 31(t);
training and, 71; and vacation entitlement, 97; workplace culture
and, 69
Jovic, Emily, 14, 15

Kanter, R.M., 85
Kemp, Candace, 13-14, 163, 165
Kubicek, H., 115

Lampard, R., 83-84
leadership: in benignly paternalistic
gender regimes, 13, 47; by men, 51;
by women, 49-51, 52-53, 164. *See
also* managerial roles
learning capacity, age and, 122-23,
143, 168; ageism and, 148-49, 152,
155; changes in, 168; and hours of
work, 152-53; life-course transitions
and, 168; older workers and, 133,
146-52; younger workers and, 143,
145, 147
life-course transitions, age and, 86;
and brotherhood masculinities, 78;
and couple relationships, 83; defined, 5; as distractions from work,
161; and flexible working arrangements, 76, 77; gender differences
in, 86; and gender projects, 14; and
learning capacity, 126, 168; and
masculinist gender regimes, 44,

68-69, 71, 72-73; and masculinities,
62; and memberships in workplace
groups, 164; older workers and, 85;
and organization of work, 172; and
skills, 126; in smaller firms, 169; in
WANE data collection, 24; and work-
family balance, 93; and workplace
cultures, 69, 77, 166, 172
linked lives: defined, 5, 62; masculinities and, 62; and workplace
cultures, 77
longevity, job. *See* job tenure

managerial masculinities: as pluralistic, 60; types of, 56; women and,
44, 51, 56
managerial roles, hiring for, 41;
men and, 31; older workers in, 78;
women in, 13, 53, 56, 92, 94, 97;
women as CEOs, 49-50, 53-54, 98,
153;
Mannheim, Karl, 114, 115, 121
marital status, gender differences in,
88, 89(t); and gender projects, 14;
in masculinist gender regimes, 65,
66-67, 70; of sample in WANE
study, 28
Marshall, V.W., 136, 137, 155
Marx, Karl, 114
masculinist gender regimes, 40-44,
55-56, 79; age in, 41, 42, 64-65, 70;
brotherhood in, 69, 72; competitiveness in, 42, 43; defined, 13;
demographic profiles of, 64-65, 67,
70, 73; education of workers in, 43;
entrepreneurialism in, 67-68, 70,
74; familial masculinities in, 68, 69,
70, 71, 74; family friendliness of,
42, 44; and family life, 41-42, 71;
and "fit" for workers, 164; flexible
working arrangements in, 66, 68-
69, 71, 73, 76; hierarchical relations
in, 68; hiring in, 41; hours of work
in, 42, 65, 75-76; human resource
policies in, 74-75; life-course transitions and, 44, 68-69, 71, 72-73; longevity in, 69-70; management style

in, 65-66, 73; marital status in, 65, 66-67, 70; masculinities in, 59-79; older workers in, 13; and parent care, 68; and parenthood, 41-42, 65, 67, 68, 70, 76; recruitment practices, 13, 41, 43, 64-65, 70; and unencumbered workers, 14; women in, 13, 40-41, 42, 43, 44, 70, 72, 73-74, 77; work-life balance in, 67, 69, 73; workplace cultures in, 13, 41, 43, 44, 64, 65, 66, 67, 69

masculinity/-ies: brotherhood (*see* brotherhood masculinities); and competitiveness, 61; in computing work, 60; craftsman-like (*see* craftsman-like masculinity); defined, 60; diversity of, 61-62; engineering and, 60; entrepreneurial (*see* entrepreneurial masculinity); and entrepreneurialism, 163; and equity, 61; familial (*see* familial masculinities); hegemonic (*see* hegemonic masculinities); and hierarchical relations, 61; intersection of, 61-62; in IT industry, 85-86; life-course perspective and, 62; and linked lives, 62; management (*see* managerial masculinities); managerial (*see* managerial masculinities); in masculinist gender regimes, 59-79; as non-static, 77; strategic (*see* strategic masculinity); traditional definitions of, 85; types of, 63-64, 165

maternity leave. *See* parental leave

McDaniel, S., 129

McGregor, J., 136

McMillan, S.J., 116

McMullin, Julie, 14-15, 137, 155, 167

men, brotherhood style of masculinity and, 13-14; and child care, 99-100; earnings of, 8, 36; hours of work, 36; individualized relationships and, 83; as leaders, 51; as nonconforming to dominant forms of masculinity, 61; occupational roles of, 31; as older versus younger workers, 9; in technical positions, 88; and work-life balance, 100, 165;

working hours of, 7-8. *See also* older workers; younger workers

Mills, C.W., 82

Morrison, M., 116

motherhood. *See* parenthood

MSI International, 26

multinational firms: and privatization, 82-83; research on, 4

NASDAQ, 6

new economy/-ies: in Canada, 3; defined, 3; IT sector and, 159-60; masculinity in, 85; qualities needed for, 168; relative age in, 156; risk in, 4, 7, 35

new technologies, age and, 115, 150; ageism and, 137, 139; and hiring practices, 144-45; and marketability of workers, 141-42; older workers and, 14, 123, 136, 137, 140, 141, 142-46, 155; and older versus younger workers, 151; organization of work and, 127; parenthood and, 126; younger workers and, 119, 123, 142, 143, 145, 168

non-IT roles/workers, 23, 30, 31, 40-41, 141; women and, 47-48, 73-74, 88, 92, 164

obsolescence, 160

occupational roles, ageism and, 162; gender differences in, 88; of sample in WANE study, 30-31; of women, 48, 163-64, 165

OECD (Organization of Economic Cooperation and Development): on migration of IT workers, 36; on older workers, 133-34

older workers, age composition of IT employment and, 9; attitudes among, 145; attitudes toward, 135-36; commitment to technology, 153; definitions of, 134, 140; effect of ageism on, 155; employability of, 150-51, 154-55; and entrepreneurialism, 154; family demands across life course and, 85; generational discourse of, 120-21; and hours of work, 136, 139-40, 152-55, 153; job searching by, 151; learning capacity, 123, 133, 146-52; managerial versus employee attitudes toward, 136; in managerial roles, 78; as mentors for younger workers, 136, 139; and new technologies, 14, 123, 136, 140, 141, 142-46, 155; and organizational change, 136, 139; and production programming, 155; and productivity, 136, 139, 154, 155; relative age of younger versus, 8-9, 134, 140; reliability of, 136, 139; retirement of, 137; and technological skills, 166-67; and training, 136, 137, 139, 140, 141, 143, 146-52, 155. *See also* age; relative age

Ontario Human Rights Commission, Policy on Discrimination, 134

organization/structure of work: and age, 105; and age and technical skill, 126-27; age-based assumptions and, 167-68; in benignly maternalistic gender regimes, 13; and gender inequalities, 161, 163; and gender regimes, 162-63; and inequalities, 162; and inequality regimes, 170; life-course transitions and, 172; masculine ethic of, 85; and new technologies, 127; and nonconformity to work requirements, 165; and parenthood, 103-4; and preferred workers, 102-3; and work-family balance, 102; workplace cultures and, 165; and younger workers, 167-68. *See also* flexible working arrangements

outsourcing, 37

parent care, 68, 69

parental leave, 101-2; in balanced gender regimes, 54; benignly paternalistic gender regimes and, 47; and hiring, 95-96; women and, 95-96, 98

parenthood, family friendliness and, 85; flexible working arrangements

and, 171; gender and, 84-85, 86, 88, 89(t), 92, 104; and gender projects, 14; hours of work and, 93-94, 101; masculinist gender regimes and, 41-42, 65, 67, 68, 70, 76; and new technologies, 126; and productivity, 99; of sample in WANE study, 28; and skills upgrading, 86; women and, 103; work organization and, 103-4; and work-family negotiation, 93; work-marriage combination and, 88; and workplace culture, 68-69; younger women and, 137-38. *See also* child care

paternalism: defined, 60; and "father figures," 47, 49, 60, 163; in masculinist gender regimes, 65. *See also* benignly paternalistic gender regimes

patriarchy: in benignly paternalistic regimes, 49; globalization and, 84; work-family balance and, 81

pay. *See* wages/salaries

Peggs, K., 83-84

permanent employment, age and, 10; of IT workers, 37; of women, 8. *See also* job tenure

Pilcher, J., 115

power relations, age relations and, 11; authoritarianism and, 60; brotherhood and, 78; gender relations and, 11; and inequalities, 159; opportunity hoarding and, 170; in social relations, 163; women and, 51

prioritization, age and, 126; of work, 98, 102, 165; work-family balance and, 100, 103, 165

privatization, and social responsibility, 82-83

productivity, age and, 116; gender differences in, 138; hiring and, 137-38; hours of work and, 98; older workers and, 136, 139, 154, 155; parenthood and, 99

project management, 13, 51, 52

Ranson, Gillian, 13, 59, 60, 61, 62, 69, 163, 164

recruitment: and employment diversity, 59; and "fit," 164; masculinist gender regimes and, 13, 41, 43, 64-65, 70; and organizational control, 170; word-of-mouth, 59
Reed, K., 156
relative age: and age identity, 156; and ageism, 134; generations and, 123-24, 161; and inequality, 15, 166; in IT industry, 140-41; of IT workers, 146; meaning of, 8-9; in new economy, 156; of older versus younger workers, 8-9, 134, 140. *See also* age
remuneration. *See* wages/salaries
Reveley, J., 117
Riach, Kathleen, 135
risk(s), concept of, 4; and couple relationships, 83; currency in sociology of, 6-7; entrepreneurialism and, 163; in expectations of career progress, 168-69; of hiring younger women, 105; IT sector and, 7, 37, 55; new economies and, 4, 7, 35; and pay, 8; social contexts of, 35; society, 4, 82; women IT workers and, 7, 98
Rix, S.E., 133
Rothman, B., 7
Rupp, D.E., 137

salaries. *See* wages/salaries
Segrave, K., 133
Sennett, R., 146
skills, age and, 122, 124-25, 166; craftsman-like masculinity and, 14; education versus, 50; enthusiasm and, 125; individualism and development of, 146; inequality and upgrading of, 161; learning of, 126; life-course transitions and, 126; older workers and, 166-67; parenthood and upgrading of, 86; personal choice and, 124; structural constraints against updating of, 155; timing/extent of exposure to technology and, 119; underappreciation for, 75; unencumbered workers and, 126; variance in, 116; of women, 56

small and mid-sized IT firms, entrepreneurialism and, 169; as gender projects, 14; and industry volatility, 169; life-course transitions and, 169; numbers of employees in, 19; prevalence of, 37; research regarding, 4, 19; resemblance to family ties in, 169-70; and risk, 55; survival during downturn, 6. *See also* IT firms
statistical discrimination, 137-38
stereotypes/stereotyping: and age, 11, 127-28; of IT firms, 59; IT workplaces and, 42. *See also* ageism
strategic masculinity, 63
supervision of others' work, age and, 10; women and, 8, 13, 51, 52, 55

Taylor, P., 135-36, 137, 138, 140
technical positions, hiring for, 41; in masculinist gender regimes, 64; men in, 88; women in, 13, 41, 46-47, 50, 56
technological skills. *See* skills
technology, adaptation to, 119, 123; age of, 150; ageism and, 14-15; crossover into private life, 162; and culture, 113-14, 115; dual character of, 113-14; generational affinity with, 14; "generations" of, 167; growing up with, 118-21, 124; innovation in, 123; masculinity in, 60; timing/extent of exposure to, 119. *See also* new technologies
training, age and, 116, 168; ageism and, 148-49; in benignly maternalistic gender regimes, 53; older workers and, 136, 137, 139, 140, 141, 143, 146-52, 155; and technology crossover into private life, 162. *See also* education; learning capacity
Turkle, S., 60
Turner, B.S., 114-15, 129

unemployment, age and, 11, 15; of older workers, 150-51; rates for IT workers, 36. *See also* job security unencumbered workers, age and, 15; as exemplary workers, 15, 161, 162, 165; gender and, 15; masculinist gender regimes and, 14; and skills, 126; as "zero-drag," 102, 161

United Kingdom, age of IT employees in, 5; age and pay satisfaction in, 10; ageism in, 141, 143, 147; benignly maternalistic gender regimes in, 52; benignly paternalistic gender regimes in, 47-48; contract workers in, 30; difference discourses in, 124, 126-28; employability of older workers in, 154; family-related policies in, 106; fringe benefits in, 10; gender of IT employees in, 5; generational discourse in, 120-21, 122; hiring of younger workers in, 144, 145; hours of work in, 10; job security in, 8; job tenure in, 30; masculinist gender regimes in, 43-44; numbers of employees in small and mid-sized IT firms, 19, 37; participation rate in, 24, 25(t); pay in, 8, 10; permanent employment in, 10; relative age in, 146; sampling strategies in, 21; visible minorities in, 28; workers' ages and new technologies in, 150

United States, age discrimination in search for jobs in, 151; age and hiring in, 149, 154; age and hours of work in, 152; age of IT employees in, 5; age and pay satisfaction in, 10; ageism in, 141, 143, 146-47, 148; benignly maternalistic gender regimes in, 49-50; child care division of labour in, 91; computing education in, 36; contract workers in, 30; employability of older workers in, 151; fringe benefits in, 10; gender differences in occupational roles in, 88, 89(t); gender of IT employees in, 5; generational discourse in, 118-20, 121-24, 167; hours of work in, 10, 152, 153; human resource policies in, 101-2; interviews conducted in, 23; job tenure in, 30;

masculinist gender regimes in, 42, 44; numbers of employees in small and mid-sized IT firms, 37; numbers of women in IT, 36; parental leave in, 101-2, 106; participation rate in, 25(t); permanent employment in, 10; sampling strategies in, 20-21; training of older workers in, 148-49; visible minorities in, 28

visible minorities, 28, 42

wages/salaries: and assessment of job performance, 8, 10; in balanced gender regimes, 54; in benignly maternalistic gender regimes, 53; education and, 37; gender gap in, 11, 36; hiring of younger workers and, 155; of men, 8, 36; of older versus younger workers, 151; and organizational control, 170; risk and, 8; satisfaction in younger versus older workers, 10; scales and technical skill, 126-27; of women, 8, 36

Wagner, R.M., 115

Walker, A., 135-36, 137, 138, 140

welfare state, 81, 82

Willms, J., 4

women, accommodations for, 7; attitudes toward other women, 164; in balanced gender regimes, 13, 55; in benignly maternalistic gender regimes, 13, 49-50, 50-51, 51-53, 56; benignly paternalistic gender regimes and, 13, 45-47, 48-49, 56; brotherhood style of masculinity and, 13-14; and child care, 91, 94-95, 98, 99-100; as "conceptual men," 164; earnings of, 8, 36; education of, 56; emancipation of, 83; as "father" versus "mother" figures, 49; generational discourse, 120, 121; hiring of, 102, 105; hours of work and, 36, 94, 98; individualized relationships and, 83-84; job perceptions of, 8; and managerial masculinities, 44, 51, 56; in managerial positions, 13, 49-51, 52-53, 92, 94, 164; masculinist gender regimes and, 13, 40-41, 42, 43, 44, 67, 69, 70, 72, 73-74, 77; as models for other women, 57; and move away from traditional family, 83; in non-IT roles, 73-74, 88, 92, 164; numbers in IT firms, 38, 163; numbers in IT sector, 28, 35-36; occupational roles of, 31, 36, 48, 163-64, 165; as older versus younger workers, 9; and parental leave, 95-96, 98; and parenthood, 85, 103, 137-38; permanent employment of, 8; in project management, 13; re-entry into labour force, 85; and risk, 7, 98, 105; skills of, 56; as supervisors, 8, 13; in technical positions, 13, 41, 46-47, 50, 56; and work-family balance, 95, 104; and work-life balance, 161, 165; working hours, 7-8; and workplace culture, 41, 44, 56, 85, 164

work organization. *See* organization/ structure of work

work-family balance, 81-106; definitions of masculinity and, 85-86; family-related policies and, 106; flexible working arrangements and, 86, 96-97, 100, 104, 165; gender differences in, 99, 103; globalization and, 102, 105-6; home-based work and, 101; hours of work and, 93-94, 100; life course and, 93; men and, 100-1, 165; prioritization of work and, 85-86, 103, 165; traditional gender roles and, 98, 103; vacation time and, 97; women and, 95, 104; work organization and, 102-3; work responsibilities and, 93

work-life balance: in balanced gender regimes, 13, 54; benignly paternalistic gender regimes and, 50; entrepreneurialism and, 69; gender differences in, 84; individualization of, 165; in masculinist gender regimes, 67, 69, 73; men and, 165;

prioritization of work and, 85-86, 165; women and, 165

Workforce Aging in the New Economy (WANE): bias in selection of firms, 19-20; case study approach, 18; characteristics of firms in, 27-28; characteristics of participants in, 28-31; data collection, 6, 20, 22-25; data management, 26-27; data storage, 26; ethics of research, 25-26; interviews, 23-25; negotiations with firms, 21-22; observational notes taken, 22; participation rate, 24-25; about project, 5-6; research design, 18-22; sampling strategies, 20-22; and self-administered web surveys, 23-24

workplace culture(s): and aging, 72, 73; in balanced gender regimes, 54; in benignly maternalistic gender regimes, 13, 48, 53; in benignly paternalistic gender regimes, 45, 46; brotherhood, 78; changes in, 69; clashes of masculinities in, 74; craftsmanship masculinity and, 63; defined, 12; divisions within, 74, 78; and employment diversity, 59; entrepreneurialism and, 63, 67; as exclusionary, 72, 73; and family-related policies, 106; fitting into, 15; and gender, 72, 73; gender projects/ regimes and, 166; generational discourse and, 14; inequality regimes and, 12; life-course transitions and, 69, 77, 164, 166, 172; linked lives and, 77; and longevity, 69; in masculinist gender regimes, 13, 41, 43, 44, 64, 65, 66, 67, 69; and men non-conforming to dominant forms of masculinity, 61; and organizational logic, 165; parenthood and, 68-69; size of firm and, 169; stereotypes about, 42; and women, 41, 44, 56, 85, 164; work environment and, 71; as youthful, 168

workplace organization. *See* organization/structure of work

World Wide Web, 116

younger workers, affinity for technology in, 168; attitudes of, 145; brotherhood masculinities and, 78; enthusiasm of, 124-25, 143; generational discourse of, 118-20; hegemonic masculinities and, 61; hiring of, 143, 144-46, 154, 155; as IT workers, 5; learning capacity, 143, 145, 147; mentoring by older workers, 136, 139; and new technologies, 119, 123, 142, 143, 145, 151, 168; organization/structure of work and, 167-68; relative age of older versus, 8-9, 134, 140; technical proficiency of, 150, 155; unfavourable treatment of, 10, 167; and working environment for women, 56; and workplace cultures, 168

Printed and bound in Canada by Friesens
Set in Stone by Artegraphica Design Co. Ltd.
Copy editor: Dallas Harrison
Proofreader: Kate Spezowka
Indexer: Noeline Bridge